MW00888559

Graciela, No One's Child

Grace Banta

iUniverse, Inc.
New York Bloomington

Graciela, No One's Child

iUniverse books may be ordered through booksellers or by contacting:

iUniverse
1663 Liberty Drive
Bloomington, IN 47403
www.iuniverse.com
1-800-Authors (1-800-288-4677)

ISBN: 978-1-4502-2527-4 (sc)
ISBN: 978-1-4502-2522-9 (dj)
ISBN: 978-1-4502-2523-6 (ebk)

Library of Congress Control Number: 2010906382

Printed in the United States of America

iUniverse rev. date: 6/1/2010

To my family

and

To abused children everywhere

"Now I am caught on one side and the other;
one bids me be silent, the other conjures me to speak."

Dante Alighieri, *Divine Comedy*

I have decided to speak.

"I will tell you truly all."

Homer, the *Iliad*

Contents

First, I would like to thank my husband for his years of understanding help with the search for my family and patience in helping me edit this manuscript.

I would like to thank my son for his encouragement and persistence, which drove me to publish this book.

I would like to thank my daughter for her understanding support and encouragement throughout this project.

Finally, I would like to thank Andrea for her sensitive encouragement and expert advice.

Preface

An Italian-American baby born in Brooklyn, New York, in late 1940, I was abducted to Mexico. Thus began what I can only describe as an odyssey. In the following pages, I tell how I dealt with the consequences of my abduction while growing up in Mexico as Graciela, no one's child. This is a story of hope and triumph of the spirit; it is also a story I had kept secret and cloaked in fabrications, even from my husband and children, until now.

My story is not about the First Gulf War or Saudi Arabia. However, it was at that time and at that place and facing my mortality that I first felt compelled to put this story into manuscript form.

We were living in Dhahran, Saudi Arabia, where my husband was employed by Saudi Aramco. It was the evening of January 17, 1991. Pieces of Scud and Patriot missiles were raining all over the compound. The Gulf War had broken out in full and I quickly realized I might not make it out alive. My thoughts went to our children, who had left just days before and who were now safely away in New England boarding schools. They were very frightened for their parents' safety.

I searched frantically for the two small, green notebooks in which, some sixteen years earlier, I had written accounts of my childhood. I had written the notes over a period of months while we were living in Cebazat, a small, provincial town in central France. Every day, I walked my children to the neighborhood school and, after, went into town. I often sat at a local outdoor café table, trying to recapture the memories, painful as they were.

I found the green notebooks, raced upstairs, and began to type the entire story into the Apple computer. Although I had very little capability in typing or using computers, I was driven to record what I could. As I started to get into the story, I suddenly became overwhelmed with emotions—the tears just flowed. What had lain dormant for almost four decades came hauntingly back in large measure.

By the evening of January 22, things had worsened to the point where many dependents were being evacuated to Rota, Spain. We were hunkered down in a huge, almost windowless, C-5A military cargo plane. I was sitting just behind the cockpit, in the front row of the top deck, a few rows apart from the other evacuees. I could see the pilot.

As we sat on the tarmac, I could hear sounds like popcorn popping all around the plane. The attendant, a young man in his late twenties, sat next to me. He realized I could hear the missiles coming down all around us. He tried to distract me so I would not alarm the other passengers who were busily chatting and unaware of what was happening.

The pilot decided to take off in the midst of the missile attacks. I guessed he thought we were safer in the air than sitting on the airstrip. As I again came to terms with my mortality, I said to myself, *It is written; it is written* ... In five days, I had tape-recorded and typed the entire story.

What I originally typed, a very rough and hurriedly written memoir, has since become the manuscript for this book. My husband first learned the details of my story as he painstakingly helped me edit the text. I often found him in tears but still anxious to press on. My son was in his thirties when he first read what I had written. He told me how very difficult it was to accept all I had gone through. At the same time, he said he had found the story to be profoundly inspiring, interesting, and worthwhile—enough so, that it should be published. My daughter felt the same.

Over time, I gathered enough courage to share part of what I had written. I asked Andrea, a family friend and writer, to read several chapters. Andrea also boosted my confidence and encouraged me to continue with the goal of publishing. Still others, with whom I verbally shared excerpts, encouraged me with comments like, "You should write a book."

"Remembrance is the secret of redemption; Forgetfulness leads to exile."
The Rabbi Baal Shem Tov

Actually writing the story was a daunting task; however, more difficult, by far, was enduring the pain of reliving a past I had kept locked away in memory for so many years.

Throughout, translations are my own. Some of the names have been changed for privacy.

I paused to decide just where to start. My thoughts soon focused on my recollections of the crucial and unforgettable moment when, as a sixteen-year-old girl, I confronted Matilde on the details of my birth, how she got me, and where I came from.

Confrontation

"Life can only be understood backwards; but it must be lived forwards."

Soren Kierkegaard

This was to be a fight for my life! I had to protect myself. In the deepest part of my being, very intense feelings told me today would be a turning point. I knew at that moment, more than ever, that I had to take full charge of my life. If I didn't get away from her now, the end result would only be in Matilde's interests. I could no longer endure her abusive control. The past sixteen years of suffering and devastation that her capricious and childlike mentality had inflicted on me had to stop!

I already knew Matilde was not my mother, and that I had been born in Brooklyn, New York. I also knew Matilde had smuggled me from the United States to Mexico. What I needed now were the details. I hoped I could persuade her to tell me enough to have at least a chance of fulfilling my dream of getting back to my country and finding my family. My whole being hungered for the truth. Deep within me, I had to know, no matter how painful the outcome might be. Where do I come from? Where is my family? Who are they? How did Matilde get me and bring me into Mexico? If my mother had rejected me, what were the circumstances? How could she have given me—a part of herself—away so carelessly, especially to someone as irresponsible as Matilde?

All my life, until now, I had been robbed of my dignity and my basic human rights. The drive to rebuild my life had swelled to the point where

I could think of nothing else. The days, months, and years of physical and mental abuse and desolation had driven me to this day. I was in this world but connected to no one. All in my life had been temporary and insecure. I was continuously haunted by a sense of urgency and had to consider the consequences of everything I did. I could never simply enjoy the moment; I always had to be ready to take the next step. I was going through life in motions, but inside myself, I was somewhere else. I had an overwhelming urge to know. My hunger had never been satisfied. I had a small amount of money and people around me who were trustworthy. Now I had to get the truth from Matilde. I knew she would likely be evasive, so I would come out empty handed—a result I simply could not accept. I had to plan my moves carefully.

I was staying with Matilde's sister, Aunt Mari, and her family at their nice home in the small Mexican petroleum town of Poza Rica. I had just left Aunt Mari's home and was waiting for the bus. I remember clearly, as if it were yesterday; it was a beautiful, bright, sunny spring morning. I looked up at the sky and said aloud, but in Spanish, "God, guide me so I can persuade her to tell me the truth." I also prayed, as I often did in my most painful moments, "*Dios conmigo, yo con El. Dios adelante, yo atras de El.* (God with me, I with Him. God in front, I behind Him.)"

I barely noticed the bus when it stopped right in front of me. Almost like a robot, I got on. I was intensely focused on the most effective ways to get Matilde to answer my questions, and on the confrontation I knew we were going to have. Nothing mattered except what I was about to do. However, I was distracted by chickens squawking under my seat. I turned to my right and saw an older woman with a gray and white *reboso* (shawl) covering her head, the ends crossed over her shoulders in a way typical of the area. A simple glance and she reached to hold the beaks of the chickens to quiet them. Just then, a child started making noise and misbehaving. Again, I simply looked at the mother. She, in turn, had only to give a stern look to get the boy to behave. Still again, my thoughts were pulled away when the bus stopped and a man with a guitar got on and started to sing. As the bus jerked forward, he held himself against one of the support poles right in front of me. He sang quite well; the song was *Besame Mucho.* After the song, he passed his hat for coins. When he got off, I was finally able to concentrate. I blocked out everything around me until the bus stopped.

When I got off the bus, it was as if my body were there, but my mind elsewhere. I looked at the sky and prayed, *Dear God, put the right words in my mouth so I can now persuade Matilde to tell me the truth. My life is in Your hands.* I looked up again at the sky and felt a little stronger, like He was with me and I was not alone. Silently, I prayed to my guardian angel, *Please protect me day and night.*

I only had to walk a short distance to Matilde's place. She was living with a Papantla Indian man on the outskirts of Poza Rica. He worked out of town during the week and came home on weekends. All around this area poorer people lived in little single-room huts with corrugated metal roofs and dirt floors. Many of these huts had a post in the center of the room where religious pictures or pictures of family members were hung. This neighborhood was quite unlike the neighborhood of beautiful chalets where Mari's family lived among the cadre, or management, of Petroleos Mexicanos.

When I got to Matilde's, I walked in without knocking. She was sitting on the bed looking into a mirror and combing her hair as she did every day. Typical of Matilde, always acting like a beauty queen, and without missing a beat, she ordered, "Graciela, clean the room and go get me some tortillas."

I was ready; I knew I had to stop her in her tracks. I took control and set the tone, "I am not here to do your cleaning or to run errands for you. I am here because I want you to tell me how you got me and, I want you to tell me all you know about my family. I have the right to know. I want to know every detail, no matter how painful."

As always, she tried to maintain control of the situation by evading me. She looked away to the mirror, "I have to talk with Pablo first; he is in on this too."

I was losing my patience and anger was building. However, I knew if I let anger take over, I would be the loser; I had to control my emotions. I insisted, "I can't wait. We have to do this now."

She called me ungrateful and started cursing me, which got me in the right frame of mind.

I said, "Matilde, listen, and listen well to what I have to say, because you, and only you, will be responsible for what I do if you don't give me the information I need."

This was the first time I had addressed her by her given name. It caught her by surprise. She was getting ready to insult me again for being disrespectful, but I stopped her with these words: "Matilde, I do not love you like a mother. I never will. If you don't want to tell me about my family for fear you will lose my love, there is nothing to lose. If you don't tell me, I will kill myself. I do not want to live without knowing the truth. Thanks to you, I have no education, and I do not want to end up like you. The only thing that has kept me going all these years is the hope of going back to my country and finding my family. For that, I need to know all you know about me and my mother."

She started crying. I knew her tears were a way to manipulate me, so I ignored her and kept the pressure on. I continued, "I just came from Mexico City and am staying with Aunt Mari. Furthermore, I have enough money for you and me to get to Tijuana. Pablo sent me the money a few weeks ago, and I am going, with you or without you!"

Even though I actually had no intention of killing myself, I had chosen the right words. I needed to shock her. Although I had chosen these words spontaneously and on the spot, they came out as if I had rehearsed them. It worked! I felt empowered like never before. For the first time ever, I felt I had some control over my life and, now, control over Matilde. I had the money, and Matilde wanted to get to Tijuana and on to the United States. In an instant, the impossible became possible. From this moment on, my resolve to get back to my country of birth and to find my family grew ever stronger.

Still crying, Matilde finally seemed to realize there was no way out. She began: "Around the first week of July 1940, we were in New York, living in a waterfront apartment on Columbia Street in Brooklyn. Pablo and I settled there after our wedding in Veracruz. Mostly Italians lived in the building. It was late in the morning on a hot and humid day when I went downstairs to see if I had any mail. I was lonely for news from my friends in Veracruz. I saw this pregnant woman, who I had never seen before, standing by the mailboxes."

I asked her, "When is the baby due?"

She said, "In three months." Then she paused and asked, "Do you want this baby?"

Matilde responded, "Why? Don't you want to keep it?"

The woman looked down, only answering, "I have to go back to my apartment."

The next morning, Matilde knocked on the pregnant woman's door. The woman did not open the door, so she told her aloud she wanted to talk more about the baby. Finally, the door opened, and the woman let her in.

Matilde said, "My name is Matilde Flores Palo. I am married to Pablo Palo, and we have no children."

The pregnant woman said, "I go by Maria, but my real name is Filomena."

Matilde asked Filomena, "Why do you want to give this baby up?"

Filomena said, "I cannot keep this baby, because I already have six children, and they have all been put in a home. My husband is a very cruel man, and I fear for my life. I am separated from him and have been living in hiding in Jackie's apartment for some time."

Matilde asked, "Does Jackie want to give this baby up?"

Filomena said, "He is a widower in his early fifties and has a twenty-six-year-old bachelor son and a daughter who is married with three little girls."

Filomena was in her mid-thirties. Matilde told her she wanted the baby, and as soon as she could, she would talk to her husband. If he agreed, she would tell her the next day.

When Pablo arrived home, Matilde was at the door, ready to tell him the news of the baby offered to her by the women in apartment C. Pablo told Matilde he did not think they would qualify for adoption as they didn't have much; he was black, and she was an immigrant from Mexico. He told her to forget about it; it was impossible to have the baby. Matilde insisted she wanted this baby, and she would think of a way to keep it.

Pablo asked her, "Matilde, what do you know of caring for a baby?"

She told him, "Eight years ago, when I was seventeen, I had a baby boy. The boy is with his father's family."

"This," Matilde told Pablo, "gives me the knowledge to care for this baby."

At this point, I interrupted Matilde. "Why," I asked, "did you want me when you had already given up your own child?"

She said, "Because I did not want to have children with Pablo. I did not want a black baby."

"What a selfish reason; how irresponsible." I said.

Of course, Pablo thought Matilde wanted me in order to get over the guilt she felt about giving up her own child.

Matilde continued with the story.

Pablo was sure there was no way she would be able to get me legally, so he told her, carelessly, as if I were a sack of potatoes, "If you can get the baby, then you can have it."

Matilde told Filomena that Pablo agreed, but they had to think of a way of turning the baby over to her without the authorities finding out. They visited each other during these three months of waiting. Toward the end of the pregnancy, they came up with what they thought was a brilliant plan. Filomena was going to turn the baby over to Matilde and Pablo at birth. Jackie, Matilde, and God knows who else thought up the idea, all tampering with my destiny—even before I was born!

According to the plan, when she gave the information in the hospital, Filomena was to give all the vital statistics for Matilde and Pablo. This way, as soon as Filomena had me and left the hospital, she would hand me over to the Palos. They would get my birth certificate, which would show them as my real parents—as easy as that, I was to be given a new identity and a new set of parents who wanted me for their own selfish reasons.

Immediately after she got me, Matilde wanted to go to Tijuana and Mexico City to show me off. She had the perfect excuse, to say she had me while she was away. Matilde was a heavyset woman, so she could have been pregnant and not shown it. All their planning was coming along fine. They thought they had covered all the angles.

The long-awaited day arrived for Filomena to go to the hospital. She started labor early in the morning, and was rushed to the Cumberland Hospital in Brooklyn. Matilde and Pablo were supposed to go to the hospital with Filomena to make sure she carried out the agreed plan and to give the correct information on the birth certificate. However, something went wrong, and they didn't arrive until after I was born. At 6:02 AM, Filomena had a baby girl and had already given the birth registration information to the nurse.

All the effort, from weeks of rehearsing what she was going to give as data on the birth certificate, was for nothing. As it turned out, whether Filomena had a change of heart or she simply forgot, the only information she gave to the hospital that they had agreed on was Matilde, the first name of the mother, and Palo, the surname. The rest was all information on Filomena and, supposedly, whoever my father was.

Matilde did not know this until she sent for the copy of the birth certificate a few weeks later. When she got the certificate, she was fuming—all the data about her and Pablo was wrong. She knew the other thing Filomena had changed was my name. Instead of being named Matilde, like her, Filomena named me Grace. I felt then this was a name just picked out of the air with no meaning whatsoever—just something to name this kid before she got rid of it.

A few days before I was born, the Palos moved to another building in the same area of Brooklyn. When the neighbors saw the Palos with this white baby girl, they assumed I was not theirs or, at least, only Matilde's child or a child left in her care.

Matilde said during my first week with her I cried day and night. I would not take the bottle. I had been breastfed by Filomena while she was in the hospital, so I wanted breast milk, not the bottle. Matilde took me to Filomena's apartment for her to breast-feed me, which she did. However, when Jackie found out, he told Matilde they had given me to her, and now I was her responsibility and not to bring me back.

As Matilde told me this, I thought, *How cruel, how indifferent!*

Matilde said I was a beautiful baby. Whenever she was out with me in Brooklyn, people used to compliment her on what a pretty baby I was. She said some middle-aged Italian women used to come to see me; she believed they might have been my mother's relatives. They asked Matilde if they could take me out for walks from time to time. Matilde said she had reason to believe they had me baptized during one of these walks, but could not prove it. As she told me this, I thought they might have done this to erase their guilt for having turned their backs on me. While they were saving my soul, they were ruining my life.

She said these ladies also brought me dresses and gifts. She told me she dressed me very well, and would never dress me in the cotton dresses that these women brought; she only dressed me in the finest materials. As she was telling me this, I could not see the importance of what dress materials I wore, but it certainly made Matilde feel good to tell it.

Matilde said, "When we went to visit you and your mother in the hospital, they gave us orange passes that identified the person we were going to visit. I kept two of them and have them with my important papers. These orange cards and a baby picture taken of you just before we left Brooklyn are the only things I have from those times."

As she was telling me this, I was hoping she would not notice how I was trembling.

I silently reasoned, *So the writing on these orange cards may be the address of the hospital where I was born.*

I felt a very strong sense of accomplishment and hope at this moment. I had maintained possession of these two cards and the baby picture since I was eight years old, and no one had been able to notice them among my meager belongings. For almost all the time I had them, I barely knew how to read or write in Spanish, let alone English. And, since I had been so busy hiding them, I did not even think of the meaning of the writing on either the cards or the picture.

Now, more than ever, I felt the importance of these two cards and this photograph in my search for my identity. I wanted to ask her more about them, but I did not dare let her know that I had them or that I had a great interest in them. Knowing Matilde, I worried she might not give me more information about my background if she knew I had them. She thought she had everything on her side and I was depending solely on her for information of my past. Up to this moment, I had never dared to mention to anyone how I had gotten the two cards and the photograph such a long, long time before.

She then told me of the difficulties she went through when Pablo left and went into hiding. Pablo felt that the war in Europe was getting worse and that the involvement of the United States in World War II was imminent. He did not want to be called for military duty.

At the beginning of 1941, with Pablo away, Matilde started working at her old profession again. She told me one of the men she was involved with at this time got drunk and threw a brick through the window of her apartment to get her attention. The brick landed on my crib, a hair's breadth from my head. My problems could have ended at the tender age of four months.

She said another time she left me on top of a table, and I fell on my head. I was only six weeks old. She also said I was often left in my dirty diapers for hours at a time, because she did not know how to care for a baby. As a result, I always had a bad rash on my bottom. To this day, I have a flat spot on the back of my head because I was not picked up from my crib, sometimes for days at a time. Only God knows how often I was fed or changed. I am amazed I survived the first six months, or even six weeks, of life with such poor care.

With Pablo in hiding, the time arrived for Matilde to move again. She made plans to go to her father's house in Tijuana, Mexico. The problem now was how to take me across the border without papers. Many people were crossing the border into the United States, illegally. At the tender age of six months, I was crossing the border into Mexico, illegally!

Matilde wrote to her father of her coming. She sold everything she had, and with the money Pablo gave her, we left Brooklyn. We were on our way, for what Matilde thought, would be a better life with her family in Tijuana.

On the train that was taking us across the border, the immigration officer was coming her way, checking papers. She got up and walked with me to another car, where the officer had already checked papers, and asked a woman to hold me while she went to the restroom. Then she returned to her seat and showed her papers to the officer. She waited until he went on, then went back to get me. She returned to her seat with me, and that is how I crossed the Mexican border—illegally!

When we arrived in Tijuana, Matilde's father, Eduardo, was living with his common-law wife, who was Matilde's first cousin, Celina. Celina was the daughter of Eduardo's own brother, his niece! Eduardo and Celina had two children. The older one, Edith, was two years older than me; the other was a newborn baby. Edith was not too happy about my arrival in her home. Matilde told me Edith used to follow me around as I was crawling around the house or the store, and when no one was looking, she would bite my behind, keeping me in tears almost all the time. She was jealous of me because people used to pay a lot of attention to me, and not to her.

As Matilde was telling me this, I thought, *Why couldn't our ages have been the other way around so I could have had some peace?*

Life in Tijuana was nice at the beginning as Matilde was showing me off to her family. Furthermore, she was trying to show her father she had changed for the better and was now a happily married, respectable woman with a beautiful child. She thought her father should be very proud of her. As I see it, Eduardo and Matilde were two of a kind.

Eduardo was a very successful businessman. Right next door to his home, he had a super market and a bakery. He also had rentals in downtown Tijuana. He was a wealthy man, and Matilde and I were not a financial burden on him. While Matilde visited her friends, the housekeeper used to take care of me. Life here was very good for Matilde—no bills and no work. She wanted to stay as long as she could.

Matilde said Pablo wanted to hide in Tijuana until the war was over. There was only one problem: Pablo could not come here and stay with her as she had overlooked telling her father that Pablo was a black man. I was white with blue eyes and blond hair and didn't look like either Pablo or Matilde. If Pablo were to come to see Matilde, she would have to move. This presented a big problem for Matilde, as Pablo was sending her money for my care and for her to set up an apartment in Tijuana so he could come and live with her. Matilde did not want this. All she wanted was the money to keep coming in, but not the man. She was ashamed of Pablo's color, and she was not about to have him meet her family. She wanted him to be just a name to them and for them never to meet him.

Pablo got tired of waiting for Matilde to get an apartment, so he threatened to stop sending money. In addition, Celina wanted Matilde to get an apartment of her own. Matilde had already overstayed her welcome. Matilde protested; she told Celina this was her father's house, and she had the right to stay as long as she wanted. Problems started, and Matilde had to move. In order to keep Pablo sending her money, she moved us to Ensenada.

Ensenada was about an hour south of Tijuana by bus, which was far enough away to keep Matilde's family from meeting Pablo. Matilde kept making excuses why she could not get an apartment or why Pablo could not come to Tijuana and join her. By this time, Pablo had gone to Puerto Rico to hide.

Pablo had quit sending money, and Matilde's money had run out. She had built up a good story about her marriage. To ask her father for money now would have revealed the truth. Facing this predicament—much of it of her own making, I thought—she would leave me with whoever would take me so she could make a living. Frankly, I don't think Matilde ever loved me. To her, I was only a means of getting money, especially from Pablo.

In Ensenada, Matilde met Señora Oro. Señora Oro was married to a general in the Mexican Army. Because they could not have children, Señora Oro was always willing to take care of me. This gave her something to do, and with her maid, she had plenty of help. Señora Oro became very fond of me, and I am sure I was fond of her too. She wanted to adopt me. They had the means to do it, and they could prove Matilde was an unfit mother.

Señora Oro offered Matilde money if she would give me up to her. Matilde kept leading her on, but at the same time she was thinking of ways to take me away without Señora Oro getting suspicious that she was leaving. She was afraid Señora Oro might call the authorities. Matilde told Señora Oro that she was planning to take me to see my grandfather in a month or so. She said that when she came back they would talk more about me staying with her permanently. I'm sure Matilde took full advantage of this lady's kindness.

I was two when Matilde went to the city hall in Ensenada and registered me as her daughter. Most likely, she bribed someone to do this. So now, if anyone questioned how she treated me, she had papers to prove I was legally hers. She told me many people did want to take me away from her. This is when she decided to move to Mexicali.

It seems it was a relief and cathartic for Matilde to tell this story. She had kept it bottled up inside for more than sixteen years. She even got to relive her past and talk about the good old days.

My First Memories

I was about three years old in a small room in the hot, dusty Mexican border town of Mexicali. I can see and feel that memory as though it happened yesterday. I woke up to hunger and the burning pain of urine and waste against my skin. The early morning sunlight filtered in from around the wooden door. I tugged in vain to free myself, cried, and looked toward Matilde's bed. She was not there; she was almost never there. Fear and helplessness were my only companions.

From the other side of the wall, I heard the sounds of children's laughter and neighbors starting their day. The familiar smell of brewing coffee and boiling milk wafting through cracks in the door made my hunger worse. I imagined people sitting and having their *café con leche* (hot milk with coffee) and enjoying freshly baked Mexican breads—on my side of the wall was nothing but desolation.

Matilde loved to go dancing, so most nights I would be left all alone. She did not ask for help because she did not want to spend the money or let anyone see my condition. Her solution was to tie me to my crib. She left me flat on my back, looking at the ceiling, with my outspread hands and feet tied tightly to each side of the crib. As far as I know, I was tied in my crib like this from the time I was an infant to the time I was five. Just as Matilde went out, she would threaten me not to make any noise. She didn't want the neighbors to know she left me all alone. At the same time, she would promise to do something nice if I obeyed—threats and promises.

I knew that when Matilde got home she was going to be tired and angry with the mess she would find. I would be beaten and cursed. She would hit me, untie me from my crib, and take me outside in the courtyard. Then, just like an animal, she would tie me to the tree. Sometimes, if she thought of it, she would give me a crust of bread or a flour tortilla, sparingly spread with peanut butter or catsup. She would leave me tied like this in the extreme heat of the day, sometimes for hours, until she got enough sleep.

Among all the unhappy and unpleasant moments in Mexicali, there were moments when I found joy in what I could do, free of Matilde. One of these moments was when I learned how to untie myself after she tied me to the tree. I was able to figure out in my mind just how long she would be asleep. I would free myself and go play. When I thought she was about to wake up, I would return to the tree and tie myself back up. This was short-lived as she soon discovered my secret and began to use a chain and padlock on one of my ankles. Sometimes Matilde would bring a man home during the day and, again, I would be put outside and chained to the tree.

Mexicali was very hot in the summer, and my back and torso were covered with red heat rash from the time I could remember. The rash made it too uncomfortable and irritating to wear clothes. I was in my underwear, always heavily dusted with cornstarch, a local remedy for heat rash. Therefore, it wasn't too demanding to take care of me. This was my daily life.

The neighbors started complaining to Matilde for tying me to the tree in the hottest times of the year. After that, she started keeping me locked in the room with her while she slept. Many times, I had to remain quiet and fend for myself. If I were hungry, all I could get for myself would be flour tortillas with catsup and maybe some *Tres Claveles* (Three Carnations) canned milk. If I didn't happen to be hungry at the time and Matilde decided to feed me, she would force me to eat. If I didn't eat, she would hit me until I did. For me, it was not a question of mealtimes; she fed me when she had time, and when she did she stuffed me. This would most likely be the only meal I would get that day. When she would bring her visitors home, I would have to wait until she and her visitors ate. I got whatever was left over.

I can remember being tied to the tree and watching children across the courtyard going into their houses to eat lunch or dinner with their families. One time, as I looked over, I remember so clearly thinking to myself, *Why don't I have a loving family like other children?*

One day, when I was not doing what Matilde wanted, she went into a rage and angrily dragged me by the arm to the *pozo* (water well) at the end of the courtyard. She grabbed me by the waist and pushed the top half of my body into the darkness to make me look far down to the shining water at the bottom of the well. She shook me roughly and threatened me, telling me that if I did not do as she said, she was going to throw me in. I remember clearly the instant I saw the shining water far down at the end of this long, dark tunnel. I was terrified she might drop me or that I might slip and fall.

My fear was intensified by my clear knowledge that she really might do just as she said. I had blocked this memory for years; it wasn't until, in my sixties and in the midst of writing this book, that I made the connection of this incident to my lifelong fear of water.

I was almost five, and I still wet my bed. I didn't have any choice, as almost all the time I was tied to my crib. In spite of the countless beatings I endured because of my bedwetting, it was hard for me to control my bladder. When Matilde realized that beating me wasn't working, she decided to stop me another way. Her remedy was to grab me, pull my underwear down, and put red pepper in my vagina. Only God knows where she got this idea. I can't find the words to explain the excruciating pain I felt—the burning was unbearable for hours, and I still feel sick when I think about it. What kind of human being would do this to a young child? What sick mind could conceive of this horror?

Matilde tried to stop my horrified screams; she was afraid the neighbors would find out what she had done. She covered my mouth, washed me with soap, and sat me in water. Finally, she promised to buy me a nice dinner if I stopped crying and asked me where I wanted to eat. All I wanted right then was to make the burning stop! What did I care about eating?

Eventually, the burning did subside, and the pain became more bearable. Matilde told me not to tell anyone what she had done, or it would be worse for me. If anyone asked why I was I crying so loud, she told me to say I fell. She then dressed me and took me out to a Chinese restaurant. I ate like there was no tomorrow, as I did not know when my next good meal would come. I especially remembered the pineapple pie I ate for desert. It was so good that, for a brief moment, the horror of the pain and burning was put aside.

Another horrific incident followed a few months later. It was a sunny, warm afternoon, and I wanted to go outside and play. Matilde wanted me to do something else. Even though I was only five, I had chores to do around the room, but I had different ideas. I could hear children playing outside, and Matilde was home and awake, so I wanted to go outside. Matilde got very angry with me and started screaming.

I screamed back, "You could not be my mother. You do not love me."

I ran to the open door. Matilde was furious and in a rage. I stood there with my right hand partly inside the hinged side of the doorway, which she could clearly see. To hurt me, she slammed the door on my finger and then yanked the door open so I could get my finger out. I screamed as if I were being killed. A neighbor heard my screams and rushed over, took me in his arms, grabbed my finger, and kept it in place. All I can remember after that is the excruciating pain and the horror of seeing half of my finger hanging by the skin. I passed out.

When I came to, my finger was bandaged, and every time the bandage needed to be changed, the neighbor was the one who did it. It is a miracle my finger did not become infected. By the grace of God, although it healed crookedly, I did not lose my finger. Even now, every time I see my crooked finger, it takes me back to that terrible place and time. The neighbor who took care of me told Matilde that if she did not treat me better, he was going to call the police. After that, every time Matilde hit me, I would scream loudly so the neighbor would hear me. I also began to answer her back.

Matilde tried to be nice to me again. She told me that if anyone ever asked me what happened to say it was an accident, but I knew it was not an accident. Matilde was screaming in rage and had purposely slammed the door closed on me. In any case, with her having shown me she could easily hurt me, what choice did I have but to do what she said?

At these times, I would eat well and I would be treated better for a while, but it never lasted long. It is a miracle I am alive today. This woman could have killed me, and no one would have known or cared.

Just as this incident happened, a circus came to town. The circus had a well-known fortune-teller. To make up for slamming the door on my finger, Matilde made plans to take me to the circus and for her to see the fortune-teller. I was filled with joy and expectation.

At last, the time came to go to the circus, and I enjoyed the show tremendously. After the show, Matilde made an appointment to see the fortune-teller. While she was waiting for her appointment, the animal trainer from the circus took me around to see all the animals—lions, tigers, monkeys, elephants, and camels. It was quite a special treat for me to see these animals up close.

Just as I got back, Matilde's turn came to see the fortune-teller, and I went in with her. As she left, the fortune-teller asked Matilde to think as much as she could of Pablo before she fell asleep that night and during the next day. He asked her to come back the next evening and bring a picture of Pablo.

The following evening, as planned, we went back to the fortune-teller. He looked at Pablo's picture and told Matilde the reason she did not hear from him was that he was out of work and living with a dancer in Chicago.

He advised her to go home and do certain things. He said at the end of two months, she would receive a letter from Pablo with money, and in three months, he would be coming to see her. I have to admit things happened exactly as the fortune-teller said. The letter did arrive with money. Pablo did come to Mexicali within the three months, even if only for a short time. He also admitted to Matilde that he was living with a dancer in Chicago. After he left, he continued to send money for several months. Because he just came and went, I thought he was just another one of Matilde's male friends. I did not think of him as the man who Matilde kept writing to and from whom she got money, and I didn't think of him as my father.

I thought to myself, *I don't look at all like him. How could he be my father?*

In addition to fortune-telling, Matilde believed in spiritualism. Whenever she didn't feel well, she would take me with her to see the *curanderos* (healers). The curanderos, both men and women, were always dressed in white. They shook sprigs of herbs over her body, spoke in tongues, and prayed for her. I would look at them and listen to their chanting and wonder why they were doing all of this to Matilde. She did not seem to change in any way. I could not understand the purpose of all these rituals. The only good thing was that I was not tied to my crib and left alone in the dark. I would behave well so I would be taken the next time. This was better for me and certainly more entertaining. In any case, these people were nice to me while Matilde was receiving her "cure."

Sometimes, when Matilde left me with other people, she gave them permission to punish me as they saw fit. Some did hit me, but thankfully most treated me well.

We used kerosene lamps for light, carried water from the well, and used a thunder pot for a toilet. We didn't have electricity or a refrigerator. Though these were inconveniences we lived with every day, some pleasant memories came from them, for instance, when the iceman came. An iceman used to bring ice for the icebox to keep our food cool. The truck was loaded with large blocks of ice, and the iceman used a pick to cut off smaller blocks for each customer. Chips of ice were prizes for the children who crowded around the truck. The iceman would even chip off small pieces just for me. I especially loved standing under the cool water that constantly ran off the bed of the truck. I let the water run down my heat rash-covered body and savored the soothing coolness. I cherished the special pieces of ice, the cooling water, and most of all, the iceman's acts of kindness.

As the ice truck would start forward to the next stop, I would hang on to the back to catch a ride. In the stifling heat, the dripping water felt heavenly. The iceman would sometimes stop and tell me how dangerous this was and to get off the truck. I would stubbornly get back on just as he would start out again. I don't remember his warnings ever being very effective.

One of my last fond memories of Mexicali happened when neighbors invited me to go with them to witness Mexicali's long tradition of celebrating with an annual bonfire. I believe this was in the fall of the year. In a desert-like area on the outskirts of town, they created a huge pile of wood and set it on fire at night. They also made a scarecrow-like figure to throw onto the fire. Just looking at the roaring flames with streams of blowing cinders against the starry blue sky was magical. After the fire died down, the children played, and the adults had a party.

Mexico City

Nineteen forty-five brought more big changes. Now that Pablo was steadily sending money, Matilde saw this as the perfect time to move. The neighbors were on to her for her poor treatment of me, so the move was imminent. She started selling off her things and made plans to leave Mexicali for Mexico City. However, before going on to Mexico City, we went by bus to stay for a while at her father's home in Tijuana.

When we arrived, Matilde's first cousin, Celina, greeted us coolly. Celina really didn't want us there for a number of reasons. Matilde and Celina did not see eye-to-eye on anything. Matilde wanted to assert herself as her father's daughter, and at the same time, Celina saw herself as the lady of the house. All of this created a lot of tension, with Matilde's father in the middle.

To add to the tension, I had fairer skin and lighter hair compared to Celina's children, so I received many compliments. This made Celina quite jealous, which became a problem for me. One time Celina took her children and me out to the theater. As we left the theater, we came across an *elote* (boiled ears of corn) vendor, and Celina decided to buy ears of corn to eat at home. The vendor put the hot, buttered ears into a paper sack. Celina could have given the sack to her older daughter or her chauffeur but instead she gave the sack to me to carry in my arms. By the time we got home, my dress was a mess, while her children's clothes remained nice and clean. This seemed to relieve some of her jealousy toward me.

After a short, tumultuous stay, Matilde told me we were going to leave Tijuana to see her grandmother in Mexico City. She said I would like it there. One place or another meant very little to me. What mattered was how I would be treated and cared for. What I did not know was that this would be a very long trip. Most of the trip was by train, with some parts by bus, and included overnight stays here and there. I remember the vendors at the different train stations selling sweet breads, tamales, *atole* (a drink made from corn), *tortas* (sandwiches on crispy-crusted rolls), and all manner of fruits and drinks. Any time I ate was a happy occasion as I was always hungry. I can still remember the tastes and smells of different fruits and foods, especially the *platanos ahumados* (smoked plantains), *platanos asados* (roasted plantains), *camotes de Puebla* (candied sweet potatoes, the white ones or the pink ones), *Cajeta de Celaya* (milk candy from Celaya, a city in Mexico), *dulce de membrillo* (candied quince)—I could go on and on. Matilde wanted me to behave well on the train, so she would buy me things at every stop. I remember, right out of Mexicali, eating delicious peaches. They were so big I could hardly hold one with my two little hands.

At last, early one morning, we arrived in Mexico City. It must have been early springtime, because it was still a very cool and cloudy day. We took a taxi to Matilde's grandmother's apartment. I remember how uncomfortable I felt in the unfamiliarity of the big city, with busy traffic and the crowds going everywhere, like ants.

Matilde's grandmother lived on the third floor of an apartment building. To avoid disturbing her, I spent almost all my time playing alone on the stairs outside the apartment. Matilde warned me that if I went anywhere else, I would get a beating. The carpet on the stairways had a musty smell, and the area was very dark, damp, and cold. All I remember is the dank, humid smell and the darkness of those stairs. I felt so lonely that I often just sat there and cried. For me, this was worse than before.

Matilde's grandmother lived with her son and other granddaughter, Minerva. There was a rumor that the son was committing incest with his own daughter, Minerva. I remember Minerva as being a very pretty woman. Matilde's grandmother's other granddaughter, Celina (whom we had just left in Tijuana), was having children with her own uncle. Matilde told me her grandmother was sick at heart for what was happening in the family.

I was unsure if Matilde's grandmother knew about Matilde's way of life. In any case, Matilde tried to appear to be a perfectly respectable, married woman when she was around her grandmother. Our days there were numbered; we could not stay for long. Matilde was used to staying out all night, coming and going as she pleased. In Mexicali, all she had to do was tie me to my crib and she was gone. Here, not only couldn't she go out as she pleased, but she couldn't leave me alone with this sick and grim-faced woman.

Matilde's grandmother always had an aloof expression, almost as if she were angry. She did not like to be called Mexican. She was part French and she liked for you to know it. She was always very well dressed and had an air of superiority about her, or least she liked to think she was superior. Matilde had great respect and fear of her and was always on her best behavior when she was around her. This was good for me, because I was not cursed at or hit as much while we were there.

Matilde quickly grew tired of living in her grandmother's apartment. She felt too restrained and wanted to go back to her old way of life. Matilde was a very heavy woman and it was hard for her to go up and down the three flights of stairs and, more urgently, she was running out of money. All of these reasons led to Matilde's decision to move on. We said our good-byes, and we were on our way to Veracruz.

Veracruz

The move to Veracruz started another nightmare of my childhood. Matilde seemed to know many people in Veracruz and often left me with them. In the first few weeks, while she was visiting all of her friends and they were feeding us, things were okay. However, when the money ran out and there was no letter or money from Pablo, Matilde had to go to work. She moved us into a hotel where she could go about her business.

Whenever she had male friends, I was put out in the hall and told to be quiet. I remember one time especially well: it was morning, and I was playing in the hall when the door across the way opened suddenly, and the delicious aroma of hot milk came toward me. A young lady called to me and asked me to come into her room. I gladly went, as I was getting bored waiting outside in the halls trying to be quiet. I was often told to be quiet or else I would get a beating, especially if the hotel owner complained. I was five years old at this time.

I looked around the lady's room where, in one of the corners, she had a big blue enameled pot of milk boiling on a hot plate. She asked me if I was hungry. Of course, I was always hungry in those days—hungry for food, for kindness, and for attention. She used a ladle to pour me a big cup of hot milk from the pot. As she handed me the cup, she asked me to wait. Then she added several tablespoons of coffee grounds to the boiling milk in the big pot to make café con leche. She stirred it, covered it, and removed it from the hot plate.

As I was waiting for the milk to cool, I looked all around the neatly organized room. Her clothes hung behind a drape in one corner. The kitchen area was in another corner, and to one side was a bowl and pitcher set, a radio on a stand, and her bed. All was very neat and orderly, which gave me a good feeling—very unlike the chaos of Matilde's room. Matilde's room looked temporary, like my whole life looked. I had a sense that this lady had been there for some time.

After a while, the lady took a spoonful of the café con leche from the pot and added it to my cup. She put in some sugar, and there I had my first cup of café con leche. To this day, this is the way I prefer my coffee. She also gave me a sweet roll. I have never forgotten that breakfast, and I will remember the kindness of this lady of the night for as long as I live. I had found a new friend, but as my life went in those times, this did not last long.

Mr. Rivera

Early one warm, balmy evening I was walking a few paces behind Matilde, and a man named Vicente Rivera, along Veracruz's famous seaside promenade, the Malecon. I heard Mr. Rivera tell Matilde that her way of life was not good for me—I needed to have a home and a family and to be in school. He told Matilde that he would like to take me back to Brooklyn to be raised with his three children. He said he had already discussed this with his wife, and she was willing to take me into their home to be brought up in their family.

Mr. and Mrs. Rivera were Puerto Ricans, and Mr. Rivera knew Pablo from Puerto Rico. They had lived near each other in Brooklyn and had worked together as merchant seamen.

While they were talking, Matilde answered in English so I would not understand what she was saying. Matilde was able to speak English because she had lived in the United States as a child.

After they finished talking, Mr. Rivera asked me, "Would you like to live with my family in the United States?"

Without any hesitation, I answered, "Yes!"

Mr. Rivera had observed our way of life on several trips when his ship came to Veracruz. He saw that there was no future for me and feared for what would become of me living with Matilde.

He gave me some money to get an ice cream, and as I walked away, I kept looking back. They continued talking, and I saw Mr. Rivera hand Matilde some money. When I got back, Mr. Rivera was about to leave. He explained to me that he would see me on his next trip and I would be going back with him to the place where I was born. He told me I would be in school, have two girls near my age to play with at home, and I would make many friends.

He asked me, "Would you like that?" It was like asking a flower if it needed the sun and the rain to live. I was elated, full of expectations, and could not wait for his return.

That day on the promenade, I was filled with hope and expectations for the future. However, a few weeks later my hope turned into sadness and hopelessness. Matilde got a letter from Mrs. Rivera telling her that Mr. Rivera had had a massive heart attack and died. When she told me this, I was devastated. This was an almost unbearable disappointment.

Not only did I have to cope with this huge disappointment but also, just at that time, the hotel owner's complaints increased. He told Matilde that he did not like it when she put me out in the hall, and if she did not provide a better life for me, he would see that I would be taken away from her. This was definitely something she did not want, not because she loved me, but because I was useful to her.

For example, Matilde used to proposition men by telling them she needed money to feed me. It was also a way for her to keep asking Pablo for money. In actuality, I received very little benefit from the money because Matilde spent it on makeup, new colorful satin dresses, costume jewelry, shoes, and other things for herself.

The complaints from the hotel owner finally pressured Matilde to make another move. She went to work in a large white house on the outskirts of Veracruz. The front of the house had a sitting room with lots of tables and chairs, a bar and a jukebox at one end, and a dance floor at the other end. In the back of the house were many rooms. The house was isolated with no other houses nearby. In a way, this was good for me—now I had room to roam.

The other ladies in the house let their maternal instincts pour out on me. They showered me with attention, care, and love—just what I craved. In this time and place, I was a very happy child. I wished that my stay here would never end.

One day, just after we got to the house, some of the ladies took me to a *charriada* (a large fiesta or fair). On a long dirt road, lined with green trees on each side, there were horse races. In other places, there were cockfights with lively betting. It seemed to me like the betting on the horses was mainly done by the *patrones* (the rich and powerful), while the rest were betting on the cockfights. There were mariachis playing and singing lively music in many places, and fireworks were set off here and there.

One memorable attraction was especially fearsome, as well as exciting. Several men ran here and there through the crowd, scaring everyone with huge contraptions decorated to look like animals. These were very elaborate constructions with wooden handles on each side. One man would get inside the head of the animal, put the entire contraption over his shoulders, and manipulate the handles this way and that while chasing its prey, especially children. Sparkling and popping fireworks were attached to the heads to add to the excitement.

Decorations made from long strings with colorful paper shapes attached were put up all over town. These colorful decorations were suspended above the areas where crowds assembled. When the races finished, the music and dancing started. The *campesinos* (farmers) came from the countryside dressed in their best traditional attire; the men all dressed in white and the women dressed in colorful dresses, which added to the festive atmosphere. Everyone seemed to be having a good time, and I was surrounded by the excitement and gaiety.

Another memory of this time occurred when they took me to the river where the laundry ladies were washing the clothes and bedding for the house. They rubbed soap bars against the wet clothes and then rubbed the clothing against a stone to loosen the soil. Others hit the clothing with a wooden paddle. Still others twisted, then doubled larger pieces, and swung them overhead in circles, striking them directly onto large, flat stones at each swing. The clothing was then rinsed by dunking it up and down in the river. After rinsing, they twisted the clothing to wring out the water. Finally, they would shake and place the cleaned clothing on rocks or bushes to dry. All different colors of clothing lay drying in the sun, like a rainbow. During these times at the river, many of the women sang popular songs. This was a very memorable scene, filled with color, motion, and sound.

In the mornings, as almost all the people in the house would be asleep, I was left alone to amuse myself. When the women woke up, they would ritually drink lemon juice, which they told me would help to fight infections. They were very kind and very affectionate toward me. My feet hardly touched the ground because they were always carrying me and hugging me. I received more attention from them than I ever had before.

In the evenings, at my bedtime, the women went to the front parlor where I could hear music and laughter. One evening, I was abruptly awakened from a deep sleep by the loud sounds of drunken people screaming, arguing, and breaking glass against the cement floor. I was so frightened that I held onto my pillow for dear life. I cried and shook in fear. Eventually, sleep overtook me, but my fear and disgust for drunken people has never left me to this day.

It became increasingly difficult for Matilde to keep me with her. She started going all over Veracruz trying to find a place to put me. I was five or six years old.

Asilo Veracruzano

Someone told Matilde about Asilo Veracruzano, an orphanage in Veracruz. I don't know how she lied my way in, because to be admitted I had to be an orphan. How could I be an orphan if she claimed to be my mother? Later in life, I received some papers from Asilo Veracruzano and discovered that she had changed my name.

On the day she took me to Asilo Veracruzano, the Mother Superior, Mother Virgo, told me that there were other children to play with and that I would like it there. Matilde patted me on the shoulder and told me she would come and see me. Mother Superior took me by the hand, and we turned away. As bad as Matilde's abusive behavior had been, at that instant I had a pang of anxiety. Then, and just as quickly, as Mother Superior and I were walking down the hallway, a kind of warm feeling came over me, and the fear went away. Instinctively, I knew this would be better for me. I also realized that, as good as this seemed to be, it just might not last long.

At bedtime on that first night, when the nuns turned the lights out, I was told we all had to be quiet and go to sleep. Just as I lay down, I was startled by very strange, loud, and frightening croaking sounds, coming from just outside the window. I was terrified. The other girls assured me these were just sounds from the frogs that lived in the narrow pond below the window. They told me the frogs were just playing and not to be afraid. It took me a while to get used to these strange sounds and this new place.

Shortly after I entered the orphanage, I began to be more hopeful. First, some of my basic needs were being met. I was eating three meals a day at set times, went to bed at a set time, and went to Mass at set times. I was with other children, and an older girl was assigned to look after me. For the first time since I could remember, I was living a life with some order.

My life at Asilo Veracruzano also had its sad moments. Every Sunday, many of the other children had relatives or friends who came to visit and bring presents to them. I had no one, and just sat and watched as the others showed off all the things they had gotten. As I sat there, I looked at the big iron gates and prayed that someone would come to see me and bring me candies and fruit too. Sadly, no one ever came.

We all slept in a long room with lines of beds and cots on each side. Because I still wet my bed, I slept on a cot. The nuns came to wake us very early in the morning and if they saw a wet spot under my cot, they would get me out of bed and push me into a cold shower. The shock of the cold water was terrifying.

To maintain strict order, the nuns each carried a ruler they held behind their backs as they walked about. They maintained an eagle-eyed watch over us. For minor outbursts, they would whack our heads or hands. If I talked out when I was not supposed to, they made me kneel for a long time in the corner of a room. Sometimes my knees were directly on the rough, unfinished cement floor. Other times, to make it even more painful, they spread grains of hard corn on the floor. To add still more to the punishment, they sometimes made me hold a heavy book in each hand with my arms outstretched. They ordered me to keep my arms up and stay still until they told me otherwise. As harsh as these punishments seemed, my life there was far better than with Matilde's cruelties.

It was in the orphanage where I discovered that singing and dancing made my world less painful. We had recreation time where we all played together. Almost all the girls my age already knew traditional Mexican children's songs and dances, which I soon learned from them. I learned songs like *Doña Blanca, La Pajara Pinta, ¡Que Llueva!, Naranja Dulce, A La Vibora de la Mar*, and others. Singing made my world seem normal.

We wore gray and white uniforms most of the time, but, on occasion, we could wear whatever other clothes we had. Wealthier ladies often brought donations of clothes that their families had outgrown. These would then be distributed to the children. I particularly remember getting a beautiful blue organdy dress. When the nuns gave the dress to me, I felt that my eyes had never seen anything so beautiful. I adored that dress.

In addition to clothing, local businessmen donated food they couldn't sell or that would otherwise have gone to waste. We always had lots of *frijoles* (beans) and *habas* (broad beans). The nuns had so many ways of cooking *habas,* and I got so tired of them, that to this day I cannot eat them.

Our bread was baked at the Asilo. I clearly remember the nun who did the baking—she was the shortest of the nuns, and her hair was always pulled back in a bun. I can close my eyes and see her now—always happy, humming a song as she was kneading the bread. I remember her putting the bread into an enormous oven using a long-handled wooden paddle. Every day I would make it a point to pass by the bakery. I looked forward to the smell of the bread, the glow of the oven, and the joy she expressed in what she was doing.

Each day we got one round, sweet bread, like a hamburger bun, and one bigger flat, salt bread, like pita bread. I often tried to exchange my big salt bread with other girls for their sweet breads; sometimes I succeeded. I would pick at the crust of the sweet bread to make it last longer. Then, little by little, I would eat the rest. I still do this today; the only difference is now I can eat as much crust as I want without having to eat the soft inside.

Sometimes, the priests who visited the orphanage to say Mass would stay for lunch. When the nuns learned that they would have lunch guests, they got busy. The kitchen exuded delicious aromas, but we only got to smell, never taste, this food.

The nuns boiled our milk in large pots and set them to cool on platforms made from old steel roof sheeting. I used to love eating the skim that formed on the surface of the cooling milk. When no one was looking, I would sneak up, put my finger in, and pull the skim off. I learned to time this operation carefully, so the milk remained warm enough to form a new skin again, thus covering up my larceny. One time I was almost caught. I heard the nun coming and raced away, catching my thigh on a sharp corner of the roofing metal. The nun, seeing my bleeding cut, asked me what I was doing.

I thought quickly, answering, "I was chasing a cat that was into the milk." I still have the scar as a reminder.

Fibs like this only worked for a time because the nuns and the older girls used to tell me fearful things. The nuns introduced me to the concepts of hell and purgatory. The older girls told me that if I lied or didn't behave, monsters, witches, and the boogeyman would get me at night. There were rumors among the older girls about children and babies being buried in the land at the rear of the orphanage. I imagined that I might join those already buried there. These and other threatening stories intensified my fear of the dark. I was in fear overload at six years old with no one to help me deal with this added burden. My only help was my continuous prayers to my guardian angel for protection.

I remember my first Christmas in the orphanage. The nuns and some of the children put on a beautiful play. I played the part of an Indian girl with a basket, asking people if they wanted to buy fruit. I had to speak like the Mexican Indians. After our religious service, we had the play, and after the play, we were given see-through bags full of colorful candies. That night, when I went to bed, I put my bag of candies under my pillow. During the night, the bag moved down my back, and early that next morning I found I had wet all over the bag and the candies. The middle of my cot was a rainbow of colors. Sadly, I didn't get any of the pleasure of eating the candy. I was very upset; the candies had been so pretty, and I wanted to preserve and savor them as I did with the sweet bread. Not only were the candies ruined, but I was also forced into a cold shower as punishment for wetting the bed.

The second Christmas at the Asilo I was again in a play. I played one of the three wise men. I was the one who brought the box of gold to the baby Jesus. I still remember how the elastic of the beard hurt my face, but I endured the pain for the enjoyment of playing the king.

The Asilo had a school, but I didn't learn much. I was still quite traumatized by my life with Matilde. We focused mainly on the first communion catechism, not on reading, writing, and arithmetic.

When I was about seven, I did receive my first communion. I was dressed in a pretty, white dress and veil and carried a missal and a rosary in my hands. The Mother Superior, Mother Virgo was my godmother for the event. After we came from church, we had hot chocolate and egg bread. Boy, was it good! After celebrating, the nuns took back our white dresses, missals, and rosaries, and we went on about our daily lives. At least I looked beautiful for a few hours. In my world, one learned early on to appreciate and never forget moments like that—they were too few and far between. I reasoned, *So what if I would never see the pretty dress, missal, or rosary again? They will remain in my memory forever.*

In God, I found hope for my unknown future. When things went bad for me, I would find a quiet place outside, look at the evening star, and pray with all my being. After my prayer, I would feel stronger to face whatever was in store for me. Because of this inner spiritual strength, I was better able to face pain and loneliness later in life. Even today, in my most trying moments, I look up to the same evening star, which has always felt like a guiding light, and pray.

The older girls looked after the younger ones. The girl who looked after me would take me with her when she went to knit and embroider with a group of girls her age. Late one afternoon, while they were working, I picked up pieces of yarn they had discarded and knotted the pieces together. Then, I found two big bobby pins, opened them to form two needles, each about six inches long, and tried to knit. The older girl, on seeing me struggle, showed me how. Using the knotted yarn and bobby pin needles, I was able to knit a little multicolored purse with a flap.

The finished artwork was displayed in a show at the end of the school year. The show was open to the public. Guests and relatives who came to the show bought the artwork on display. There were prizes to the best, second best, third best, and most original. I won the prize for most original with my little purse—I was in seventh heaven. They displayed my little multicolored purse with the two bobby pins stuck into it. I can't remember what I won, but I still remember the wonderful feeling I had when I saw my little purse among all the other beautiful works of the older girls.

When I was left at the orphanage, Matilde was supposed to send whatever money she could. However, time went by and no one had heard from her or knew where she was. One time I got very sick and they could not locate her. She had apparently moved to another town.

I had a very high temperature, and they couldn't seem to bring it down for some time. Eventually, I did get better.

After two years in the orphanage, and not hearing from Matilde, Mother Virgo started looking for someone to adopt me. She had found a well-to-do family in Mexico City and had started arranging for the papers. Mother Superior told me of her plans for finding a loving home for me. I was filled with hope for a new life. I wanted desperately to go to school, to have a home, and to be like other children. These things would have meant the world to me. I longed for a life, free of Matilde, where I would not be left alone, locked up, tied to my bed, or chained to a tree.

Just at that time, however, Mother Virgo received a letter from Matilde, saying she had saved money and was coming to get me. I think she also sent some money in the letter. A short time later, guess who appeared out of the blue—Matilde! Mother Virgo told Matilde that there was a family in Mexico City who wanted to adopt me. She told Matilde she should give me up; it would be better for me. The family could provide for me, and I would want for nothing.

Matilde had other plans. She didn't want to let me go, probably because she wanted someone to care for her in her old age. This was an old custom of the time in Mexico. She told Mother Virgo she was taking me out of the orphanage and would be able to care for me because she was going to open a small business selling candy, peanuts, gum, and fruits. She also said that Pablo had sent her money and had promised to send money each month. History repeats itself; once again, my dreams were destroyed.

Return to Chaos

With the money Pablo sent, Matilde rented a single, dirt-floor room, near the corner of Peru and Circunvalación. During the time Matilde was busy organizing things, I got a few minutes to be by myself. Across the street, there were trees with large, strong hanging vines. Matilde had just taken me to see one of the Tarzan movies that were quite popular at the time. I got the idea to pretend that I was Tarzan, swinging on those vines. I would climb up a tree, grab a vine, and yell like Tarzan as I swung. At the end of the swing, I would be a long way off the ground. It was a miracle that I didn't fall or hit another tree. In any case, I had some moments of fun and excitement during those few days, and even survived it all.

Here begins yet another painful period of my childhood. Matilde got an idea to use some of the remaining money Pablo had sent for my care to buy traditional Mexican candies like *dulces de calabasa* (candied pumpkin), *dulces de camote* (candied sweet potato), *dulces de leche* (milk candy), *dulces de coco* (coconut candy), Chiclets gum, and bags of warm roasted *cacahuates* (peanuts). She put these in a big basket on a wooden stand at the entrance of the railway station. I sat nearby or walked around looking at all the people coming and going. I remember wishing I could go with them, I was seven years old.

Often there were soldiers and old men around the train station who, like me, had nothing better to do than sit around, watching the trains come and go. One time I witnessed a tragic event directly in front of me. A young man, clearly and knowingly, walked right in front of an oncoming train. His body was torn into pieces and strewn all over the tracks. It was not an accident.

In that terrible instant, I was overcome by a wrenching feeling from the trauma and shock of the gruesome sight. Almost uncontrollably, the thoughts flashed into my mind, "He's in heaven. He's in heaven." Then I heard someone say, "He's at peace; no more suffering, no more pain." I suddenly realized that a person could choose to live or die.

Horrified, I rushed to the entrance of the railroad station where I found Matilde sitting calmly behind the huge basket. She already knew about the incident. Most certainly, she knew I needed desperately to find comfort and to ease the terror of the frightful incident I had just witnessed. Instead, Matilde took full advantage of the situation. She simply dismissed my needs by coldly and insensitively warning me, "That can happen to you if you don't behave!" During all of the time I was with her, Matilde never showed me any true affection or tenderness.

I had horrific nightmares of that incident for the longest time. The scene was seared in my mind forever. I had just been taken out of the orphanage and had no one, especially not Matilde, to help me deal with any of this.

There was a café in the train station run by a man and his wife. They had two girls who came to the cafe each day after school. They wore their blue and white school uniforms and came to do their homework. I looked on longingly, wishing I could be like them.

Their father, seeing me walking by myself around the tracks, was afraid I would fall into the path of a train. He became especially concerned after the tragic accident. He made his concerns known to Matilde. After he left, she gave me a beating and told me to sit by her all day. She angrily added, "You are good-for-nothing, always causing problems."

Well, the nobility of Matilde's new life soon got old, so she decided I had to help. She gave me two big one-gallon tin cans, with wires for handles, and sent me to the cargo port to get leftover food that the foreign ships gave away after meals. The port was a few blocks from the train station, and I walked there every day for food. Whenever the cooks would see me coming, they would make sure to give me food first. This is when I first tasted tapioca pudding. I thought it was made in heaven—I still wonder if it was that good or if I was just that hungry. This was 1948.

During this time, a salesman was living with Matilde. Whenever I brought the food, she would take the best of the food for her and her man; I got their leftovers. Looking at my situation from a child's point of view, I quickly figured out a way to take care of the problem. I simply ate whatever I wanted before I handed the food over to Matilde and her man. At a very early age, I knew I had to take care of myself, because this woman only thought of herself. Instead of her taking care of me, I was taking care of her. This became very evident when the café owner and his wife started to be nice and offered to help me. Matilde, fearing to lose control of me, closed up shop at the railroad station, got me a small basket, and sent me to an area called *los Portales* (the porticos).

I was sent out each day to sell little brown bags of peanuts for ten centavos a bag. I also sold little packages of Adams Gum, but I can't recall the price. Matilde told me that if I wanted to eat, I had to sell all the bags of peanuts that day because they would not be fresh the next day. If I didn't sell out, I would get a beating. Sometimes I would be out all day trying to sell all of the peanuts. Because of Matilde's size and strength, I was black and blue for days after she beat me. She was very careful not to hit where it would show, so she hit me a lot on my head, bottom, and back.

This area was called los Portales because there were large buildings on two sides of the *Zocalo* (main square) of Veracruz, each with *portales* (porticos). The large arches faced the street and there were wide sidewalks inside with lots of nice restaurants, bars, and shops. I think Café Parroquia was the biggest restaurant of them all. The cathedral and a large, beautiful government building were right across the Zocalo from los Portales.

Matilde allowed me only one peso a day from my sales to buy food. When I finally sold all of the peanuts, I would go to a *fonda* (a small food stand) and buy *sopa de fideos* (a soup made with vermicelli pasta). The *sopa de fideos* was very filling for the price; I could get four bowls for one peso. This would be my only meal that day. I learned very early to be resourceful with my meager allowance.

My meals were very irregular. I never knew when I would be able to eat, no matter how hungry I became. I remember telling Matilde that I was not feeling well one day. She said it was only an excuse because I did not want to go sell peanuts. She called me lazy and good-for-nothing as she forced me out of the room. As she closed the door, she yelled out for me not to come back until I sold all of the peanuts. I did not do very well that day. So, when it got dark, I went behind some bushes and spent the night. I was so sick and so tired that I must have fallen asleep as soon as I hit the ground. The next morning, by the grace of God, I felt better, and I was able to sell almost all of the peanuts. I treated myself to two *huevos estrellados y bollitos* (sunny-side up eggs and a bread roll).

I called attention to myself because of my blond hair, light brown eyes, and fair skin. People, especially tourists, often asked me about my mother and father. Many of them took me for a Spaniard. Some of the Americans would give me money, even if they did not buy anything. Thanks to their generosity, I did not always go hungry. In addition, some of the waiters used to give me more food than I could afford with my meager allowance.

One of the pleasant memories of this time was listening to music; especially a song that was very popular—*Begin the Beguine.* It seemed every tourist played this song in the jukebox. In addition, there were musicians at many of the restaurants playing the traditional music of Veracruz. Some groups with large instruments like harps and marimbas stayed in one place, while others with guitars strolled about. Music was very much a part of the Portales area of Veracruz.

When I went to sell at los Portales, I had to take a bus. Many times, I would leave for home very late at night, so tired I would fall asleep on the bus. Thank God, the driver would see how tired I was and would wake me up so I could get off at the right stop. As tired as I was, I still had to cross a two-way road without streetlights. It is a wonder I was not run over by a car. It is a miracle I am alive today. This way of life went on for about a year.

Gabriela Mistral

I met Gabriela Mistral in 1948 at the Café Parroquia. When I first came to her table, she immediately took an interest in me and asked if I wanted something to eat or drink. She took my basket and sat it in another chair, and then she sat me next to her.

She started our conversation asking, "Why are you not in school?"

I answered, "Because Matilde does not send me to school."

She continued, "Do you know how to read and write?"

I answered, "No."

She asked me, "Would you like to learn?"

I answered her strongly, "Yes!"

She asked, "Where is your mother?"

For the first time, I felt I was talking with someone I could trust. I said, "The woman I live with, who is married to a man named Pablo, claims to be my mother. I know she could not be my mother because of the way she treats me. Also, I don't look at all like her or any of her family."

Then she responded, "Maybe you look like Pablo."

I answered, "No, I don't look like him either."

She asked me, "When did you last see Pablo?"

I told her, "I have only seen a picture of him. He is a dark Puerto Rican man."

I think what I had to say sparked Gabriela Mistral's curiosity. I thanked her for the yogurt and fruit.and told her I had to try to sell the bags of peanuts or else I would be in a lot of trouble. She asked me what kind of trouble I was talking about, so I explained to her how I had to sell all of the bags of peanuts in order to receive my allowance to eat, and how I would be beaten if I failed. Because I trusted her, I tried to answer all of her questions as well as I could and with no fear of what Matilde would do to me. Matilde had told me that if anyone asked about my mother, I was to say she was sick at home.

As I picked up the basket to go, Gabriela Mistral told me that she would be there at the same time at the same table the next day if I wanted to join her. I told her I would like very much to join her. As I was leaving, she bought some of the bags of peanuts. After that first meeting, she would buy all of the peanuts so I could visit with her freely.

As I was walking away, I felt that this lady, whoever she was, wanted to help me. Here began another ray of hope. As long as I had hope, I had all I needed to endure the suffering.

I later discovered that Gabriela Mistral was awarded the Nobel Prize for Literature on November 15, 1945. She was the first Latin American woman ever to win the Nobel Prize for Literature. She had become a member of the *Cuerpo Consular* (Consular Body) of the Chilean government in 1932. The Chilean government gave her a type of roving consular post, which allowed her to represent Chile wherever in the world she chose to live. She began her diplomatic missions in Italy and Spain but also worked and lived in Brazil, France, the United States, and Mexico. Of course, I did not know any of this at the time. I didn't even know what a Nobel Prize was or what it meant. However, even though I didn't read or write, I had seen her picture frequently in the local newspapers.

The next day I could not wait to get going—even Matilde noticed it and asked me why I was so eager to go out. I pretended I didn't hear her and just left. For one thing, Gabriela Mistral would buy me something to eat, but more importantly, I had also found someone I could talk to and to whom I could tell all my fears and worries. At first, I did not confide in her completely. I had learned very early in life to distrust everyone. However, Gabriela Mistral knew how to build trust, bit by bit.

As time went on, she asked me all sorts of questions. If she sensed that I was afraid to answer, she would change the subject and talk about something more pleasant. Little by little, I told her all about my life. I told her about Mr. Rivera, who had offered to take me to live with his family in the United States and then died of heart attack before that could happen. I told her about my life in the orphanage, about all of the things Matilde had done to me, and about her way of life. I don't think Gabriela Mistral believed everything I told her; however, she never made me feel that she didn't believe me.

Meeting Gabriela Mistral at this time in my life was a godsend. I desperately needed someone to give me hope and courage. After that first meeting, I met with her every day. Sometimes I would go to her apartment and she would tell me about New York, Europe, and all the places she had lived around the world. She had a nice collection of beautiful picture books from each place. I was especially interested in New York. I would look longingly at the pictures, wishing I were there.

Often, during our visits, she tried to teach me how to read. She had a small book just for teaching children to read. She took my hand in hers and made my finger point to the letters as she coached me with the sounds. She would put consonants together with vowels, *bah, beh, bee,* and so on, to form small words or sounds in Spanish.

Sometimes during my visits, she would be very busy with visitors or preparing for her upcoming duties. At these times, I would often be with a young lady named Doris Dana, Gabriela Mistral's traveling companion. I sensed Doris Dana was very protective of Gabriela Mistral. However, she did spend time teaching me math. As far as I can remember, this was my first exposure to mathematics and using numbers. Those lessons have remained very helpful to me throughout my life. I also met writers, poets, painters, and intellectuals of the time who visited Gabriela Mistral, although I was too young to appreciate who they were.

During one of our visits, Gabriela Mistral asked me to go for a walk with her. After we had been gone longer than we should have, Doris Dana became worried and came looking for us. When she finally found us, she asked me if I had been unable to find the way back. I explained that I didn't know my right from my left and had no sense of direction. Doris Dana sighed, "Oh my God, this is like asking the blind to lead the blind." Apparently, Gabriela Mistral didn't have any sense of direction either. We had gotten so involved in our conversation that we had lost our way. Between the two of us, we became hopelessly lost.

Gabriela Mistral lived near the beautiful seaside promenade, *el Malecon* (the promenade), and *el Faro* (the lighthouse). When Gabriela Mistral had company, I would amuse myself by looking at the sea, especially Fort San Juan de Ulúa, from her apartment. I used to imagine being on a ship, passing by Fort San Juan de Ulúa, on my way to a better life with Gabriela Mistral.

I also enjoyed the action and people watching on the Malecon. I especially enjoyed watching the handsome navy cadets in their white uniforms as they strolled by. Other things I enjoyed seeing were the small boys who would dive for coins and all the other people who, much like me, were trying to make a living selling things. They sold ice cream, fried or roasted bananas, fresh fruits, popcorn, *tortas*, and coconut water. They also sold a variety of traditional craft objects made from tortoise shells or seashells. All these sights and aromas were a delight, as were the different sounds of the vendors as they advertised their goods.

I also enjoyed watching *los novios* (the sweethearts) who would walk hand-in-hand and once in a while sneak a kiss when the chaperones were not looking. These were happy moments, because I could escape Matilde's world, where I only found abuse.

I loved to hear the sounds of the children at play and whole families enjoying life the way I wished I could. When I saw children with their loving families, I used to wonder how it must feel to be one of those children. I still ask this question. I guess I will never know; that part of my childhood was rubbed out of my life forever. I felt then, as I do now, in situations when others describe their happy childhoods and family experiences, that I know nothing of these experiences. I always feel on the outside looking in.

The place where we lived was a row of rooms with thin wood walls and dirt floors. The cracks in the wooden walls were covered with pages of old calendars or pieces of newspaper. There were three rental rooms in a row, and after that, there was a big room with a cement floor and a big open window with black iron bars. This room was used as an eating and cooking area for doña Josefina's family. The room I shared with Matilde was on the end opposite the big room.

A lot was happening in my life at this time. Unfortunately, I remember one morning particularly well. Matilde had been out all night and was sound asleep in her bed. I lay sleeping on the floor directly across from her. I was awakened abruptly by Matilde's lover, a salesman who had moved in for a while. He was rubbing himself against my side, one hand rubbing my inner thigh. I wanted to scream out, but he covered my mouth so quickly and with such force that I couldn't make a sound; I couldn't breathe. For an instant, I thought I was going to suffocate. Then with his other arm, he grabbed me and forcefully hauled me out of the room. Pain shot through my face as he crushed my mouth with his rough hand. He took me outside so I would not wake Matilde.

When we were outside, he threatened me, "If you tell anybody about this, I will deny it. You know Matilde will not believe you. She will side with me and ask me to give you a hard beating for accusing me."

I knew this would be the case, so I did not tell anyone. In the past, Matilde had often asked him to beat me whenever I hadn't sold all of the bags of peanuts that day. He had shown pity by not beating me too hard. That morning, I think it was a miracle that I woke up to stop him. Matilde slept soundly the entire time. Even today, the anger and the fear overtake me when I think of all the dangers I was constantly exposed to.

My only salvation was that this creep left the next day. He was a traveling salesman who sold dress materials and undergarments. I prayed every night he would not come back, and at the same time, I lived in fear of whom Matilde was going to bring to our room next.

In spite of these horrific experiences, I always held dear to my dreams and my faith. God was my constant confidant, the only one I could talk to without fear. In light of the low-level values of people I was constantly exposed to, I often wonder how, by the grace of God, I dared to think differently. The values of those around me were like day and night from my own.

At times, when I felt I could go on no more, I would walk alone to the canal near the place we lived. I would sit on the bank, cry my heart out, and look at the sky—especially at the brightest star, the evening star. I wished for the day when I could get away, go back to the United States, and find my family. I put all my hopes on this happening. I lived for this even though I did not know the circumstances of how Matilde took possession of me. There was no doubt in my mind whatsoever that she was not my mother, and the hope of going back to the United States and finding my family is what gave me the strength to carry on.

This was not to say that I did not continue to have my dark moments. Sometimes I found myself thinking that if there were ever a time when I knew for sure I would not find my family, I would just end it all by walking in front of a speeding train. One thing that held me back from quitting on life was that I was taught in the Asilo, as a Catholic, that to take one's own life was a mortal sin and that I would go to hell if I did so. I did not see the sense of exchanging the hell I was living in only to go to another. I reasoned that I knew what hell was like in this life and that the other one could even be worse. In my young mind, I had covered all the bases. For me, every day of living was a test of endurance.

I was almost nine years old and I was beginning to defend myself against Matilde's beatings and verbal abuses. She could be very cruel, constantly cursing and calling me stupid or good-for-nothing. One day a man was visiting her and she was cooking, which was very rare. She knew how much I liked pasta and was cooking macaroni. I was really looking forward to it so I did everything she asked. I cleaned the floor, brought water, washed my clothes, and cleaned the dishes. At last, just as I was finished and savoring the macaroni that was almost ready, Matilde called me to go to the store. I knew it would take a long time as I had to walk there and back. I did not want Matilde to get angry with me, so even though I had hunger pains, I went without protest.

When I got back, the man was gone. I could hardly believe my eyes. Matilde and her man had eaten all the macaroni. All that was left in the *cazuela* (a clay casserole) was the burned macaroni stuck to the bottom. When I asked why she had not saved any for me, she dismissed me, saying, "You can eat what is left. If you are still hungry, eat some tortillas." There are no words to express the anger I felt.

I yelled at her, "You could not be my mother. A mother does not do this to her hungry child."

At that moment, she looked at me and said, "You look just like her." I could see rage welling in her eyes, because she just realized what she had said.

Instantly, I demanded, "Tell me how you got me."

I stood by the open door in case she tried to hit me. She was cursing and fuming with rage. I kept insisting that she tell me the truth, and she called me all sorts of names and told me how ungrateful I was.

Cursing at me, she screamed, "Get out of my sight."

I yelled back, "Tell me about my mother and my background. If you won't tell me for fear you think I won't love you any longer, don't worry, because I have no love for you at all."

This really set her off. Now, in a full rage, she screamed, "I am going to kill you, you ungrateful, no-good so-and-so!"

In a flash, she grabbed something and threw it right at me. I was quick too, thank God. I raised my right arm to protect my face. When I looked at the blood pouring out of my arm and the big knife stuck in it, I passed out.

When I came to, Matilde was holding half of an onion and pressing it to my nose, a home remedy to awaken people to consciousness. Next, I remembered Matilde crying and telling me not to tell anyone what happened because it would be very bad for me and for her. At this moment, I couldn't have cared less what happened to her, but I did care what happened to me.

Just then, doña Josefina, Matilde's landlady, appeared with gauze, disinfectant, and some adhesive tape. Between the two of them, they cleaned and bandaged the wound. When doña Josefina asked how it happened, Matilde quickly said I had been playing with the knife and had accidentally cut myself. Matilde was right there next to me, looking me in the eye. Out of fear, I said nothing. I still have a two-inch-long, quarter-inch-wide scar on my arm—a clear reminder of that terrible incident.

When doña Josefina left our room, Matilde started begging me to forgive her. She promised me that she was going to change and be good to me. It was good to hear but very hard to believe. I did not know what I could do. She had just lied to doña Josefina, who seemed to believe her. In any case, whom could I tell? In my pain, I did not think of Gabriela Mistral. And, if I remember correctly, she was very busy at this time, visiting various schools and colleges with the officials of Veracruz.

Matilde would not let me go out until my arm healed. My injured arm was the one that I used to carry the heavy basket of peanuts and gum. When Matilde told me I would not go to sell peanuts for a while, I was happy and sad at the same time; happy I had some relief from having to sell peanuts and gum, and sad because I would not be able to see Gabriela Mistral. I was also anxious because I had no way of letting her know what had happened. Painfully, I knew I would not see her for a while.

During the time my arm was healing, Matilde was not as mean to me and she did not force me to do housework. She kept her word until my arm was almost healed, and then life returned to what it had been. Looking back, I guess she was doing nothing more than making sure I was well enough to continue to sell peanuts and gum.

When I was finally able to see Gabriela Mistral, she saw my arm and I told her what had happened. She could not believe what she was hearing and asked me if I would like for her to take me with her when she left Veracruz.

I do not have to tell you my answer—it was an emphatic, "Yes!"

At that point, I saw another ray of hope on the horizon. I prayed this would turn out well. I was filled with hope and confidence again. The next time Matilde tried to hit me I held the belt. My defiance made her even angrier. For the first time, she realized I was going to try to defend myself. She cursed me, and I ran from her. She asked doña Josefina to hold me so she could punish me.

After this, whenever I was to get a beating, doña Josefina, or her husband, would hold me so Matilde could hit me in the right places where it would not show. The only thing I could do was to scream loudly so the neighbors in the next housing area would hear me.

One time, when my mouth was not covered and I cried out, the neighbors came and said, "One of these days you are going to kill that child. If you do not stop, I am going to call the police."

Matilde stopped beating me and when they left she said, "See, it's all your fault. You are a no-good, and you are always causing me problems."

Whenever something like this would happen, Matilde would stop beating me and change to another method of abuse, like twisting my ears or pinching my arms.

In the next lot to our left, there were more rooms for rent. Here lived a black couple. The lady told me to come to her room whenever Matilde was trying to hit me. Sometimes she would offer me something to eat. Normally, all she had was boiled white rice. For breakfast, she used to add black coffee to her boiled rice. These people were very, very poor, but they would try to share with me what little they had. I will never forget this lady and her generosity.

There were other kind and generous people; for example, two ladies, a mother and her daughter, who lived next door, and an old man who made his living by making candy in a large copper pot. He made *turrón* (a nut-brittle candy) and some clear candy balls. He always gave me some of the candy and let me have whatever was left in the pot. I knew, when needed, these kind people would help any way they could.

One day, someone, I have always felt it was Gabriela Mistral, called the authorities to question Matilde. However, when the detectives came, she was out. When she returned, doña Josefina told her that two detectives had come looking for her and that they would be back the next day. I was not there, or I could have told them a thing or two. I could have shown them the evidence of the most recent beating. In those days, parents could do just about anything to their children in the name of discipline. In this case, some of the people who wanted to help were scratching for a mere existence for themselves, and I don't think they knew where to go for help for themselves, or for me. In any case, with the knowledge that the police were looking for her, Matilde left the neighborhood and left me to work for doña Josefina. Here starts another period of desolation for me.

I had to work all day, every day, at doña Josephina's place. I had no money for the bus, so I was trapped and could not get away to see Gabriela Mistral. My day at doña Josefina's house started with going to the *tortillaria* (place where tortillas were made and sold), making coffee, setting the table, cleaning the kitchen, and bringing the drinking water in from outside. It was quite a walk from the water faucet to the kitchen, and I had to use two metal buckets to carry the water. I had to fill the *tinaja* (a large clay container for drinking water) about twice a week. I also had to build the fire for cooking, which was done on a *brasero* (charcoal-fired brazier). The *brasero* had three burners, a red tile on top, and wood all around it. It was about two feet wide and three or four feet long. I had to get on a chair to reach the top to put the charcoal in the burners. Then I had to fan the *brasero* until the charcoal glowed red.

During the day, I also made salsa. This was a lengthy process. I ground hot chili peppers, garlic, onions, and tomato with a *tejolote* (pestle) in the *molcajete* (a rough-surfaced, three-legged mortar made from volcanic stone). The juice from the hot peppers stung my fingers intensely. In any case, I had to continue until the salsa was finished.

At night, I would be very tired from the work. On days when I filled the big *tinaja,* my arms would be painfully sore. When I finished with the kitchen, I had to clean the bedroom where all of us slept. Rolando, doña Josephina's son, was two years younger than I was. He slept in a double bed, and doña Josefina and her husband slept in another double bed, while I still slept on the floor, just as I did when I was with Matilde. I folded my bedding every morning and put it under doña Josefina's bed.

It was during this time that I experienced yet another troublesome fear—fear of the outhouse. In Matilde's room, I had been able to use the thunder pot, but now I only had the outhouse. The outhouse was a run-down wooden shack with a door. Inside was a rickety wooden floor on which was built a raised seat with a hole. The very first time I went in, I saw the sea of waste, and the fear grabbed me that I might fall in. I quickly devised methods to avoid using the outhouse. I went behind the outhouse, by a banana tree and a papaya tree, to urinate. Otherwise, I went across the road behind bushes and trees growing in the empty field. Doña Josephina used to remark how delicious the fruit was from the trees by the outhouse. I wondered if my personal irrigation made the fruit taste better.

I also had to feed and care for the two big German shepherd guard dogs, Titan and Tarzan. Whenever I had to go to the store, I took them with me. I would walk between them; I was so short, and they were so big, that they almost came to my shoulders. This must have looked odd to people who would see me with the dogs—they used to call me *la niña con los perros* (the girl with the dogs). When those dogs were with me, no one would bother me. This gave me a sense of security when I had to be out alone. Tarzan and Titan were not cuddly dogs. They respected me, and I respected them. They knew I was the one who fed and cared for them and, in return, they protected me; we had a symbiotic relationship. They were guard dogs, not pets.

Doña Josefina told people that I was her niece, and she told me to say the same if I were asked. The truth was that she treated me very differently than a family member would be treated. Every day began another day of slavery. This was ever so evident when Rolando would get up and eat his big breakfast of fruit, eggs, milk, and bread—as much as he wanted. I, in turn, only had tea with a little milk and two pieces of bread—the cheapest food. When Rolando finished breakfast, he would go on to school, and I would go to work. At other meals, while I worked, I would see him eat whatever he wanted and as much as he wanted, while I had only small portions of whatever they gave me from the leftovers. I only saw them eat the better food—none of it ever touched my mouth. The only thing that changed for me was that I was able to eat at regular times, even though doña Josefina was still rationing my food.

Doña Josefina, like Matilde, believed in superstition, spiritualism, and herbal folk medicine. The superstitions were many. For example, if she saw an owl near the house, she became very agitated because she believed this signified the pending death of an immediate family member or a neighbor. After I came to know this, I would shoot rocks with a slingshot at any owls I saw to chase them away, thus avoiding becoming a victim of her agitation. If she spilled salt, she would sprinkle water on it with her hand, while making the sign of the cross.

One day, while cleaning the bedroom, I innocently put a pair of slippers on her bed. On seeing this, she went into a rage and started cursing and hitting me. I thought she had lost her mind. I dodged away with the broom in my hand, but she started to hit me again. I yelled, "Why are you hitting me? What have I done?"

She screamed, "Don't put shoes or a hat on a bed; this brings bad luck." I was cursed, yelled at, and beaten for not reading her mind. I couldn't avoid her abuse no matter how hard I tried.

Her belief in spiritualism surfaced whenever I would see her crush fresh basil in a big bucket of water. Then, while chanting, she would sprinkle the mixture around the house to drive away the evil spirits. I can remember thinking that she should sprinkle the green mixture on herself, because she was the evil one.

She also frequently used herbal medicine. If she had a toothache, she would chew on cloves; for upset stomach, chamomile tea; cramps, cinnamon. If she had a headache, she would lick basil leaves and paste one of them on each temple. She had an herb for whatever ailed her.

During this year, life and death went hand-in-hand. A young couple who rented the room next to doña Josefina's dining room had an infant who cried a lot. Early one afternoon, I heard painful cries coming from the parents and asked doña Josefina what happened. She said that the couple's only child had just died. Their piercing sobs made me feel so sad.

Toward evening, I followed doña Josefina into their room. The entire scene shocked and startled me. I focused on the small child, dressed in white and lying on his back on a narrow table, which was covered with a white cloth. I could clearly see the child's yellowish skin and protruding stomach. Many tall, lit candles were placed around the child's still body. I believe they may have been homemade, possibly tallow candles. The candles gave off a smell much as I had experienced in the church at the orphanage. There were so many candles, and the flames so high, I was afraid the body would catch on fire. I was frightened by the sight and didn't get close. I had never been to a wake, and the scene was so unexpected and dramatic, that I got out of the room as fast as I could. Even decades later, I can recall the sights, smells, and sounds in that room.

Once outside, I looked at the starry sky and said an *Our Father.* Then I began praying and talking to God. I was desperately trying to deal with all I had just seen and felt. As always, I didn't have anyone around with whom to share any of these thoughts and feelings, or to comfort me. My only comforts at the time were praying and talking to God. After my prayer, I asked God, *Why would You take a child who is so much loved by his parents—why?* Just then, the tragic scene I had witnessed at the train station, not so long before, flashed into my mind. I remembered clearly the bystander's words: "He's at peace, no more suffering."

Life soon returned to normal and our daily routines continued. During the 1940s in Veracruz, we had daily contact with vendors who passed the houses, calling out to advertise their goods or services. Some made daily deliveries of milk, eggs, and bread. Others—like the terra cotta dish man, the knife and scissor sharpener, the gelatin man, the Indians with fruit and vegetables, and the *carbonero* (the charcoal man)—came less often. I particularly remember the gelatin man with his glass case full of custards and colorful squares of gelatin. From every angle, you could see the gelatin dancing from side to side as he approached. I rarely got the gelatin. However, whenever I could afford it, I did buy the custard, which was my favorite. The whole daily scene was often quite colorful.

To add to the color, doña Josephina had about a dozen singing birds in cages. Each day she hung the cages just outside the dining area. I must say, I did enjoy their singing. She also had a big talking parrot that caused me a lot of grief. Sometimes the parrot would call my name, and when I went to see what doña Josephina wanted, she would tell me she hadn't called; it was only the parrot. If I thought it was the parrot, and didn't respond, doña Josephina would become angry that I hadn't answered her call.

One day I remember particularly well. Doña Josephina had left me in the house alone. But, before she left, she asked me to tell the carbonero to leave two sacks of *carbon* (charcoal), which is what we used in the brasero as fuel to do our cooking. The carbonero came later while I was playing, but I hadn't noticed him When he didn't see anyone, he called out to ask if we wanted any charcoal. The parrot, imitating doña Josephina perfectly, said, "No."

When doña Josephina came home and found the carbonero hadn't left any charcoal, I got a beating. She sent word to the carbonero, asking him why he didn't leave any charcoal. The man explained that he had come to the house and called out to ask if we wanted any charcoal. He said she shouted out, "No." At last, she figured out what happened; she knew the parrot imitated her voice. Nevertheless, I still got a beating, not for what I did, but for what the parrot did!

Another time, doña Josefina became angry with me because I did not mop the floor to her liking. She hit me very hard on the head and told me I was not only left with her to work for my room and board, but also in exchange for the rent for the room in which Matilde left a lot of her things. I suddenly realized I was not only supporting myself, but I was also paying Matilde's rent! To add to the injustice, I was always required to refer to this cruel and abusive person as *doña*, a title of high respect in Spanish-speaking society. I did not respect this woman at all.

After weeks of working for doña Josefina, she agreed to allow Rolando and me to go to the movies. Normally, as was the custom in those days, I would have had to stay with Rolando as my chaperone. However, as he wanted to be with his friends, it was easy to make a deal with him to go off on my own and for us to meet up later. Instead of going to the movies, I went straight to Gabriela Mistral's apartment. When I went in, I saw boxes strewn all over the floor. Several women were putting things, mostly books, in the boxes. They were getting rid of what was left in an otherwise empty apartment. As I looked at all of this, I had a sinking feeling in the pit of my stomach. Gabriela Mistral had left, and I wasn't with her. I just stood there watching my hopes and dreams die in front of me, again.

I was fixed to the spot where I was standing when a lady came to me and said, "Oh, you must be Graciela. Gabriela Mistral left this for you."

She handed me what seemed to be the most beautiful doll I had ever seen. However, not even the beautiful doll could diminish the deep despair I was feeling. The lady sensed my deep sadness and tried to console me, putting her arm around my shoulder.

She continued, "I was going to take this doll to you if you did not come here before I closed the apartment. Gabriela Mistral made arrangements with some friends of hers to teach you to read and write and they will talk with doña Josefina to ask her to let you attend the lessons. Gabriela Mistral decided to leave because of her poor health. She and Doris Dana departed only yesterday."

After leaving Gabriela Mistral's apartment, I was filled with feelings of deep loss and despair. Sobbing almost uncontrollably, I somehow made my way to the church right across from the Café Parroquia—the very place where I first met Gabriela Mistral. In the midst of the candlelight and faint scent of incense, I let it all out. The tears and emotions were unstoppable, and I cried my heart out. Finally, when I could cry no more, I started another conversation with God. Still in shock, I somehow made my way back to doña Josefina's house.

When I got back to doña Josefina's, she saw the beautiful doll and right away took it from me. She told me she was going to put it away for me. She always took things away that were given to me, and I never saw them again. Not even this cruel act added anything to the weight of despair I was experiencing. Nothing, but nothing, could compare to the feelings of loss at Gabriela Mistral's departure from my life. This experience made me guarded. From that time on, I could never trust or hope so completely the same way again.

After a while, by the grace of God, I mustered some hope and did go forward again. How the women from Gabriela Mistral's apartment did it, I do not know, but doña Josefina did allow me time off to go to my lessons. I usually went two afternoons a week. I walked about three miles roundtrip, because I did not have money for the bus. I was nine years old and had to get up early each morning and work all day before I could leave, and I had to continue working after I came back. It is difficult now to imagine how much I could have learned. I was always exhausted when I arrived for my lessons. Nevertheless, I went. Nothing was going to stop me.

When I got to my teachers' house, they were always very pleasant to me. When I did well, they would reward me with a big red apple or an orange. Whatever they gave me I would devour before I got home. These lessons only lasted a few weeks and, too soon, I found myself back in the every day drudgery of life with doña Josefina.

Precious Possessions

Early one afternoon, doña Josefina asked me to go to the store. I was walking to her room to get money from her nightstand. Just as I put my foot in the door, I heard Matilde, who had just come back for a visit, talking to doña Josefina's older daughter, Tolla. They were in the adjoining room, and Tolla was asking Matilde for my papers, so they could send me to school. She told Matilde people were asking why I was not in school while Rolando, who was younger, was going to school, and to a private school at that.

So I could hear them better, I quickly and quietly picked up the money and walked a few steps to hide behind the door between the two rooms. This was brave of me; if they had found me eavesdropping, I would have gotten a severe beating.

Matilde told Tolla I was born in Brooklyn, New York, at the Cumberland Hospital, but she could not use that birth certificate because it had some errors. She said she also had two orange visitor passes from the hospital and a baby picture of me taken before she took me out of Brooklyn.

Then she added, "I registered Graciela in Ensenada, Mexico, in 1942. I could send for those papers."

Tolla said, "Send for those papers; we need them."

By this time, I had enough information, and I had to get back to doña Josefina and on to the store. I had to do it in a way so Matilde and Tolla would not notice me leaving. Quiet as a mouse, I tiptoed out of my hiding place.

On my way to the store, all I could think about was how to retrieve the orange cards and the baby picture. Even at this early age, I knew intuitively that it was critical to get possession of them—at any cost. I decided that when Matilde went dancing that weekend I would get into her room and look for the pieces of my past. The only question was, *Where to look?*

The days leading up to the weekend seemed so long. I waited four days. On Friday night, Matilde took about an hour to get ready for the dance. This meant that she would be out all night, perfect for my plans to play detective.

Night came, and after finishing my chores, I told doña Josefina I was going to play with the girl across the way. I went to the end of the row of rooms; the last one was Matilde's room. I went in. I was so nervous that I could hear my heart beating and my hands were sweating. I knew very well that if they caught me, I might not live to tell about it. Between doña Josefina and Matilde, I would have been hurt badly. In any case, nothing was going to stop me.

The first place I decided to look was in a basket Matilde hung from the middle of the ceiling. I put a stool on a chair to reach the basket and free it from the wire hook. I climbed precariously up onto the stool. Just as I freed the basket, the stool started shaking. I felt I was losing my balance and quickly thought to take aim for the bed, instead of falling on the floor, where I would have surely injured myself. My quick thinking landed me safely on the bed, basket in hand.

With the basket firmly clutched in my hands, I carefully got down from the bed and sat on the dirt floor. I sat the basket on my lap and, with a flashlight in one hand, anxiously started to search. My hands were trembling as I went through the papers and photos, one at a time. I did not know how to read or write so all I had to guide me was the orange color of the cards and an image in my mind of a baby who might look like me.

At last, near the bottom of the papers, I got to a square, white envelope. I opened it, and behold, I found two orange cards and a baby picture. The baby picture, with writing along the side, was mounted on the back of a mirror. I felt like my heart stopped for a moment. I wanted to scream for joy, and at the same time, I wanted to cry. I could only cry quietly, so I sobbed. I was holding in my hands some tangible proof of my birthplace. The sad part was I couldn't read what was on the cards, or the photo, or share my joy in finding them.

From that moment on, I became obsessed with guarding these precious possessions, and that obsession continues even to this day. First, I hid them among my meager belongings in an orange crate under doña Josefina's bed. Next, I devised a way of hiding them more securely in the springs under doña Josefina's mattress. Other times I kept them tied to my waist using the strings on my underwear. To this day, I habitually tie a string around my waist for no apparent reason; I just feel insecure without it.

Even though I was filled with the new hope the orange cards and the baby picture gave me, I still had to deal with doña Josefina. She was having increasing problems in her marriage and, in turn, took her anger and frustrations out on me. Fortunately, just at this time, Matilde got a better offer and hired me out with a family that had a two-year-old boy. As usual, Matilde asked for my pay in advance; I never saw a dime of it. This was only temporary, about three months, until the lady found a nanny for the child. They were a well-to-do family, and my stay there was nice—any place was nicer than being with Matilde or doña Josefina. Unknown to me at the time, the Laras, a family who would soon mean a great deal to me, lived nearby.

When I returned, doña Josefina picked up where she had left off and continued to abuse me. For a while, my only defenses were to give her looks that could kill or to scream loudly every time she hit me. Just as before with Matilde, I knew if I screamed, the neighbors would sometimes come to my aid and demand that she stop or they would call the police. When this would happen, she would pretend she loved me and would tell them I was her niece, which could not have been further from the truth.

One time, she was about to hit me with a belt because she said I left some dust on one of Rolando's nightstands. Just as the belt was about to strike, I grabbed it with every bit of strength my body could muster. The next thing I knew, there was doña Josefina on the floor in a very unladylike position. I could see her underwear. When I saw her on the floor and realized what had happened, I ran for my life. She was calling me every curse word she could think of.

I ran across the street to a long stretch of land that went for miles. It was hilly and had a lot of trees and brush. On the other side, there were more houses. I hid there most of the day. However, I was afraid to stay after dark, so I went back in the hopes I could spend the night hiding behind the outhouse or on the *lavadero* (used for washing clothes by hand).

The lavadero was built up off the ground. It had a large, grooved stone washing surface that sloped to a drain hole at one end. The washing surface was surrounded by a shallow concrete wall, just high enough to conceal me.

I headed for the lavadero. Just as I turned the corner, there was Tolla! She had just arrived from a trip with one of her male friends. Tolla made her living like Matilde. However, unlike Matilde, she was discrete and hardly ever brought any of her men home with her. When she was at her mother's house, she passed herself off as the respectable daughter who worked away from home, coming to see her mother on her days off.

Tolla had already heard what had happened that morning. She came closer to me and told me I should not have done what I did to doña Josefina. I explained that I was tired of being beaten and called all those nasty names and did not care what happened next. I told her I just came back for my things, and after I got them, I would go away.

Frankly, I couldn't have cared less about my old clothes; all I was after were the two orange cards and my baby picture, which were well hidden between the mattress and the springs of doña Josefina's bed. These three things had become my most valuable possessions. I felt sure they held proof that I was in the United States when I was born, and perhaps they held clues to help me find my family. Reluctant as I otherwise was, I knew I had to risk going back. No matter what happened, I had to retrieve them. This had been my secret for some time now, and I was ready to risk my life to get them.

Tolla told me to go to doña Josefina and ask for forgiveness and to promise her I would try to do a better job and obey her. I had to do this, even if I did not want to, because this was the only way I could retrieve my precious possessions. By this time, doña Josefina had time to cool off; I guess she had learned her lesson. She now knew that I had more strength than she realized, and that I was not going to be passive and just let her continue to hit me any time she felt like it.

When I went to doña Josefina's room, she was acting like a martyr. The moment I saw her in bed, I realized there was no way for me to get the baby picture and the orange cards. I would have to ask her forgiveness and do as she asked until I could get them out from under her mattress. At this point, I was not sure when this would happen; she might decide to play sick so her husband would pay more attention to her, or she might be up right away and back to her old ways.

Even though I wanted to hit her more than apologize to her, I told her I was sorry for what I did and didn't mean to pull her so hard and cause her to fall. I promised I would try to do my work better, and I knew she loved me like her daughter, and I loved her too. Normally, even at that young age, I couldn't tolerate two-faced people, but I was playing the part to perfection. I could have won an award for playing that part. She said she would forgive me, but I had to pay more attention to the way she wanted things done. If I did a good job, I would be given twenty-five centavos every Sunday, so I could go to the movies. Of course, all this remained to be seen; she had made promises to me before, and she never kept her word. Why should she now? I did not have much of a choice. I had to stay and see how much I could endure.

The Laras

Life with doña Josephina soon went back as before and I did get to continue the lessons that had been arranged by Gabriela Mistral. I was nine or ten years old.

On my walk to and from the lessons, I passed by a house with a huge mango tree in the yard. I often paused and looked longingly at the mangos. The lady of the house must have noticed me, because one day she offered me some mangos and asked me where I went each day. I told her I went to school for an hour, two afternoons a week. Because there were no schools in the area, I explained to her that my schooling was at the home of two women who were friends of Gabriela Mistral.

The lady introduced herself and said her family name was Lara. We started to talk, and she asked me about my family. I told her about Matilde, a woman who claims to be my mother, and how she had always left me here and there. I told her I did not believe Matilde was my mother. I also explained my situation with doña Josephina. I told her I worked to earn my keep and to pay rent for Matilde's room. After hearing this, Mrs. Lara told me she and her husband did not have any children and would pay Matilde to have me as her companion. Mrs. Lara was about twenty years younger than her husband. She said all I had to do was run errands and go with her when she went out. She said she loved shopping, eating in restaurants, and going to the theater.

This all sounded unbelievable. Here was another person who wanted to help me. However, as I was listening to this, I thought, *Be careful, Graciela, don't go dreaming again. So far, nothing has come true, and besides, Matilde may not agree to this.* I told her I could not stay long, because if I were late getting home, doña Josefina might not let me continue my lessons.

I waited until Matilde came back, and I told her I had met some people who wanted to meet her and offer her a deal with good money. This is how I got her to meet the Laras. When we met, they were very nice to Matilde. They told the maid to set the table for four and to let us know when all was ready. While Matilde and the Laras were talking, Mrs. Lara asked if I wanted to play in the garden. I gladly said yes.

Here I was in this beautiful garden with fruits, vegetables, birds, chickens, flowers, and my favorite, the huge mango tree, and I could not enjoy any of it. I was a nervous wreck. My body was in the garden, but my mind was on what was happening in the living room.

I was afraid Matilde would not agree to let me stay, and the prospect of going back to doña Josefina's house was unbearable. Doña Josefina was still having problems with her husband, which meant all of her anger and frustrations would continue to be channeled my way. More and more frequently, she did not like the way I did anything, so she would hit me quite often on the head with whatever happened to be handy. I went around with big swollen bumps on my head, black-and-blue marks on my upper arms, and swollen belt marks on my bottom. She also pulled my ears so hard they would be sore for days. History repeated itself, because doña Josefina had permission from Matilde to do all this. After all, one was getting a slave, and the other was getting her rent paid!

I was apprehensive as I was called back to the living room where the three were sitting. With one hand, Matilde motioned me to come to her, in her other hand she had a drink. She held me by the waist and told me of her decision. Matilde had made a deal; obviously, her quick decision was influenced by money. Unbelievably, unlike deals in the past, this one turned out better for both of us—Matilde got more money and I went from being a slave to being a princess! She said I should obey Mrs. Lara and be a good girl. She even said she loved me. She was the perfect picture of a loving mother in front of the Laras. I found out later that the Laras had agreed to give her two months' allowance and allow her to be able to come see me and take me out.

As Matilde was walking out, she told us she would bring my things the next day. Instantly, I burst out, so fast and so strongly that Matilde was not even finished with her sentence, "I want to get my things and say good-bye to doña Josefina and the neighbors."

I startled everyone with the force and urgency of my request. I was the only one who knew that under doña Josefina's mattress was hidden what I valued most. I was terrified by the thought of Matilde finding the orange cards and the baby picture. Even though I could not read at the time I found them, I knew instinctively, and felt deeply, that these cards and the baby picture would play a crucial role in my future. They gave me a sense of comfort and security. Without them, I felt sure I would have lost all hope.

I had been very nervous while I was out in the garden praying to God to make it possible for me to be left with the Laras. I reasoned to God that anything would be better than being with Matilde or doña Josefina. I had suffered enough, and I needed some help.

I used to talk to God as I imagined a child would talk to a most trusted friend or parent. This was usually a one-way conversation. Only when I got an answer to my prayers was there a two-way dialogue. When that happened, I was in heaven, and when it did not happen, I would reason that God was too busy. This faith is what carried me through.

Matilde agreed that I could get my things at doña Josefina's place. On the way, I was deep in silent prayer asking God to keep doña Josefina away from the bedroom while I was there. When we got to the house, I asked Matilde to wait until I got my things before telling doña Josefina I was leaving. I said I wanted to be present when she told her. By the grace of God, she listened to me.

As we arrived, doña Josefina was watering her garden. When she saw me, she said, "I need some matches. Get the money from my night table." I thanked God because the bedroom was precisely where I wanted to be at the time, and time was of the essence.

I moved as fast as my feet would take me. I went into the bedroom, took the money, and went under the bed to retrieve my orange cards and the picture, all the time praying for doña Josefina and Matilde not to come in. I was having some difficulty freeing the cards from the mattress springs—I was all thumbs and so nervous that my heart was beating twice as fast as usual! Suddenly, the cards and pictures were free. At that instant, I looked up to get out from under the bed and saw doña Josefina's feet.

"What on earth are you doing down there?" she demanded. "I thought I asked you to get matches from the store."

For a brief second, I could not speak. I felt like my heart was in my throat. Then, as if I had preplanned what I was going to say, I answered, "I dropped the money because I was trying to hurry. A coin went under the bed to the far corner and I just found it."

Once more, luck was on my side. All she said was, "Hurry, I need matches so I can light the fire."

I quickly put the cards and picture at my waist, just under my blouse. They were held in place by the tie string of my underwear. When I emerged from under the bed, I was relieved to see doña Josefina facing the other way. If she had looked, she would have seen the fear and the sweat on my face. If she were close enough, she could have heard my heart pounding. I got out of the room as fast as I could. I almost flew to the store and back; I wanted to get to the Laras as soon as possible.

When I got back from the store, Matilde was talking with doña Josefina, telling her about me leaving. As I was handing the matches to her, she turned to me and said, "Remember all the things I taught you, and if you don't like it there, you can always come back."

I thanked her, as I had learned not to burn bridges along the way, but deep inside I was hoping never to come back. *I am rid of her*, I thought to myself. *Now if I could only get away from Matilde.*

I thought I may have a chance in life to better myself, but as long as Matilde was around, she would take all she could from me and give nothing in return. How could I get away from her? I was only ten, almost eleven, so she was still in control of my life.

Only God knew how this new arrangement would work out; I could not put too much hope in it. I remembered so clearly how Mr. Rivera, the Asilo Veracruzano, and Gabriela Mistral had all departed from my life, and how my hopes and dreams departed with each. I knew I had to dream again of the day I could go to New York, and that dream made me go on. I knew a new place in America would be better. I gathered my meager possessions and took a bus to the Lara's house. It was only minutes from doña Josefina's house to the Laras', but it seemed like a lifetime.

Mr. and Mrs. Lara were waiting outside their door so they could see the minute I turned onto their street. As I appeared, Mrs. Lara walked quickly to meet me, took my hand, and said, "You will see; you will be with us and will like it here. You and I will do many things together. Tomorrow we are going to get you a new dress."

The warm welcome quickly eased my fears. Before, I had only talked with the Lara's, now I was moving in. I prayed all would work out for the better. I prayed, as I had so often done before, *Dios conmigo, yo con El. Dios adelante, y yo atras de El.* To this day, I continue to pray this very powerful prayer in times of need.

When I asked Mrs. Lara where I could put my things, she showed me to my room, next to hers. Oh, it looked beautiful and, just imagine, a room to myself and my own bed! I had not slept on a bed since I left the orphanage, and even then, it was only a cot. When I saw the bed, I knew I had to tell Mrs. Lara I still wet my bedding occasionally. She responded as though it was the most natural thing to do. She told me she would have the maid put a protective covering on the bed if that would make me feel better. I could not believe all this attention and kindness. I had to pinch myself a couple of times, because I thought I must be dreaming. I was not expecting any of this. She asked me if I was hungry, and I told her I was a little hungry.

She took me to the dining room, and I swear the cook put what seemed like a banquet before me. This was almost too much to absorb in one day. I felt like I had just left the devil in hell and had passed through St. Peter's gate into heaven! For the first time in memory, I could eat whatever was on the table and I could have as much as I wanted, but I was in such emotional overload that I couldn't do either. I even had my own room and, for the first time in my life, a real bed of my own. I could not believe I was going to sleep in a real bed at a decent hour without dropping from exhaustion. I didn't have housework, and I wasn't being beaten and cursed. At doña Josefina's and with Matilde, I always lived in fear of the next beating; here I was in fear this would all end.

The school year was almost over, so Mrs. Lara immediately started looking into a school for me to attend in September. Little did she know how many problems she would encounter. She did not have any papers for me and, in those days, to get into a Catholic school, in addition to a birth certificate, you needed to show papers from your baptism, confirmation, and first communion, as well as the parents' marriage certificate. Public schools required at least a birth certificate. I only had my two orange cards, my baby picture, and the belief that Matilde was not my mother. I was not about to tell them about the orange cards for fear they would take them away from me, tell Matilde I had them, or try to get more information from her about me. I knew from experience that they would get nothing from her, only lies.

The Laras had a very elegant house, beautiful furniture, and a big patio with a huge backyard. Where the mango tree was, they also had chickens, so they could have fresh eggs every morning. One of my favorite things was to gather the fresh eggs for our breakfast. Having just been laid, many of the eggs would still be warm. The chickens laid brown eggs and they tasted so good. Mr. Lara used to have a drink made with *Jerez* (liquor, like dry sherry) and four egg yolks, which he took every morning. Sometimes I would take a freshly laid egg, crack the top gently, and drink it. I still prefer brown eggs, and every time I eat them, it brings back those warm memories of this brief and happy period in my childhood.

I also loved sitting at meals with the candelabras, the candlelight, and, most of all, the company and stimulating conversation. Sometimes, as I was sitting at that beautiful table with a napkin on my lap, I would wonder when it was going to end and when the bad things would start happening again.

So far, the time with the Laras had been good for me, and I wondered if it were actually possible for people to live like this all of their lives.

The reflection of the lights from the chandeliers on the table setting, especially the crystal, made it seem all the more magical, like a scene right out of *Alice in Wonderland*. I felt like I was Alice and that Matilde was the wicked queen who was always after me. Each time I would sit at the dinner table, my eyes would wander all around, taking in the paintings, the furnishings, and the pure elegance of the house, and each time, I discovered something I had overlooked before.

Mrs. Lara would often ask me what I was thinking. In those moments, she would startle me, because I would be so deep in thought, observing every object around me so very deeply. The whole time I would think to myself that this is how I wanted to live forever. I would imagine never having to worry about where my next meal was coming from or how poorly I was dressed.

Every time the maid came by, I looked at her with kindness and always thanked her for everything she did for me. I had no reason to feel sorry for her, because she was well paid, well dressed, and treated with kindness and respect. Materially, her living conditions were better than doña Josefina's were. I knew the maid missed her family because every month she went to see them for three to four days.

I used to love the way she would call me to the table. She would say, "*Niña Graciela, lávese las manos; ya es la hora de comer.*" Which meant, "Little Graciela, go wash your hands; it is time to eat."

She spoke ever so softly with an Indian accent, so it was like music to my ears. All I had ever known before were the screams of Matilde or doña Josefina, cursing at me all the time.

The maid cooked things I liked and would scrub me when I took a bath. Oh, life was so good for me then. On the good side, unlike with the witch and Alice, I felt like Cinderella, and my fairy godmother was Mrs. Lara.

Mrs. Lara took me to my first play. It was *Caperusita Roja* (*Little Red Riding Hood*). She also took me to my first ballets, *el Lago de los Cisnes* (*Swan Lake*) and *Cascanueces* (*The Nutcracker*). I loved them all. After the theater, we would go to the Café Parroquia for pastries and cocoa. I would sit there, remembering, ever so clearly, when I had to sell peanuts and gum to get money to eat. Whenever vendors came to our table, I asked Mrs. Lara for money to give to them, especially if they were children. At other times, I would offer them whatever I had on my plate, and silently I would ask God to find them a lady like Mrs. Lara to care for them. My heart ached for them and always will, for I have known how much cruelty an orphaned child can find in this world.

After the Café Parroquia, we used to walk to the Zocalo. The Zocalo was in the center of town, right across from Café Parroquia. People, especially young people, would meet in the evenings and, as was the custom, stroll in a circle around the Zocalo. The parents or chaperones sat on benches placed all around the park or followed a few steps behind, always keeping a watchful eye on the young ladies under their charge. On Sundays, cadets dressed in crisp, dress white uniforms would be there. They looked ever so handsome, and I thought that when I grew up I would marry a cadet.

Before we left for home, we used to stop at the cathedral. I would light a candle thanking God for sending me to the Laras and ask Him to help find a way for me to get to New York so I could look for my real mother. No matter how bad or how good things were for me, this remained my fervent prayer. I could not tell this to the Laras, because they wanted me for their own. To them, I was the child they could never have, and I could not disappoint them, I was in constant conflict.

The only links I had to help me regain my real family at this point were the two orange cards and the baby picture. The baby picture was actually a small purse-sized makeup mirror with a plastic cover onto which the photograph was printed, which was very typical of the time. The edge of the plastic cover had writing, which someone told me said, "Roubain Studio, 262 Columbia Street, Brooklyn, New York." That little bit of writing was not much to go on, but the burning desire within to find my mother and family did not diminish for a moment, even though I had more than I could ever dream possible with the Laras.

After a few months of living with the Laras, Mrs. Lara and I took a trip to Puebla, a city in the mountains, one day by bus and northwest of Veracruz. We visited with Mrs. Lara's family for a few days. Puebla was beautiful, but the weather was cold, which was quite a change for me. There seemed to be a beautiful church on every corner. I was told that in Puebla there is a church for every day of the year. There were beautiful decorations with colored tiles on the churches and public buildings.

Every morning during our stay in Puebla, I got up early and stood on the balcony facing the busy street below. I loved to experience the mist in the air and to watch the Indian ladies with their rosy cheeks carrying big baskets on their heads and little babies on their backs as they rushed to the *mercado* (market). Puebla is known as "The City of Angels." Its people, with their rosy complexions, looked like angels, and the white mist, which hung ever so gracefully in the air, looked like I imagined heaven should look.

That first morning, I could not wait to explore the town, but at that moment, Mrs. Lara could not go with me. I asked her if I could go to the bakery with the maid and afterward explore the city. She said I could go but cautioned me to stay close to the maid so I would not get lost.

She gave me some money to get what I wanted, and we eagerly took off. While at the bakery, I wanted to choose the breads. When it was my turn, the young man asked me what I wanted. As I began to call out the names of the breads, everyone laughed. I couldn't understand why they were laughing at me and I became upset. Seeing this, the young man handed me a tray and tongs to choose what I wanted.

The maid was trying to tell me something, but I was too upset to listen. When I asked the young man what was so funny, he asked me where I was from. I told him I was from Veracruz, and he explained that in Puebla they used different names for the breads than the names they used in Veracruz. He used the local name for each piece I had pointed to. The big laugh had come when I had first said I wanted *dos novias* (two sweethearts)! When I realized what had happened, I felt better.

The trip to Puebla was fun—I got new clothes and visited some of the churches and other sights. Upon our return, we found Mr. Lara in poor health and angry with Matilde because she had come to ask for more money. By now, I realized that she had collected a lot of money ahead of time and probably thought she had found a gold mine. The Laras kept giving her money so she would not take me away from them. I knew how overbearing Matilde could be and lived in constant fear that the Laras would get tired of her and, to get rid of her, give me back.

Adding to the problems of Matilde's ongoing demands for money was the problem of me not being in school. Life had gone on, and two or three months into the new school year, I still had no papers to meet the school's requirements for documentation. The Laras had asked Matilde to bring my birth certificate or some legal document that would state the place of my birth. Matilde kept telling them she had sent for the papers and said I was born late in September 1940, in Ensenada, Mexico. When I heard this, I wanted to go for her throat and was so upset that I left the room.

Matilde's visits became more frequent. She would sit for hours talking about nothing and expecting to be fed and served drinks. I wanted to tell her, in front of the Laras, to go away and never come back; I did not want to see her again as long as I lived. However, I knew I could not do this because first I needed to get the information out of her. I had to know what she knew about my family and how she got me out of the United States. Most of all, I needed names. What was my family name? What kind of people were they? Why did they give me up with so little regard for my well-being? It would have been more merciful to let me die than to do what they did. I wanted to find my family not only for love but to resolve my anger and resentment. I could not wait to see whether or not Matilde would bring the documents from Ensenada she said she had for me. I believed that she had no such papers and that she was just buying time to get more money from these good people.

One day, lo and behold, who do you think appeared at the Laras' front door? Very early in the morning, Matilde arrived with a large brown envelope, eager to show the Laras proof that she was my mother and that she had been telling them the truth all along. I was called to the living room where Matilde and the Laras were sitting. I sat on my favorite French provincial chair—it made me feel like royalty. It was just as well that I felt like royalty at that moment, because I was about to be dethroned! When Matilde showed the papers to the Laras, I felt like my heart went to my feet. I could not breathe. I could not utter a word, even though I felt in my heart that those papers were full of lies. To console myself, I thought, *At least I will be able to go to school.*

Mr. Lara read parts of the documents aloud so I could clearly hear what was written, which I would have rather not heard. The words that stay in my mind were "daughter of Matilde and Pablo Palo." To me, that was criminal. It was an insult, a great injustice. To have a legal document that identified this woman as my mother was almost more than I could bear. The sadness I felt at the knowledge those papers existed stayed with me for a long while.

The instant I heard those horrible words I cried out, "Oh no!"

I began crying very hard. I cried out of the deep feelings of hopelessness at not having anything or anyone to help me undo this lie. Mrs. Lara tried to console me; she could not understand why I was crying so hard.

She kept telling me, "Now you will be able to go to school. Don't you want that?"

I answered her between sobs, "Yes, I am very happy I will be able to go to school."

"Please dry those tears," she said and handed me a candy dish.

I always thought that those papers did not really exist. Now, with them right in front of me, I felt Matilde's hold on me more than ever. It was devastating to know this woman could do with me what she wanted and that the law would back her up, even though the papers were falsified. If she wanted, she could take me from the Laras now. There would be nothing that they could do to stop her. People say that you should be careful of your fears, because the more you fear something, the more the possibility of it coming true.

Mr. Lara asked Matilde why she had waited two years to register my birth. Matilde's answer was that she just forgot. This question, and the trip I had taken with Mrs. Lara to Puebla, made Matilde very uncomfortable, which is why she produced these papers now and was coming so often to see me. I did not consider Matilde to be an intelligent person, but when it came to me, she could always sense when someone was trying to help me or give me a better life. She would show up at the worst moments to ruin my future and to maintain her control over me, just as she was trying to do now.

After Matilde left, I never again felt as happy at the Laras as I had felt before her visit. I was always in fear that my new way of life would be taken away; I just did not know when. Weeks went by and I was still not in school. Even though I had a birth certificate, the other necessary papers were still missing.

Again, the Laras asked Matilde for the papers. Matilde said she would have to send a request to the Church of Guadeloupe in Tijuana for the baptism and confirmation papers. There was more waiting because the school would not take me without the papers. I think the name of the school was el Josefino. It was known then to be one of the best in the area, and expensive too. I dreamed of going to school, and the possibility of going to el Josefino was more than my poor little heart could bear; it would have been a dream come true.

Suddenly, Mr. Lara's health took a turn for the worse. His doctor recommended that he see a heart specialist in the United States as soon as possible. They said the doctors in Veracruz could do nothing more for him. Mrs. Lara was faced with many problems now—one of them was Matilde.

It was in the early part of the year that Matilde appeared at the front door with doña Josefina. I was in the garden gathering fresh tomatoes and other ripe vegetables when I heard Mrs. Lara call. She used to call me Gracielita. I will never forget the look of sadness on her face as I approached. I could tell she had been crying, so the first thing that came to my mind was that Mr. Lara was getting worse.

As she took my hand, Mrs. Lara said, "Your mother is here. She wants to talk to you." As she said the words "your mother is here," I instantly felt a sick feeling in the pit of my stomach. When we got to the living room, Matilde was all smiles and doña Josefina was by her side. I immediately asked myself, *What is this woman doing here with Matilde?*

Then, Matilde said to me, "I got a letter from your father, he wants us to go to San Francisco to live with him. He has a good job, and next month he is sending us more money for our trip and our brief stay in Tijuana while we get our visas, then to the United States. You will see; you will like living there. I am coming to take you now so we can be ready to go as soon as I get the money."

As I heard her speak, I was petrified with fear over my whole being. I was numb; transfixed to the floor by what she was saying. I could not utter a word, cry, or realize the pain those words were causing. I wanted the earth to open up under my feet, swallow me, and release me from this woman forever. This would be a blessing compared to life with either of these two women. In any case, I had heard those shallow promises about Pablo sending for us before.

Mrs. Lara left the room and asked the maid to gather my things, which were quite a few by that time. I had the most clothes and shoes since I could remember. Most of all, they all fit perfectly and were to my liking. Mrs. Lara had already asked Matilde to leave me with them until she got the money. Matilde refused and insisted she would take me right then. I guess that is why she brought doña Josefina with her—in case there were any problems in getting me. Matilde told them that if she did not hear from Pablo in two weeks, she would bring me back. She said that the money Pablo had sent was on its way and she didn't want to lose time.

When I finally came out of my numb state and realized my hopeless situation, I wondered if, for once in her life, Matilde was telling the truth. That is how my stay at the Laras came to an abrupt end and Matilde's hold on me began once again.

I knew there was nothing in the world Matilde wanted more than to go back to the United States. In fact, she had some relatives in Los

Angeles. What kept me going was the thought that I would be going to the United States, and once there, I would have a chance to get away from this woman and maybe find my real family soon thereafter. Oh, how naïve I was!

As we were about to leave, I hugged Mrs. Lara, kissed her, and told her I would get away to come see her if I could. We were all crying—Mrs. Lara, the maid, and even Mr. Lara. How I hated to be the one who was causing those tears for these wonderful people who had made me so happy and who only wanted the best for me. I was also sad because of Mr. Lara's deteriorating health. It was evident, even to me, that he was progressively getting worse.

As we walked out of the house, I kept looking back at the Laras and the maid. I will never forget Mrs. Lara's expression and that scene. Here were people who loved me, and Matilde, just as she had many times before, was taking me away. I could hardly stand to be around Matilde and there was nothing that they or I could do to stop her. I thought about how unfair life could be to those who needed protection the most.

I was taken back to doña Josefina's and not let out of sight for one minute—not even to go to the corner by myself. I was worse off than before; in prison under their watchful eyes. How I missed the Laras' kindness, love, and all the luxury and comfort in their home. It was so very hard to come back to all the abuse and deprivation that I had been free of; I was very depressed. All I could do was pray that I could somehow get back to the Laras.

Jalapa: Into the Fire

Shortly thereafter, Matilde and I went by bus to Jalapa, to the house of doña Josefina's married daughter, Maria. Maria had two children, a six-year-old boy and a five-year-old girl. Matilde told me we were to wait here for Pablo's money to arrive. One week went by and no money. Then, Matilde left. She said she was going back to Veracruz and would come back to get me when she got the money. I was almost twelve and wouldn't see her again for more than three years.

Maria's husband, Alfonso, was a native Indian from Jalapa. His family owned a large parcel of land on which they had a compound where most of the family lived. In fact, all of his married brothers and sisters lived on the compound, except Alfonso and Maria. They lived elsewhere because Alfonso's mother did not like Maria. In those days, the mothers had a strong influence on their sons, even after they married.

Maria was expecting her third child. She had an Indian maid for the housework, but she wanted me to babysit her children. That was the deal she had made secretly with Matilde. Here began another terrible period in my young life, and I had no means to get away. Again, I was left with total strangers, and again, Matilde got the money for my work.

As soon as I left the Laras, I started wetting my bed again. Right away, Maria had reason to begin verbally and physically abusing me. They ridiculed me cruelly for this. To add to my misery, the climate was much colder in Jalapa and even in the winter months I had to sleep on the cold, cement floor. I began suffering from severe sinusitis, especially in the coldest part of the winter. Several times, I came down with a high fever that made me so weak I could hardly get up. Each time, Maria called me all sorts of names and told me I was only being lazy.

One of the reasons for my frequent sickness was that I did not have winter clothes or shoes. I had quickly outgrown the nice, well-fitting shoes and clothes the Laras had given me. Because I had no shoes, I had to go barefoot most of the time. In desperation, I tried to wear Maria's old shoes, but they were hard to walk in because they were so big. I had gone from having anything I needed with the Laras to having nothing with Maria. This sudden change in my life was taking away my will to go on. Even in my prayers, I now only asked for my misery to end.

One day, the aches became so bad I cried continuously; aspirin would not help. As sick as I was, they would not call a doctor. I had to walk by myself to the clinic in the center of town; no one would take me. It was a long way to walk, especially as sick as I was. It took me a long time to get there because I had to stop often to rest along the way. When I arrived at the clinic, I fell at the door. A nurse ran over, picked me up, and called a doctor. The doctor asked to see my mother. Of course, my mother could not be found, and by then I was too sick to talk. They laid me down and gave me medication to try to bring the temperature down. Finally, they gave me penicillin. A few hours later, I felt better. I stayed in the clinic all day. I got there early in the morning, and I did not get back to Maria's house until late that evening. The doctor also gave me some pills to take every day for two weeks, so I had some proof as to where I had been all day so Maria would not curse at me. She was not happy that I had taken all day.

I felt alone and depressed and I didn't see a way out. To make matters worse, the skin on the front part of my lower legs, feet, and ankles became very dry and cracked with the cold weather, which made it very painful to walk. The cracks in the skin bled, and when the cold air would hit, the pain became worse. On cold mornings when I had to walk uphill, the pain became unbearable. Through all of this, Maria remained cruelly indifferent and would not do anything to help; it was as if I were made of stone and had no feelings. At night, I buried my head in the pillow and cried myself to sleep. Each time Maria vented her anger and hit me, I would pray to God to make her stop. I did not think I could endure much more. Even the hope of finding my family now seemed impossible. I felt so alone, so cold, and so very sick.

One day, on the way to get the morning bread, a kind lady saw me crying and asked me what was wrong. All I could do was to point to my swollen and cracked feet and ankles. Right away, she took me into her house and put some ointment on the cracked and bleeding wounds.

The kind woman asked where I lived, and I told her that I lived in Alfonso and Maria's house, a few blocks away. When she asked if I was related to them, I explained that they claimed that I was their niece, but it wasn't true. I also told her that a woman, who calls herself my mother, left me to work for them. The kind lady looked at the old dress I was wearing and just shook her head. She offered me something to drink, which I eagerly took. Then I thanked her for all she had done. I told her I had to get going or else I would be punished. She asked me to come back the next day so she could put more medication on my skin.

As I walked out of her house, I looked up at the sky and said, "Thank you, God. I thought that You had forgotten me." The ointment lessened the pain.

Near the bread store, I found a twenty-five centavo piece, which I eagerly exchanged for two pieces of my favorite bread. I devoured the bread so fast that it surprised the sales lady, and she commented that I must be very hungry.

I thought to myself, *Well, a long walk on a cold morning when you have not been given enough to eat would make you hungry.* Aloud, I only answered, "Yes, I am."

She asked if I wanted another piece of bread; she said she would not charge me for it. I asked her if I could have it the next day, and she said, "Certainly, you may have it tomorrow."

I hurried home with the bread. Maria only gave me a piece of bread after everyone else had chosen his or hers. I had mine with a cup of warm *atole*, a hot drink, often flavored with different fruits, and made from corn flour, water, milk, and sugar It is a very nice drink, especially on cold mornings.

Maria had just birthed her baby, a boy, and her husband had been drinking heavily. Some nights he didn't even bother to come home. When Maria would ask Alfonso where he had been, he would say, "At my mother's."

Thinking back, this guy had the perfect excuse. Since his mother and Maria were not on speaking terms, Maria could never find out if he was telling the truth. This made her very angry, and she took her anger out on me.

This morning, two good things had happened to me and I was in good spirits. Maria asked me to fry some dried red peppers for making her husband's favorite dish, adobo. She put the peppers in the pan and asked me to stir them, which I did. She did not say when to take them out, so I kept on turning them. When she came back, she started screaming at me, grabbed the pan, and held the edge to my face. She cried out, "You good-for-nothing, can't you see they are burning?"

At the same time I was screaming, she was burning my face with the frying pan! I freed myself from her hold and ran, crying, to pour some water on the burn. The burn was just in line with my cheekbone on the right side of my face. Thank God, I got free from her in time to prevent it from becoming a deeper burn, or it would have marked me for life. At the time, I did not know if I had been permanently scarred or not. I went around looking like an Indian with two lines on my face until the skin fell off. Maria put some medication on the wound and had the Indian maid do many of my duties for a while.

The most severe beating I ever got from Maria was the day I cut her children's hair. The children wanted me to do it because they had stuck bubble gum in each other's hair. First, I just cut a little, but it didn't look even, so I cut a little more. I kept trying to make things better but they got worse. That night, when Maria went to check on her children, all hell broke loose. She grabbed me by the hair and started screaming that I could have cut a vein and killed the children. Maria was the one I would have liked to do that to, not the children. She gave me such a beating, I could not sit down for days. To make matters worse, she tore my dress as she was pulling me back and forth. I only had two dresses at the time and the one that was not torn was getting too small for me. A few days later, she brought out one of her old dresses and cut the length to my size. It took a beating for me to get another dress.

One day Maria asked me to iron a white blouse using a flat iron, the type that we had to put onto the fire to heat. Then she went to another part of the house where she had a big argument with Alfonso. When she came back to where I was ironing, she was fuming. She began to curse me very angrily for not ironing properly. In a flash, and with no warning whatsoever, she grabbed the iron from me. With the hot, sharp edge of the iron, she struck me hard on the face, just above my left eye. Blood started pouring down my face.

I was in shock at her sudden turn of anger toward me. This happened for no apparent reason. Even though I had been ironing precisely as she had instructed me, her anger at Alfonso was vented on me. She yelled, "You are not doing this right, you stupid so and so." The wound was a painful open cut as well as a burn. I still have the scar to remind me of the pain and shock of this incident. My body is like a roadmap; it still bears traces of the abuses. Whenever I glance at the scars, I am transported instantly to those horrible times and places.

Alfonso and Maria were not poor. To this day, I cannot understand Maria's indifference and cruelty toward me. As I write and think back in time about these unhappy periods of my childhood, I can't continue because the tears make it impossible for me to see what I am writing. I knew that writing my story was not going to be easy—I just didn't know I would relive the scenes of pain and humiliation so very vividly. It is as if I were there again. Some nights I can't go to sleep, and if I do sleep, I have unpleasant dreams about what I am writing. I have to tell myself it is all in the past, it is only a memory, but the sadness remains.

Not only was I exposed to cruelty and indifference, but I was twelve or thirteen and had no one my own age to be with. I was completely isolated from people, other than Maria's family. We never even went to church on Sundays. My only companions were Simba, Alfonso's prize hunting dog, and two goats, a white one named Blanquita and a black one named Negrita.

I used to take the goats to graze in the hills. When I could not be seen from the house, I would get on the white one and ride it like a horse. I use to love these quiet moments I spent alone in the fields with the animals. Sometimes I could see the *pastores* (shepherds) coming back with their flocks of goats and lambs. I loved to hear their bells as they went by.

Simba was a beautiful dog with large ears and an upright tail. He was white with big spots of gold and black on his body and face. I believe he was a beagle. Alfonso told me he didn't want me to play with Simba because he was a hunting dog. I could not resist, so whenever I was alone with Simba, we would play. I still have a scar on my left hand where he scratched me while playing roughly. Whenever I glance at this scar, it brings warm memories of Simba.

One happy occasion was the night when Alfonso took Simba and me hunting for armadillos and rabbits. I remember I was following Simba in the dark and fell down the side of a hill. I hardly noticed the scrapes and scratches on my legs because I was enjoying the excitement of the hunt and the beautiful clear starry night. Alfonso got several rabbits and one armadillo. When the armadillo was cooked, I thought it tasted like pork.

I also loved to go to the nearby *fincas* (orchards) and eat as much as I could of whatever fruit was in season. I would eat until I thought my stomach could hold no more. While grazing the goats, I would sometimes go to the *cafetales* (coffee plantations). The shiny red coffee beans were irresistible. I picked a few of the reddest ones and sucked the sweet nectar; this was nature's candy. I did this even though I knew I could have been shot for trespassing.

Another thing that was nice was when I was sent to buy *chicharrones* (deep-fried pigskins). The part I especially liked was that the vendors usually gave me a sample before buying. Oh, they were so good when freshly cooked. I also enjoyed the almond candies I bought from the nuns. They made the candies into shapes of fruits and animals. Each Sunday I was given fifty centavos. Even though they were younger, Maria's children were allowed to buy anything they wanted. I had to save two or three weeks to buy the almond candies, but they were worth it. I used to take only small bites to make them last.

The nuns also sold the leftovers from cutting the Holy Communion bread. They put the pieces in brown bags. It was very light, but it looked like a lot. I was always looking for a way to get the most for my money. One thing I remember about the nuns is that they never asked anything about me; they were purely business. They gave me what I asked for, took my money, and that was that. Sometimes I would try to say something, but the door closed before I could finish the words. Oh, how I needed to have someone I could talk to—some kindness, some understanding, and some compassion. From these nuns, I got nothing.

In spite of the constant isolation, there were infrequent diversions. I loved to see the smaller children fly their kites on Sunday afternoons.

A family that lived on a nearby hill made the kites. Kids would buy kites from them and fly the kites from the hill. Occasionally, when I had saved enough money, I would get a kite to fly too.

Almost everything positive that happened to me happened when I was alone. One day while I was making a bed, out of the blue, I spotted a large calendar on the wall and, for some reason, started trying to make out the sounds of the letters. Then I started trying to sound out the words. In a flash, the vowels and consonants seemed to go together and I began to sound out the combinations as they formed syllables.

I started quickly sounding *Sa … ba … do.* Then together, I sounded *sabado*! This struck me so hard and so effectively, I was ecstatic! For the first time, it all came together. I was finally starting to see the results of those hours of drill I had spent in Veracruz with Gabriela Mistral and, later, with her friends. At the time, the drills hadn't had clear meaning to me; however, for weeks I had so painfully and stubbornly kept attending and trying.

I tore through the calendar: *Do … min … go, domingo! Lu … nes, lunes!* I was having a veritable epiphany! In just a few compact minutes, it had all gelled, for the first time, into reading. I was so excited—I was reading! My thoughts turned again to Gabriela Mistral and those warm moments when my hand had been held so steadily by the great teacher while taking my first footsteps toward literacy—if she could only see me now.

Suddenly, I was ten miles high. I felt so powerful I thought I could conquer the world. For just a fleeting moment, everything else in my life seemed trivial. Sadly, I had no one who would understand or with whom to share my elation. I was twelve.

Another part of my extremely limited education, mathematics, also came to me at this time. Alfonso had a trucking business. When he was not there, I gave out the keys to the truck drivers. When the drivers came back from jobs, they checked in with me. I took in the truck keys and the payments, counted the money, and recorded the amounts in a notebook beside the number of each truck. Even though I often had dealings with the drivers, not once were they disrespectful or out of line with me. Sometimes they called me *la niña guerra* (the fair-skinned girl). Other times they called me *guerra pelo de elote* (the light-complexioned girl with light-brown "corn" hair) but thank God, they were always respectful.

I was able to do this job mainly because I had a natural ability with numbers. However, I had also been given the meager beginnings in mathematics during the times that I spent with Doris Dana and at the lessons that I had attended for a few weeks in Veracruz with Gabriela Mistral's friends. By this time, I was a teenager and had not attended school. My total education to this point was next to none.

Maria had planned to take her children on a week-long trip out of town. This time she took her children with her. The maid was on her days off and was supposed to come back the same day Maria left. While Maria was away, my duties were to feed the pigs, feed the chickens, feed the dog, and, of course, my favorite thing—take the goats out to the fields. I was also to bring water into the house and collect the eggs. Because none of this seemed so hard to do when Maria was telling me, I wondered why she hadn't decided to take me along; the maid could have done all of her own duties, as well as all of my duties, by herself. Then I put it all together. I knew how very tight Maria was with money. I realized that I did not have a decent dress or shoes and, to save face, Maria would have had to buy these for me. In addition, she would have had to pay my bus fare.

The day came for Maria to leave. Alfonso was already on a delivery trip out of the state. Maria told me they would both be back at about the same time. She left me all alone and told me the maid would be back that afternoon. Well, the maid did not arrive that day. All that night I was scared at every sound. I thought someone was trying to get into the house. I took a big hunting rifle down from the wall and put it next to me, just in case. I am glad I did not have to use it, but if I had needed to, I would have—I was that scared.

The following day, the goats got into the kitchen, climbed onto the counter, and broke several of the red clay cooking pots. I was very afraid of whatever punishment I might get from Maria when she got back. I stayed there alone for two more days and nights.

The morning the maid finally arrived, I told her I had not slept well for several nights, so she told me to go to sleep. She said she would do what needed to be done. My head hit the pillow and I was out in an instant.

When I woke up, the maid prepared *huevos rancheros* (eggs sunny-side up in hot sauce with a fried tortilla on the bottom and one in between). It tasted so good. There was no one to ration me to one egg or to have only two tortillas, so we ate well. I showed the maid how to make the milk not show you had taken some out of the pot; I took two glasses of milk out of the pot and replaced them with water. Then I boiled the milk, let it cool, and put it in the icebox where a new skin quickly formed back on top. No one was ever the wiser.

We sat down together and enjoyed two delicious cups of hot chocolate. Frankly, I was wishing Maria would never come back so I could keep on eating like this. But, as they must, all good things come to an end.

The next day, when I went to feed the pigs, one became untied. I tried to pull him back with a rope—I dug my heels into the ground to stop him, but he kept on dragging me, my rear end bouncing on the hard ground, until I was finally able to wrap the rope around a tree. Even though my rear was bruised and sore, it was a miracle I was not hurt more. This pig was huge, much bigger than I was; it was a monster!

I imagined what Maria would have done to me if this pig had gotten loose. Someone could have had *chicharrones* (deep-fried pigskins) that evening, and she probably would have nearly killed me. When animals got loose, you seldom found them because others, if they were not honest, would catch, kill, and butcher them right away to get rid of the evidence. A pig, as big as this one, would have provided a year's supply of food for an entire family. They could have gotten bacon, sausages, ham, headcheese, and fat for cooking. That is why I hung on for dear life to that monster of a pig, no matter how much it hurt.

After gathering the eggs and feeding the animals, I took the goats to the fields. I had a fun time riding Blanquita, the white goat. There was no one to be afraid of now; I was alone. Then, the time came when Maria was supposed to be back, but no Maria! It is not that I minded, or missed her, but the maid and I had no money left. The next day, Alfonso appeared and I told him there was no money for food. He told me to follow him and he would give me some money.

He went into the room, a long room where all of us used to sleep, pulled a key from his pocket, and unlocked the middle door of the *ropero* (wardrobe). The ropero was a big, tall piece of furniture with three mirrored doors and three small drawers under the middle door. The middle door was the smallest and was locked. When he unlocked and opened the door, I could not believe what I was seeing. Money fell to the floor! It was crammed full of hundred peso notes! My eyes were bigger than my face when I saw that. Here I was going hungry, did not have shoes or clothes, except possibly some of Maria's hand-me-downs, and Alfonso had plenty of money.

Alfonso told me not to tell Maria about the money. She did not know he had sold property from his inheritance and he had no plans of telling her. Now here I am in the middle. He gave me the money and told me to get whatever the maid needed to cook *adobo* (method of cooking meat in a spicy sauce made with *ancho* chili peppers, onions, etc.), his favorite dish. For just an instant, I sadly remembered the day Maria went into a rage when I burned the peppers while preparing adobo. Then, as quickly, I realized she wasn't here and I could see we were going to eat well that day.

Alfonso locked the door, put some money in his pocket, and left. As I was turning to leave, I looked down, and there under the dresser was a one hundred peso note! I picked it up and started to give it to Alfonso, then held back. I rationalized to myself, *Why should I? He is not going to miss it. He doesn't even know how much he has, and it is all in such disorder. But, if he asks for it, I will give it to him. In any case, I had more than earned it.*

I did have the perfect excuse. I could not possibly give it to him in front of anybody as I was the only one, other than him, who knew of the money. Well, he never asked about the money, and I never told him. I hid it with my other treasures: my two orange cards and my baby picture. When I got back from the store, I gave Alfonso the change and told him that while dinner was being prepared I would go with the goats to the pasture. I said I would be back in about two hours. On the way to the open fields, I prayed that Maria would not get back before supper, as she would spoil it for me. She always rationed my meals, and I knew I might not get any *adobo*. For sure, she would find something to scream about. Life for me was better without her.

With great expectations, I ran out with the goats. When I got out of sight of the house, I rode Blanquita then played with Negrita. I looked around, sat on the grass, and just looked up at the cloud formations. I felt good. Maybe it was the realization that I finally had some money of my own. Before it got dark, I started for home. On the empty land across from the house, I stepped on a broken bottle and cut my foot badly. It was bleeding profusely by the time I got to the house. Just as I arrived, I saw Alfonso talking with two men. He looked very worried. One of the men saw I had blood all over my leg and skirt. With a look of fear, he ran to me. I quickly told him what had happened. He cleaned my foot and tied it with his handkerchief. He told me they would take me to the clinic. He was afraid the cut was too deep and might become infected.

The next thing I remember was seeing the maid crying convulsively. I asked, "Why are you crying?"

Between sobs she uttered, "Señor Alfonso."

The men put the maid and me in the car, and we drove away. I was preoccupied with the deep and painful cut on my foot and held it on top of my other knee. I thought they were taking me to the clinic, but instead we arrived at the hospital. The nurse examined my foot, then cleaned and dressed it before the doctor came. After the nurse left, another lady came in and started asking about my family and about Alfonso. She asked if he had ever touched or hurt me.

I said, "No, but Maria had."

She asked, "What does Maria do to you?"

I answered, "When I don't do what she wants, she beats me."

Then she asked, "Have you ever seen Alfonso touching the maid?"

I said, "No, never."

Apparently, while I was out grazing the goats, Alfonso tried to rape the maid. I never did know whether he did it or not. All I can figure is that he did, because I was held several days at the hospital. They fed me with the rest of the patients. It was all great, because they were taking good care of me and my cut was healing nicely and did not hurt as much.

I did not ask the nurses when I was leaving because I was being treated much better in the hospital than I would have been at Maria's house. I reasoned, *Who wants to face screaming Maria and her spoiled children?*

Alfonso had given the authorities the address for doña Josefina and Matilde. The reason they were keeping me in the hospital longer was that they were waiting for Matilde to come. They had sent a telegram, and within six days, Matilde was there. When I saw Matilde and Tolla together, I was surprised and disappointed because I knew this could only mean I would be going back with them to Veracruz.

The instant I realized I was going back to Veracruz, I told Matilde and Tolla I wanted to say good-bye to Maria and the children before we left. This was not true, what I really wanted was to get my most precious possessions. I silently and fervently prayed, *God, Please do not let anyone find them before I get there.*

God was listening, because no one had even touched my clothes. I gathered my meager belongings, so few I could wear everything I owned. I put my valuables, including the hundred-peso note, in an old white sock, put a string through, and tied it around my waist. I was ready to go. As long as I had those cards and my baby picture with me, I felt there was hope. Hope of what, I did not dare to think, for at that moment my future still looked grim.

Whoever had spoken with Matilde and Tolla before I was turned over to them, must have really given them a good scare, because they were uncharacteristically nice to me. During the bus trip back to Veracruz, Matilde told me Pablo was sending money and writing regularly. She promised that as soon as we got to Veracruz she would buy me a new dress and shoes. I could have passed out when I heard that, but I never put much hope in her promises. She told me I was to go back with doña Josefina only to wait until she got all the right papers ready to send for our visas. She said if I did not want to stay with doña Josefina, I could stay with her. What a choice, Matilde or doña Josefina, the two people I most wanted to get away from. The only thing that made the thought of going back to doña Josefina or Matilde bearable was the hope of seeing the Laras again. I immediately wondered why she had not mentioned the Laras.

My brain was going a mile a minute thinking about my situation. My only hope was the Laras, and at the first opportunity, I was going to see them. It would be good to be with them again. I knew I could not discuss any of this with Matilde or doña Josefina, because if I did, they would not let me go.

So ended three years of bleakness, pain, and abuse in Jalapa.

Back to Veracruz

It was 1955. I was almost fifteen and hadn't seen Matilde or Tolla for more than three years. Right away, they remarked at how well developed I was for my age. I was surprised when they said this, as I had just been through three years of abuse and desolation and had been mainly concerned with my survival, not the size of my breasts. I had been isolated from any contact with girls my own age and had no way of comparing. Also, within months of first arriving in Jalapa, I had outgrown the lovely, well-fitted clothes and shoes the Laras had bought for me and had since worn only Maria's old, baggy hand-me-downs. Thinking back, it was probably a blessing that I had to wear these old, loose-fitting clothes; it may not have only been the maid Alfonso raped, or attempted to rape!

To my amazement, just after we arrived in Veracruz, Matilde kept her word and took me to buy a new dress, some underwear, a pair of shoes, and a pair of sandals. I even got my hair done at a beauty shop and had my photograph taken. Having my hair done and my picture taken was unbelievable. I kept wondering why all of this was happening. It turned out that Pablo had asked for photographs—one for himself and one to apply for my ID. Thanks to Pablo, I was treated like a human being, if only for a moment.

I chose to stay with doña Josefina, instead of Matilde, because I thought Matilde might start living with another man. If this happened, I did not want to be around her. Besides, doña Josefina knew by now that if she tried to hit me, I would defend myself, so the beatings were not as bad as before. I believed she also felt I would probably be leaving soon, and if she treated me better, I might stay longer. Doña Josephina had hired a maid while I was in Jalapa. The maid mainly lightened the load on doña Josephina, but I was still expected to work to pay for Matilde's room and my meals.

Tolla gave me some of her bras. She had some pretty ones in pink, blue, white, and yellow, all made of satin and lace. These were my first bras, and I was very proud of them; they fit me perfectly. She also had her seamstress alter some of her dresses to fit me, and one of her boyfriends brought me two new dresses with elastic in the middle. How good it felt to have new clothes.

Now, when I went to the store, young boys began to say *piropos* (flattering and flirtatious sayings). For example, if a girl they liked passed by, they would start saying things like, "Oh, beautiful one, you are like an angel. I would work for you for the rest of my life!" Others would say, "I cannot live without you; have mercy on me and be my girlfriend."

They had more sayings, or piropos, than I can remember. I would just keep on walking and thinking to myself that they must have a book with all these sayings. In fact, all of them were made up on the spur of the moment. I guess it depended on how inspired they felt when they saw you. If this were the case, I must have inspired them a lot! It sure was good for my morale.

Another good thing that happened was that I was placed in a public school. It was just across Avenue Circunvalación, so I could walk there easily. The classes were very hard because I was almost fifteen and had had very little school up to that time. I was lost most of the time, but it was great just being able to go to school. I used to say to myself that when I could read and write like the teacher, I would be the luckiest girl in the world. I had to work very hard at doña Josephina's to be able to continue in school. When I came home, I still had to do chores before I could start my homework.

I wish I could remember the name of one particular teacher—she was so nice to me and helped me a lot. When there was a school play, she wanted me to participate, but I couldn't because I needed money for the costume. She put me in a dance called *Jesusita in Chihuahua (Little Girl Named Jesusita in Chihuahua)*. She got me a cowboy hat, boots, gun, and whip. She borrowed everything from friends, and I had a great time. The other girls were a bit jealous because I danced with six boys, and during the dance, I had to flirt with them. I still have a picture of myself on this happy occasion.

Just as in the play, boys were becoming an issue in my life. During this period in Mexico, virginity was highly prized in a bride. All young girls were closely chaperoned wherever they went and all contact between young girls and boys was closely guarded.

The groom's family would pay for everything to do with the wedding. If a young woman was found not to be a virgin on her wedding night, she would be returned to her family in great shame and humiliation, and the marriage would be voided. If her family was wealthy and she had an education, she had a future—if not, all she could look forward to would be menial jobs.

From the time I returned to Veracruz, I was not allowed to go anywhere by myself. I usually had to go with Tolla, doña Josephina, or Rolando. I knew I needed to get away by myself, so I made a deal with Rolando that whenever we went to the movies I would go my way and he would go his. Then we would meet somewhere so we could arrive back together. He was happy with this arrangement because he wanted to be with his friends.

One Sunday, I was eager to get going because I saw an opportunity to go to the Laras. I had made up my mind that when I got to the Laras' home, I was going to tell them about the orange cards and the baby picture and request their help and advice on how to write to the hospital where I was born. Rolando and I made our deal, and I was off. I was so eager to see the Laras that I was not walking; I was running. I felt strongly that they were my only hope now. I wanted to stay with them, if they would let me, so I came prepared with my most precious possessions. I did not care about the rest of my things, I just did not want doña Josefina to get suspicious that I was leaving and try to stop me.

As I approached their house, I noticed a big black bow above the door. I felt my heart skip a beat. That could only have meant that Mr. Lara had passed away. By the time I reached the door, I was crying so much I could hardly see. I knocked, but no one answered. I sat on the steps and cried for I don't know how long. I cried for Mr. and Mrs. Lara, and I cried because I felt so alone and helpless. The only thing that had made my coming back to doña Josefina's house bearable was the hope of being with the Laras again. Now that hope was gone.

After a while, I went to ask the neighbors if they could tell me where Mrs. Lara had gone or if they knew of someone that could. They said they did not know, but they thought Mrs. Lara went back to her family in Puebla; another hope vanished. I did not know her family's address or last name. If I had known, I would have gone to her. I still had the hundred-peso note with me, which was more than enough for the bus ticket.

When I met Rolando again that evening, he could tell I had been crying and asked me what had made me cry. When I told him I had seen a sad movie, he wanted to know which one. I told him *Nosotros, Los Pobres, y Ustedes, Los Ricos,* which was the title of a very sad Mexican movie that was popular at that time. In English, the title translates as *We the Poor and You, the Rich.* When we got back to doña Josephina's, she too asked why I had been crying. Rolando answered for me.

I was so sad that, for a long time, the only thing that gave me any joy was going to school. I went to church and prayed before the main altar for God to show me the way to find my family or to send someone who could help me. I knew if Matilde were asked for my hand in marriage, and there was money or free room and board for her, she would jump at the opportunity, no matter what I thought or wanted. The last thing in the world I wanted would have been for her to live with me and to be married to someone she chose for me. I could not think of anything worse than that.

To keep trouble away, doña Josefina had always told others I was a relative. To make matters worse, one time Tolla's older daughter came to visit and I went out with her to a neighbor's house. One of the neighbor's girls asked Tolla's daughter if her cousin could come with them. Tolla's daughter answered, "She is not my cousin; she's just *una arrimada, la gata* (a servant girl)."

This was very painful. These few cruel words during this girl's short visit meant very little to her, but did a lot of harm to me. Now, knowing my real status, the neighbors no longer let their daughters associate with me. Their daughters went to good parochial or private schools; I had just started in a poorer public school. Moreover, my education to this time had been almost nonexistent.

After this incident, my life became almost entirely grim and monotonous. I had no friends of my own. Sometimes I did get together with Rolando's friends, but they were all boys and almost two years younger than I was.

When things around me became unbearable, my two outlets were running and singing. I would run with the dogs around the property until exhaustion would dull the pain of my existence. I would lie on the ground and let the exhaustion overcome my thoughts.

There were, however, a few breaks from the monotony. Neighbors used to show off whenever they would get new records. They would open their windows wide and turn up the sound so the entire neighborhood would hear and know they had just acquired the latest music. I loved this, and during the day, I tried to memorize each new song that came out.

At night, when I finished all my work, a group of Rolando's friends would often meet right in front of the house. We stood around or sat on a large cement and iron standpipe. We tried to see who could sing the songs the best. I could release my pain by letting my voice open up and fly to the wind. I felt this was just about the only thing I could control in my life, and it was my only outlet besides running. I always felt better after singing. I can still sing almost all those songs, word for word. I remember in particular the songs *A Los Quatros Vientos* (*To the Four Winds*), *El Tren Sin Pasajeros* (*The Train Without Passengers*), *Por Un Amor* (*For One Love*), and *Cu Cu Roo Cu Cu Paloma* (a *paloma* is a dove). I was able to do imitations of Lola Beltran, Lucha Reyes, and Amalia Mendoza. Amalia Mendoza was also known popularly as *La Tariacuri*. Sometimes the neighbors would even applaud our singing. Today, this period is called the Golden Age of Mexican Music.

During those rare moments I had free after doing all my work, I also used to play games of skill. Almost all the games I played were boy's games. I guess I was a bit of a tomboy, but I really didn't have any girls my age to be with.

I never had any real toys, as I didn't have the money to buy them. On the rare occasion anyone did give me toys, doña Josefina would take them away from me and give them to Rolando or her grandchildren.

What I did play with were very cheap, often handmade toys, like wooden tops or yo-yos, which I could buy in the mercado for a few centavos. I became quite skilled at throwing a top and working the yo-yo.

Our ping-pong, which we made ourselves, was a very exciting game. The ping-pong ball was actually a small piece of broomstick, about three inches long, that we whittled to a point on each end. The players each had a foot-long piece of the same broomstick.

The game would start by putting the small pointed piece on the ground. With the bat, you would hit the small pointed piece on one of the ends, making it fly into the air. Then, while the piece was still in the air, you would try to hit it as far as you could with the bat. We would measure the distance the small piece was hit by the number of lengths of the bat. The one who hit it the farthest was the winner. This was a fun game and required a lot of interplay and skill.

Another game was marbles; we called them *caniqas*. If you played hard, you could win a lot of marbles, and I did. We often traded marbles. If I knew someone had a great agate, for instance, I could get it by trading a lot of my less valuable marbles. Although I became highly skilled at playing the game, the collecting and trading was the part I liked best.

Riding bicycles was another one of our activities. For a month or more, I would save my meager allowance of one peso per week to go with these boys to rent bicycles. We would walk to the bicycle rental place, get the bikes, and, to get our money's worth, pedal as fast as we could to wherever we were going to ride.

I remember we would each do as many daring things as we could; I did all of the same things as the boys. For example, we would ride to the top of a steep hill, pedal as fast as we could downhill, and then coast with our feet out to each side, letting the bikes just fly. There was a busy cross street at the bottom of the hill, where we would zoom across without slowing. All we did was ring the bells, blow the small battery-powered bicycle horns, or scream—if a car had come, we would have been killed!

We also enjoyed hanging onto the backs of the busses—a truly daring and extremely dangerous feat. When the bus would stop, we would ride up and hang on to whatever we could so the bus would pull us along to the next stop. Sometimes the drivers would stop the bus to warn and scold us. In a way, I am glad that I didn't have enough money to rent bicycles more often, or I may not have written this story.

As I began to develop more apparently into a young woman, it became less proper to play these games and my normal, everyday life became quite bleak. However, I was becoming old enough to participate in some of the much-loved holiday celebrations in Veracruz. One of my favorites was Carnival, a huge celebration just before Lent, which goes back to the early history of the city. People come from all over the world to celebrate Carnival in Veracruz.

I remember fondly the first time I saw the celebration and the effect it had on me. Rolando and I were standing on the side of the street when four young men, carrying a coffin on their shoulders, started running toward us. They were running all through the parade route. For a moment, I thought this was a funeral in progress. Then I read the sign behind them, "This is a burial of bad humor." The week-long party began.

Carnival lasted for one week; however, I was allowed to go during only one day that week. I had to work very hard and behave very well to be allowed to go with Rolando for just a few hours. Though the time was short, I was able to get away from my problems and get caught up in the fun and joy of the moment. I treasured these few moments, as they came so rarely.

In Mexico, November 2 is *el Dia de los Muertos* (the Day of the Dead). This was the one event I always looked forward to. It was traditional at that time in Mexico to start preparing a week before *el Dia de los Muertos*. Doña Josefina would set up an altar in the room right next to where I slept. Each day she would prepare more preserves, sausages, egg breads, candies, and fruit to be added to the growing pile of food already on the altar. This was done so the spirits of the departed would have plenty to eat.

Doña Josefina always rationed my food, and I never had enough. To correct this injustice, I decided I would eat with the spirits! I sneaked into the room while no one was around and very carefully picked whatever I could from under the pile of goodies. I was very careful to make it look as though nothing had been touched. All along, I prayed I would not be caught. I was certain the spirits did not mind, as there was always plenty of food for the spirits, and me. On the second day of November, people would go to the cemetery with the food from the altar and have a picnic by the tombs of their loved ones.

As Christmas season approaches, it is traditional in Veracruz for children to get branches from pine trees and decorate them with multicolored paper chains. A decorated branch is called *la Rama*. They would then go caroling in groups. As a reward for caroling, people would open their doors and give the carolers an *aguinaldo* (Christmas treat or reward), which was a small gift of money or candy. I once went with Rolando and his friends.

Nearer to Christmas, Rolando and I were allowed to go on a very special and traditionally Mexican Christmas celebration called *las Posadas* (the inns). *Las Posadas* goes for nine evenings, ending on Christmas Eve. Each evening the procession started with everyone holding a candle. We went to a different house, representing an inn, on each night. When the procession arrived at the chosen house, we sang songs and eventually the door opened. Then we reenacted the story of Mary and Joseph just before the birth of Jesus.

Someone in the group would ask, "Is there room at the inn?"

The people in the house always answered, "No, go away, no room."

Then, after a while, we would be invited in. There was always a nativity set as the main center of attention. A miniature baby Jesus would be ceremoniously put into the nativity scene. A few prayers were said, and then the party started—piñatas, food, tamales, tostadas, desserts, etc. The next night, the procession started at the last house from the night before. It moved on to the next house with a repeat of the enactment, the ceremony, and subsequent party. The mood was purely festive. The occasion—the birth of the baby Jesus—was celebrated in high fashion.

The ninth night of *las Posadas* ended in a midnight Mass on Christmas Eve. Afterward, everyone went home for a big feast and party in their own homes. Only the best was put on the table at this party. They served *lechone* (roasted piglet), tamales, and *pavo* (turkey). The pavo and lechone were slowly roasted with red condiments. Most people did not have large ovens in their homes, so they took their pork or turkey to a local bakery, an establishment set up just for this purpose. Many people cooked lamb in a pit dug in the ground outside their homes. They placed burning coals in the pit. To prepare the lamb, they added spices, wrapped it with banana leaves, and put it onto the coals in the pit. Then more coals were added on top. Finally, everything was covered with dirt and left to cook for hours. Lamb cooked this way was truly delicious. They also served champagne. The evening was so very festive, and everyone came to celebrate.

This was the most important religious celebration of the year. However, there were no gifts exchanged at this time. Instead, the custom was to exchange gifts on the sixth day of January, Epiphany, the day of the revelation of Jesus to the world. Epiphany was marked by the arrival of the three Magi bearing gifts for the baby Jesus. In Mexico, the evening before Epiphany, children used to leave their shoes at the foot of their beds. They went to sleep with hopes that gifts would be placed in the shoes the next day. Rolando always got lots of presents; I got very few.

Birthdays are another important time of celebration in Mexico. One particularly important birthday celebration occurs when a girl turns fifteen. It is traditional in Mexico to have a very big social celebration of her coming of age. The party is called a *quinceañera* (a girl's fifteenth birthday party, similar to the traditional coming out party that used to be popular in American high society, but more religious in nature). The girl would invite fourteen of her best girlfriends, each accompanied by a boy, to be her attendants, and all would dress formally for the occasion. The fifteen-year-old girl would dance the first dance, a waltz, with her father, and then the party would start. The celebration would go all night and into the next day.

My fifteenth birthday came and went unnoticed except by Mother Nature; I got my first period on that day. Tolla had promised me a new dress for my birthday, but she became angry with me for something, and I did not get the dress until weeks later. It was a pretty, pink dress in princess style.

Although my special day may have gone unnoticed by them, I had a secret admirer who lived nearby, a nice nineteen-year-old boy named Jesus. He brought the *mariachis* (traditional Mexican musical group) to serenade me on my birthday. Tolla thought the *mariachis* were for her, so I was able to listen to them in peace and let her think they were singing to her. Jesus hid behind a tree so they would not see him. He knew if they saw him, I would get in trouble. Tolla had already insulted and slapped him and told him not to see me again. After that, he asked me to run away with him. He said we could go to Orizaba, another city in the state of Veracruz, get married, and live at his aunt's home. He said he could get a job in a photo lab. Thank God, my life was not too unbearable at doña Josefina's, or I may have seen Jesus's proposal as a way out.

Deep inside, the hope of going to the United States became stronger than ever. I could not see myself marrying anyone, no matter how good looking or wealthy. That was not what I wanted. I was an attractive young girl with fair skin and light hair. Most men liked that because they felt by marrying someone with lighter skin, their children would also have lighter skin, which was considered an improvement. In other words, I was very worried I would end up in Veracruz for the rest of my life.

Just across the street, there was a young military man who had asked permission to court me in the afternoons. Because his family was well-to-do, doña Josefina agreed right away. I did not even like this young man, so when he came to see me, I would sit so doña Josefina, as was the custom, would have a good view of both of us. I was chaperoned at all times. During these visits, Jesus would ride by on his bicycle. He gave looks that could kill, but there was not much else he could do. I would not take him up on his proposal. While everyone around me more or less accepted his or her lot in life, I did not; I always looked to the future. Somehow, I knew I could do better.

During this time, Matilde was living it up. On weekends she would go dancing at Villa del Mar, the Mocambo, or Boca del Rio; these were dancing and nightclub areas near the sea.

There was a very rich and powerful man in Veracruz; I'll call him "*el Jefe*" (the boss). He had four wives and many sons and daughters. The first wife had four sons, the youngest three years older than me. Wherever he went, he had four *pistoleros* (bodyguards) with him. In Veracruz at that time, it was said that there were three laws to live by—civil law, church law, and el Jefe's law. Whatever el Jefe wanted, he got—by agreement or by force.

I was fifteen years old, and Matilde was waiting for money from Pablo to take us to Tijuana. One day I went with the maid to the mercado to buy *jaibas* and *camaronnes* (crabs and shrimp). As we were leaving, a young man, one of el Jefe's pistoleros, approached us and offered to take us to our home. I refused, saying that we would wait for the bus, but the pistolero said, "el Jefe prefers I take you to your home."

Surprisingly, the maid seemed to be okay with this. I somehow felt she knew who this person was. She said, "Niña Graciela, it's okay to go with him; we will be home in no time. It is too hot to wait for the bus." I did not feel threatened, so I agreed.

Later, I found out that el Jefe liked me for one of his sons. If el Jefe had gotten his way and I had been forced to marry his son, Matilde would have come to live with us as "the mother of the bride." Thinking back, I still cannot contain my feelings of fear and anger at this close call, which could have altered my entire life.

Thank God, Pablo had sent the money to Matilde, just in time. Matilde started selling and giving away her things and packing for the trip. Just days later, we were on our way to Mexico City. In a way, I was glad to be going away with Matilde. I shudder to think what would have happened if the money had not come when it did. These two greedy women, doña Josephina and Matilde, would have forced me to marry for the benefits they would have derived.

I saw this as the help I had been asking God to send. Matilde told me that from a hill in Tijuana I would be able to see the United States and the lights of San Ysidro. She said that in Tijuana we would get our visas for the United States. I cannot describe my joy and, at the same time, my apprehension at this news.

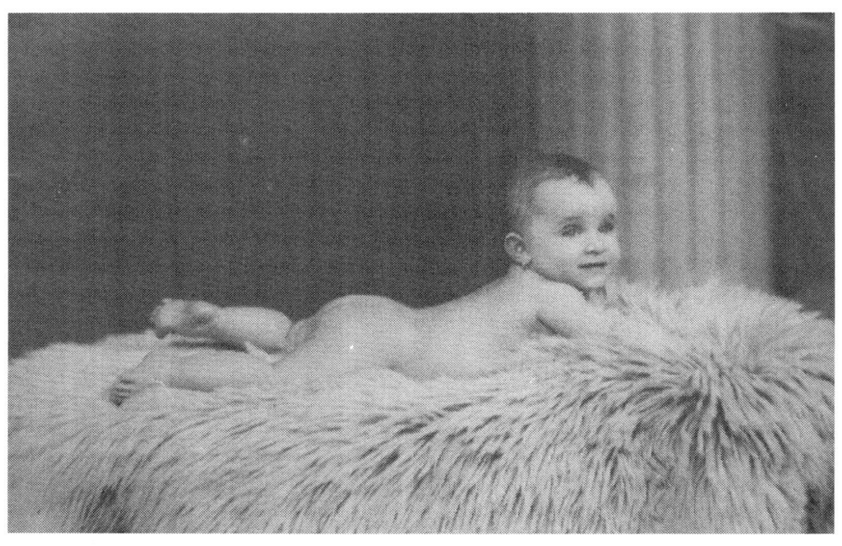

My baby picture—I was six months old
Brooklyn, New York

Department of Hospitals
Cumberland Hospital
VISITOR'S CARD
(Maternity)
Name of Patient .... Matilda
Ward ...56...
Admitted ...9-40...
THIS CARD MUST BE SHOWN AT DOOR

Department of Hospitals
Cumberland Hospital
VISITOR'S CARD
(Maternity)
Name of Patient .... Matilda
Ward ...56...
Admitted ...9-40...
THIS CARD MUST BE SHOWN AT DOOR

The orange visitor cards—I still keep these

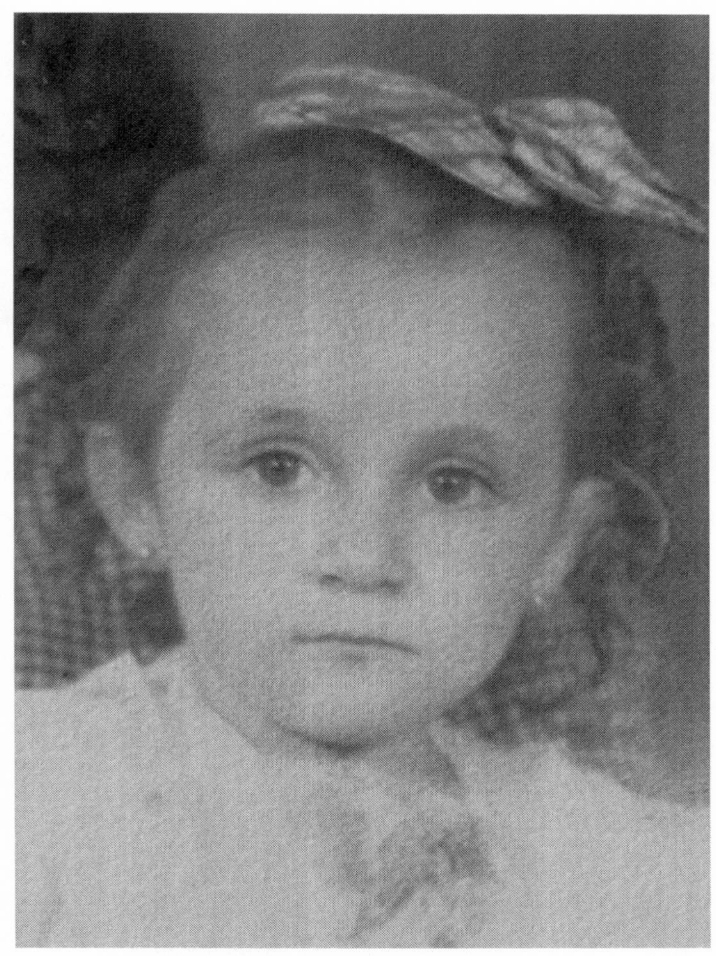

My second birthday
Ensenada, Mexico

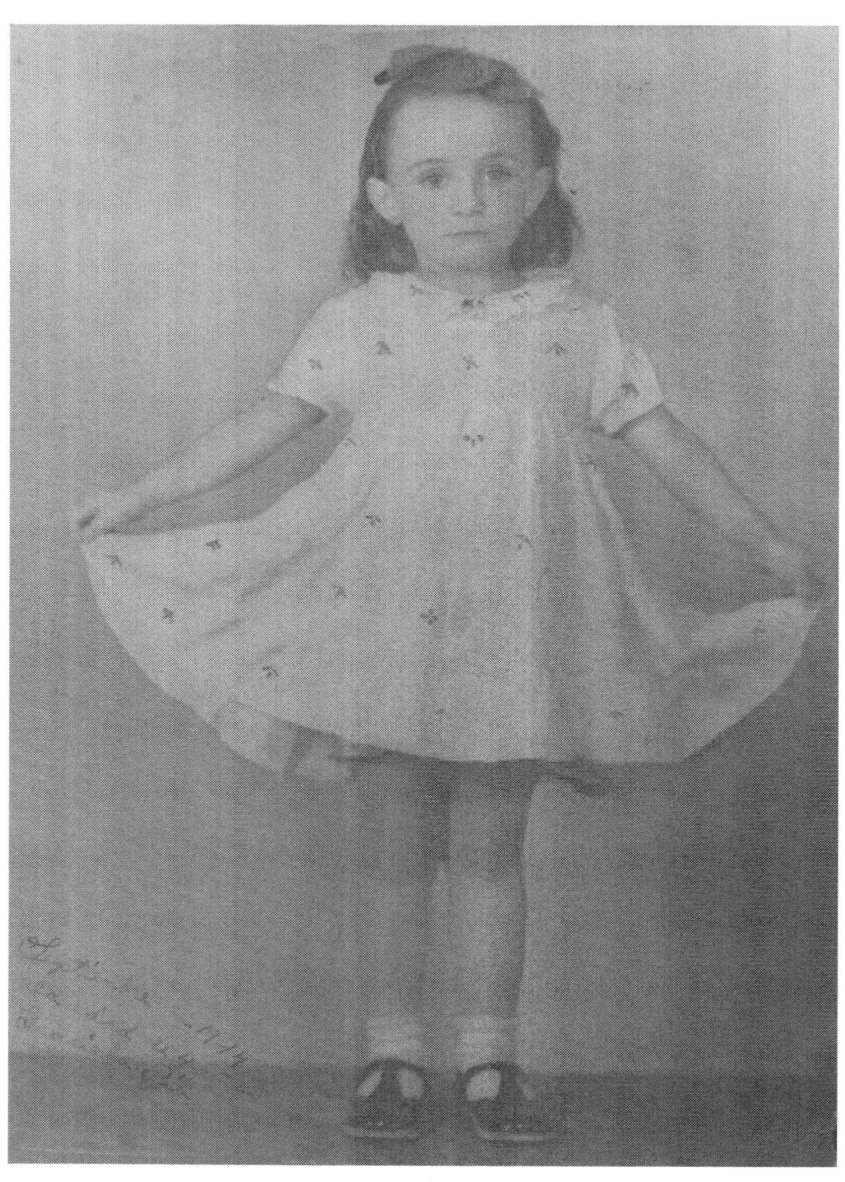

My fourth birthday
Mexicali, Mexico

Doris Dana (left) and Gabriela Mistral as I remember them from Veracruz in 1948

After my fifteenth birthday
Veracruz, Mexico

Me (third row, second from right) in school I attended for two months in Mexico City. Aunt Mari bought the uniform for me.

Me at fifteen years old,
in cowgirl costume provided by a kind teacher
for a school dance program, Jesusita y Chihuahua
Veracruz, Mexico

Me (left) and Cristina Baranda
just before I graduated

Receiving my high school diploma
Benjamin Franklin Adult Business School
San Francisco, California

Just married

Our wedding party,
just after we were married
Alawai Yacht Harbor, Honolulu, Hawaii

Pranks on our wedding day

(from left) Doris Dana, me, Margit Varga,
and my children
Bridgehampton, Long Island, 1976

SELECTED POEMS OF

Gabriela Mistral

Dearest Graciela —

Remembering all the love that Gabriela Mistral & I felt for you in Veracruz and knowing all that you suffered, this book comes humbly to you — with great love,

Doris Dana.

April 14, 1976 - (el día que me llamaste)

Penned inside the book, Selected Poems of Gabriela Mistral, on the day I called her in 1976. The book was a gift to me from Doris Dana, the author.

Luisa and I walk the Brooklyn Bridge together for the first time

Matilde and Pablo at their wedding

Closer to My Dreams

"One does not love a place less for having suffered in it."

Jane Austin

Matilde wanted to stop in Poza Rica, Tuxpan, and Mexico City, to see her relatives before we left for Tijuana. I had not met any of these people, and frankly, all I wanted to do was go straight to Tijuana; the rest was something I had to endure along the way.

We said our good-byes, and doña Josefina told Matilde to send her address as soon as we got to the United States. It seemed I would never get away from these two women—what a terrible thought.

Jesus lived only one block away, so doña Josefina and Tolla were always on the lookout for him. Whenever they saw him, they would insult him and tell him to stay away from me. In spite of their efforts, I somehow managed to see Jesus before we left. As he had done several times before, Rolando was acting as a lookout. He would whistle if he thought Tolla or doña Josefina might see us together. He thought Jesus was all right, so he would often help us so we could see each other. Rolando was hurrying me.

Jesus cried when I told him I was leaving. He said he wanted to marry me. I told him I had to go to the United States before I would ever think of marriage, but I promised to write, and we quickly said our good-byes.

Finally, we were on our way to Mexico City. When we arrived, we went to Matilde's uncle's apartment. Uncle Gustavo Sr. lived in a nice apartment with his wife, Aunt Guigermina, and their daughter, Rosa, who was two years younger than me.

A few days after we arrived, I told Matilde we had better be going. Reluctantly, like a child who had something to hide, she told me we didn't have enough money to get to Tijuana. She had overspent on clothing and other luxuries for herself so she would make a good impression on her family. I wanted to slap her when I heard this. By now, I knew Uncle Gustavo Sr. wanted us out.

Matilde asked Uncle Gustavo Sr. if I could stay with them while she went back to Poza Rica to see her sister, Mari, and wait for more money from Pablo. Uncle Gustavo Sr. was not happy at all with me staying, but he wanted Matilde out in a worse way, so he agreed. Here I go again, left with people I had just met, and who didn't want me there. What choice did I have? The only saving grace was that Aunt Guigermina was very nice to me; she understood my situation and how badly I felt.

Gustavo Sr. had three adult sons and a teenage daughter. Gustavo Jr., was from his first wife; Javier, Enrique and Rosa were all from his present wife. They all came to meet me, and afterward Gustavo Sr. accused his sons of being nicer to me than to their own sister, Rosa. This made me feel even more unwelcome.

Later, Uncle Enrique and his wife, Aunt Perita, offered to take me in, since they had two daughters several years younger than me. They welcomed me into their home and the girls introduced me to their friends; we all got along well together. At last, I was with girls my same age; this was very important to me at the time. Often, there would be five of us at one time. We used to walk arm-in-arm in the evenings, singing and going to parties together. At least here, I felt welcome.

Aunt Perita, who worked as a nurse, had a maid who cooked and took care of the apartment. I was enrolled in school, but I couldn't attend because I needed a uniform. I had just met Matilde's sister, Aunt Mari, who was visiting from Poza Rica. Although we had just met, she bought me a uniform. She knew I had no money of my own and saw my need. From the time we first met, she always treated me with love and kindness. I will always be grateful for what she did.

In spite of my more comfortable situation, I still felt completely lost and uncertain about my future. I sat down and wrote Pablo a very strong letter. I told him about most of the things I had been through in the past fifteen years, and I blamed him for my situation. I explained that I did not want to end up in Mexico with Matilde causing me more harm than good. I closed the letter by asking him if he could find it in his heart to send money so I could get to the United States. I asked him to send it to me and not to tell Matilde. I was desperate, and I saw him as my last hope.

Even though I struggled to write at all, I must have written a very convincing letter. Within two weeks, I received an answer from Pablo with two precious checks—one in my name for one hundred dollars; the other in Matilde's name for twenty-five dollars. I could have hugged and kissed the mailman when I got the letter.

Now I had to find a way to cash these two checks without Matilde knowing I had gotten them. I told Uncle Gustavo Jr. all I had done and that I had received a letter with the checks. Somehow, I knew I could trust him.

Right away, he told me, "Until you are ready, don't tell Matilde about the money, and don't tell anyone you are leaving."

I asked him, "How am I going to cash the checks, especially the one in Matilde's name?"

He said, "I will take you to my bank. We will say you are my niece, Matilde is your little sister, and you are signing for her."

We went to the bank right away, and since they knew him, they cashed the checks. At last, here I was with thirteen hundred and fifty pesos, all my own.

I asked Uncle Gustavo Jr., "Now please will you help me tell Uncle Enrique I am going to Poza Rica to get Matilde so we can go to Tijuana?" He agreed and explained to Uncle Enrique and Aunt Perita what I was doing. I took the money, hid it in a little white sack, and pinned it to my under garments. I was on my way to Poza Rica.

Poza Rica is several hours by bus northeast of Mexico City. When I arrived in Poza Rica, I went to Aunt Mari's house first. Uncle Gustavo Jr. had been in contact with her and she already knew about the money, so I gave it to her to keep for me until I was ready to leave. I told her I wanted to see Matilde, but it was the weekend, and I wanted to wait to see her when her man would be at work.

Aunt Mari and her husband had seven children, four boys and three girls. Inez, the eldest girl, was younger than me. Aunt Mari's husband did not like Matilde around his house or, more specifically, his three daughters. I knew he did not want me there either. He felt that as long as I was there, Matilde would be coming to the house while he was at work. In spite of this, Aunt Mari and her family treated me like family, especially the daughters, Olivia, Carmen, and Inez. I was closest in age to Inez, but somehow Olivia and I spent the most time together.

When I got there, the home was buzzing with preparations for Inez's upcoming quinceañera. There were girls my age coming and going to the dressmaker and beauty shops and shopping for new shoes and accessories. Some girls were trying on their new dresses—Inez's dress was all white, and her fourteen girl attendants were dressed in pastel colors. Each dress was a different color, like the colors of the rainbow—a delight to the eyes.

Here I was, in the midst of all the excitement, but not part of it. This was made ever more evident by the question I was asked by several of Inez's girlfriends, "Why is it you are her cousin, and you are not one of her fourteen attendants?" All I could say was that this was a surprise visit. The truth was I had to save and didn't have extra money for a dress, shoes, and all the accessories.

After the weekend, I went by bus to confront Matilde. During our showdown, I had somehow convinced her to tell me all she knew about where I was born, my family, and how she got me. As our confrontation closed, I told her if she wanted to go with me to Tijuana, she had better be ready soon. She told me she needed at least a week so she could sell her things. She was going with me, now all I had to do was wait. I went back to Aunt Mari and told her we would be leaving in a week or so. Her husband was elated to hear the news of our departure. However, just before the quinceañera, Matilde sent word that her man had become ill, and she would have to wait a few more days.

Then came the evening of the quinceañera. In a photograph of the quinceañera party, I saw afterward, I was in the background standing on a chair so I could get a better view of the festivities. The look on my face said it all—I was on the outside looking in, but not part of it.

Although it was not a pleasant evening for me, I was thankful I was there rather than at Matilde's place. I did not want to cause trouble for Aunt Mari with her husband. Aunt Mari was always very nice to me, and I know that if she had had money of her own, she would have gotten me a dress. All the money Aunt Mari had was what little she could save from her grocery money. After buying food for a family of ten, I am sure there was little left.

A week later, the man finally went back to work, and Matilde sent word she had to have yet another week to get ready. It was so difficult, after counting on only one week of waiting, to have to endure yet another week. I was agonizingly suspended in time. Even though I was a little afraid of the unknown, I always held the hope things would be better for me the closer I got to the United States. I felt I could overcome whatever misfortune came my way as long as there was hope for a better future.

Finally, Matilde was ready to leave. The day before our departure, I needed to make the reservations and buy the tickets from Poza Rica to Tuxpan, and on to Tijuana. I asked Aunt Mari for the money she had been keeping for me. She handed me the money, and before leaving, I separated it so Matilde would see I had just enough for the expenses of the trip. This way she would not know how much additional money I had. Off I went to the bus station.

After a few hours, I returned with the bus tickets and the schedule for the trip. The next day Aunt Mari gave me a gold medal of the Blessed Virgin to save me from all harm. I still have this medal. For added protection, she also put a clove of garlic in my belongings to keep evil away. She packed some *anonas* (large tropical fruit) and something to eat along the way. We hugged, and she wished me good luck.

Aunt Mari, in the short time I had known her, showed she loved me like her own niece. However, she had no idea of my plans, as she was completely unaware of the horrors of my childhood or the story Matilde had just told me of how I was born and how she got me; she did not know Matilde was not my real mother. At the time, I could not share any of this with Aunt Mari or her family; it would have been too much for them. In any case, I know she would have done more for me if she could have.

We said our good-byes, and I headed for the bus station. I met Matilde and, as we got on the bus, I felt a sense of personal freedom and an even stronger sense that I now had some control over my life. This was 1957; I was sixteen. I had neither a family nor an education, only a strong desire for a better life pulling me toward Tijuana and, more importantly, the United States. As I sat down in the bus, I touched the waist of my dress to assure myself that my baby picture and two orange cards were there. As I felt them, it gave me comfort and hope, somehow diminishing the fear of the unknown. I was ever surer these were key proofs I had been born in the United States, almost seventeen years earlier.

We made our stop in Tuxpan, where Matilde had some family to whom she wanted to say good-bye. Tuxpan was a pleasant little fishing town, and someday, I want to take my family there. At my insistence, the visit was short and sweet, and we were on our way again. After leaving Tuxpan, my thoughts turned to what might be waiting for me in Tijuana. I was contemplating how I was going to break the news to Matilde as to what my plans were and that I had the orange cards and the baby picture in my possession.

One of the benefits of traveling by bus is you get to see the countryside. The panoramas were beautiful, especially Lake Chapala, near Guadalajara. The fishermen equipped their boats with huge nets that looked like butterfly wings. All these years later, I can still close my eyes and see this beauty. I cannot recall the names of all the cities we passed through; however, I can recall the marvelous scenery and majestic countryside.

Matilde thought that when we got to Tijuana we were going to wait until the papers were ready for us to immigrate to the United States. However, I intended to enter the United States as a citizen, not an immigrant. My biggest problem was to prove that I was born in the United States. The how, when, and where I would do this remained to be worked out. In any case, I could not talk to Matilde about these things. I did not know if there was more information about me she might be withholding. I would have to approach her at the right moment, and this was not the right moment. I knew I had to be very careful so she would not suspect my plans. I had to make her believe that I was going to do what she wanted, right up until the last minute.

After almost a week of travel, we arrived in Tijuana. It was morning, and Matilde seemed to be very happy to be back. We took a taxi to her father's house, the same one we had left some ten years before. It was a depressing sight. Matilde's father had died a few years earlier, and Matilde's cousin, Celina, had gone through the entire fortune he had left to her. She had squandered it all. She had had a few lovers who stole everything from her, and now all that was left of those days of servants, fur coats, chauffeurs, and the best that money could buy was the property where the house and the bakery sat. The only reason the property remained was that Matilde's father left it to Celina's mother, and Celina could not sell it.

I could not believe my eyes at the condition of the house—the beautiful, ornate furniture was gone, and in its place was cheap, worn-out furniture. The floors, which had been richly carpeted before, were bare. The walls were empty of their paintings, and the rich velvet curtains were gone. According to Celina's daughter, Edith, things had gotten so bad that she had used some of the curtain material to make dresses for her and for her children. Edith was a little more than two years older than me. She already had two children and one on the way. She got pregnant by one of the helpers in the bakery when she was fifteen. Would you believe she had a great party, her quinceañera, when she turned fifteen? She was presented to Tijuana society, and her picture was in the local newspaper. Now, four years later, she did not have enough to eat!

Celina was working as a bar maid in Los Angeles and only came home two days a week. Her present lover, Rafael, took care of the smaller children during the week. Rafael appeared to be in his late twenties or early thirties; Celina, in her late forties. I could not believe Celina had squandered all the money and the businesses in such a short time. It was hard to see the way they were living now and to remember the opulence in which they had been living when we saw them last. It was incredible.

Matilde asked Celina what she had done with all her father's money. Celina told her it was none of her business. This created bad feelings right from the start. I told Matilde not to ask Celina any more questions. I told her if her father had wanted to leave her something, he would have put it in his will. He apparently left everything, except the property, to Celina and their children.

I began to inquire about who still lived in the neighborhood from the early forties. I found two families still there. I started asking questions of the ladies in these families and found one lady who remembered me as a little girl. After more discussions, I felt sure I could confide in her. I told her my story and my plans. She told me I did not look anything like Matilde or her family. Because they had never met Matilde's husband or even seen a picture of him, they had their doubts about Matilde's claim of being my mother.

I was under a lot of pressure now, as Rafael would appear everywhere I went. If I sat outside in the evening, he would be there, trying to make conversation with me. He even had the audacity to ask me to go out with him. I looked forward to Celina coming home so Rafael would stop bothering me. I started spending more time at the house of the lady I had come to trust. She lived only four houses away from where I was staying.

The lady introduced me to her married daughter and son-in-law, both of whom knew English. Her son-in-law carefully examined the orange cards and the writing on the baby picture. He suggested I go to the mercado in downtown Tijuana and have a letter typed to the Cumberland Hospital in Brooklyn, New York, requesting a copy of my birth certificate. He suggested I enclose one of the orange cards, give them my name and date of birth, and wait to see what happened. He said I should have an answer within a few weeks.

I almost flew to the mercado and found the place where they typed letters in English—it was actually an orange crate turned end-up with a typewriter on it. I think I paid the young man two pesos for typing my letter and addressing the envelope. When I put the orange card in the envelope, I felt as if I were missing part of myself. I felt incomplete and frightened. What would happen if I never heard from them? What would I do next? I looked up at the sky and prayed that I would have an answer soon. I continued to pray, *Oh, God, let it be.* My only consolation was I still had the other orange card with me, just in case this one got lost.

I rushed to the post office, arriving just minutes before closing time. My hand was trembling as I let the envelope drop out of sight; the *clank* of the metal door on the mailbox signaled the finality of my decision. In any case, it was done; I had parted with one of my precious orange cards. I felt weak because I was putting so much hope in this letter. I felt as though part of me was going with the letter.

I knew I had to get out of Tijuana soon. No matter how careful I was, the money Pablo sent me was running out. I did not buy anything that was not absolutely necessary. I made my pesos stretch as far as they could.

I used the return address of the lady's home so Matilde would not have a clue as to what I was up to. I went every day to check the mail. I was becoming very anxious as each day passed. As I was on my way to the lady's home on the twelfth day, I caught sight of her waiting outside, waving a big white envelope. I flew to her. She was as excited as I was. I was shaking as I opened the envelope—no birth certificate and no orange card, only a letter. The letter was written in English, so we had to wait until her son-in-law arrived to know exactly what the letter said. I believe it was a Saturday morning, and she said he was due any time.

She asked me into her home. I was in such a state that she asked me to sit down while she made tea. I must have looked terrible, because she appeared very concerned. She kept trying to reassure me. She told me not to worry; it was probably good news. I was worried because I didn't see a copy of my birth certificate or my precious orange card, and I could not read the letter.

When her son-in-law finally arrived, he did not even get into the house before I thrust the letter in his hand. He quickly scanned the letter, smiled, and said, "They just want two dollars so they can send you a copy of your birth certificate."

I could not speak; the tears just flowed. I sobbed uncontrollably. I felt as though I had found part of myself. I felt overpowering joy. I was thankful I was with people who understood, so I could just let my feelings flow.

After a pause, the lady said, "This calls for a celebration. You are having lunch with us!"

I looked at her and thanked her, but impatiently asked if we could celebrate after I went to the bank. I explained that I would still have time, if I hurried, to exchange my Mexican money for American money, have another letter typed, and send the two dollars. She told me she had some American dollars and could exchange the money right then. She handed me the two dollars, and I flew out of the house.

Mercifully, the bus arrived just as I got to the bus stop. I rushed off the bus to the mercado where I found a young lady to type the letter and address the envelope. I paid her and raced to the post office. Again, I arrived just minutes before closing time. I paid the airmail postage and paused, just a second, before I let go of the envelope. The feeling returned that part of me was going along with it. Now I was faced with another agonizing wait.

Matilde was getting suspicious of my visits to the lady's house. Every time I said I was going to this lady's house, she thought I was meeting a boyfriend. In my situation, who in the world would have the time or the inclination to have a boyfriend? All I lived for and thought about was getting away from Tijuana and Matilde. This time the waiting was even more unbearable. The minutes seemed like hours, days like weeks.

As soon as I got my birth certificate, I planned to tell Matilde and ask her to go to U.S. immigration with me. I knew I would need someone to help me with all the questions I thought I most certainly would be asked. I reasoned she would know the answers better than anyone would. I was almost sure she would do this for me.

In the meantime, through Matilde, I met a lady named doña Altagracia, and through doña Altagracia, I eventually met her daughter, my godmother, Nelly. Nelly and her father, Canuto, stood for me when I was baptized and confirmed at the Parroquia de Nuestra Señora de Guadalupe in Tijuana, when I was two years old. Nelly lived in

Escondido, California, and came to Tijuana most weekends to visit her mother.

A few days later, I was standing outside just looking around, killing time. I was trying to get away from Matilde and away from the house. Just then, Rafael drove up and asked me if I wanted to go with him to meet Celina at the border. He said she was arriving soon. I knew Celina was arriving that day, so I got in the car. Instead of going the direction he should have, he went out of the way and stopped the car. He pulled me to him and tried to kiss me. I resisted. He forced me down onto the seat and again tried to force me to kiss him. I managed to knee him in his privates, and that knocked some sense into him. I told him he better turn around and take me home, or I was going to tell the police he tried to rape me and also tell Celina about him bothering me to go out with him. I also told him my godfather worked for the police department.

It worked; he knew this incident might affect his chances of ever crossing the border. He took me home, and on the way, he told me he could not help himself because I was pretty and that I was driving him crazy every time he saw me. He said he did not love Celina and was with her only so she could help him with his papers so he could go to Los Angeles to work. This explained why he was living with her.

I told him he had a terrible way of showing he liked me, but if he promised to stop following me and not to bother me again, I would not tell anyone about this incident.

The next day, feeling the need to have one of those heart-to-heart talks with God, I went to the Parroquia de Nuestra Señora de Guadalupe and prayed for the speedy delivery of my birth certificate. I also thanked my guardian angel for keeping me safe from the close call I had with Rafael. I had a lot of extra pressure on me with this creep living in the same house and in the next room from Matilde and me. I desperately wanted to get out of this house and away from him as soon as I could. *Where to go* was the big question.

Matilde wanted me to look for a job. She thought I would be good as a waitress. She was not worried about my safety at all; she could only think about me supporting her. I could just imagine myself, a sixteen-year-old girl working as a waitress in Tijuana. I feel sick now just thinking what would have become of me if I had listened to Matilde.

As usual, every time I have felt my lowest, hope has come from somewhere to lift me up. It had been almost two weeks since I had sent the letter and the two dollars for my birth certificate. I went every day to the lady's house to check the mail. One morning, just like the few mornings before, the feeling of expectation was driving me on. I went out as I knew it was about time for the mail to arrive. As I started toward the lady's house, all I could see, just as a few weeks before, was a hand with a large envelope waving back and forth. I started to run—no, fly—toward her. She anxiously handed me the envelope and asked me to sit down. She sat right next to me as I tore into the envelope. There was my orange card! Instantly, I felt whole again, like recovering a part of myself. There, with the card, was an official paper with an important and official-looking embossed seal in the corner. I looked and looked, trying to figure out what all of this meant. I could clearly see my name. I had always been called Graciela in Spanish, but Matilde had told me my name was Grace in English. I knew for sure this was my birth certificate.

I looked at the lady. She was excited for me and at the same time seemed to be observing all of this and taking in the emotions of the moment. When she asked what I was going to do next, I told her that I needed to figure out how to tell Matilde and then how to cross the border.

Then I looked at her and asked, "Could you please keep this for me? I don't want to take it to Matilde when I'm telling her, because she might try to take it away from me or destroy it. She doesn't know all I have done, and this is going to be a big shock."

The lady put my birth certificate on a shelf in her china cabinet and locked the door. I thanked her profusely for all her help and moral support and said, "Now I have to think carefully about my next step."

I left with the feeling I had just held the whole world in my hands. I knew I had the key to many of the answers to my past and, hopefully, my family. Soon more of my questions would be answered. I felt newly confident that I would have answers to the burning questions I had painfully held inside for so long.

I stopped and pondered how I could have just been given up so casually and with so little regard for my future, especially to a complete stranger like Matilde.

Overjoyed and full of hope, I went to the Parroquia de Nuestra Señora de Guadalupe to give thanks to God for my birth certificate. In the excitement of the moment, I hadn't realized that this was the very church where I had been baptized and confirmed some fourteen years earlier. I was probably crying then too.

I refer to the kind woman who helped me as *the lady*, because I cannot remember her name. I would really like for her and her family to know how much her simple acts of kindness meant to me. She, her daughter, and her son-in-law were there when I needed them most, and they asked nothing in return. For this, I will forever be thankful to her and her family.

Looking back, I believe I cannot remember her name because at the time I was dealing with so much stress, making so many moves, and meeting so many new people. A lot of the stress came from being in such close contact with Matilde. It also came from Rafael, from the uncertainty of my future, and from seeing the money run out with no hope of getting more unless I went to work. Most stores, where I had asked for a job, wanted proof I had been to school and that I had finished at least the tenth grade, which I had not. This too, added to the stress. Working as a waitress and housekeeping were looking like my only options. I felt I could do better, no matter what little education I had. I guess this feeling of always trying to do better was now what kept me going. I thank God for that inner drive and faith that was always with me.

I went into the church, lit some candles, and knelt at the altar. I prayed to God, thanking Him for this tremendous miracle of getting my birth certificate. This impossible dream had come true.

As I left the church, I realized that I had to tell Matilde. I walked in to find her sitting around, beautifying herself as usual, and told her that we needed to talk. She immediately asked if I had received a letter from Pablo, and I told her I had not. She probably thought he had sent money to me for the visas.

I said, "No, what I have to tell you is that I sent for a copy of my birth certificate and I got it." I looked at her—it was as if something hit her hard. She was instantly stunned and in shock—time seemed to stand still. She didn't curse me; she didn't say anything. I could sense her big disappointment as the finality of the end of her control over me had abruptly jolted her senses.

Finally regaining her composure, she asked, almost too calmly, "How did you do this? What did you tell them? How did you get it?"

I went on, "Matilde, remember those two orange cards and my baby picture? I have had those with me for the past eight years. I have been hiding them from place to place. Remember those times when I wanted to go and say good-bye to doña Josefina in Veracruz and when I wanted to say good-bye to Maria in Jalapa? It wasn't that I wanted to say good-bye, what I really wanted was to retrieve those orange cards and the baby picture. Do you really think I wanted to say good-bye and thank them for all the beatings and abuse I had gotten from them? No, I had to retrieve the cards and the baby picture."

At this, Matilde asked, "How did you know I had them?"

I continued calmly and carefully, "One afternoon, when you had been away for quite a long time, you came back and you were talking to Tolla in her room. I started to walk in and overheard what you were talking about. I quietly hid behind Tolla's door. I don't know how you didn't hear my breathing or the tension I was in, but I was there. I knew I was taking my life in my hands because I felt sure if you had caught me, all three of you would have beaten me short of my life. In any case, I somehow knew that was a chance I had to take.

"Tolla was asking you for my papers so they could send me to school. She said the neighbors were complaining at how Rolando, who was younger than me, was going to school every day, but I wasn't. Tolla told you they needed my birth certificate and my other papers, and you told Tolla I was born in Brooklyn, New York, and the only papers you had were the two orange cards that were issued by the hospital to visitors and a baby picture taken just before you left Brooklyn with me to come to Mexico. However, you told Tolla you had registered me in Ensenada when I was two years old and that she could use those papers. You said you would send for them. I was listening to all of this."

I continued to explain, "With this information, I made a plan. I waited until you went dancing that weekend. When the time was right, I told doña Josefina I was going to play. Instead, I went into your room with a flashlight. I put a stool on a chair, reached the basket, and got the cards and the baby picture and have been hiding these things amongst my meager possessions ever since."

As she heard this, Matilde had a look of disbelief and shock at my audacity. All of these years, she hadn't noticed that the cards and the picture were missing. It was too much for her to comprehend. To me, Matilde always had a child's mind. Even though I had kept this secret from her, she did not ask me for proof. I guess by now she knew better than to doubt me. To my surprise, Matilde did not blow off her usual verbal abuse.

In a seemingly civil manner, all she asked was, "Pablo knows what you have done? You know he was planning to fix us papers as immigrants. Now you have ruined that."

I told her, "Why should I immigrate to the country where I was born in the first place? I did not choose to leave it. I was taken out illegally, and I want to go back as an American citizen, not an immigrant."

"What about me?" she asked. I told her that Pablo could fix her papers and she could go as an immigrant.

With barely hidden anger in her expression, she calmly asked me, "What do you plan to do now? Are you going to tell Pablo about the birth certificate so he can get us a place to live in the United States?"

I quickly decided that I didn't want her to become more upset. I told her that I wanted her to come with me to the checkpoint on the border. I needed her to help me answer all the questions they would ask, and if she were with me, they would be more likely to believe me.

She became agitated and asked, "When do you plan to cross the border?"

I told her, "As soon as possible. I have been waiting for this moment all my life!"

Even though she was obviously upset, she calmly and cunningly said, "Give me a couple of days to get all of my papers ready, and I will go with you."

I figured that was fair, as I also had to get my things ready and say good-bye to friends. I thought this would also give me a little more time to see if we would hear from Pablo. Maybe he would send us some money.

By now, I had nearly run out of money to buy food. What little I had, I wanted to keep in case I needed it for something important.

Matilde was eating with Celina's family. Raphael was eating there too. Because of the incident with Raphael, I wanted to avoid being around him. I was eating mostly bread or tortillas; these were the cheapest food I could buy to satisfy my hunger. I left Matilde with her thoughts.

By the time I left Matilde it was late afternoon, and I decided to go to doña Altagracia's house to give her the good news of my birth certificate. She was very happy for me and said this called for a celebration. To celebrate, doña Altagracia invited me to have dinner with her and asked me to buy some tortillas. When I came back, we sat down to a very nice dinner. She had prepared a delicious pork and chili dish, a salad, and beans and rice. All of this was served with the fresh tortillas I had just brought. We had *jamaica* (Mexican drink made from hibiscus flowers) to drink. It was heavenly; I had not had a good meal in weeks and must have eaten like there was no tomorrow.

Doña Altagracia, obviously noticing how I ate with such gusto, asked me, "When was the last time you had a complete meal?"

I told her that I did not have much money and that for the past few weeks I had been eating very poorly, having some canned things and mostly bread and tortillas. When she heard this, she told me I was welcome to stay with her. She said she always had more food than she could eat and, at times, it even went to waste. She said I could also help her by going to the store and delivering the dresses she made.

I thanked her for her offer and told her I would be glad to help because I especially did not want to stay at Celina's house. She assured me that even if I were unable to cross the border the first time, I would have a place to stay. I said to myself, *Thank God for this woman.*

After we celebrated, we settled into a nice discussion of my plans. I told doña Altagracia I had known for some time that I was not Matilde's real daughter. I always suspected this, and before we left Poza Rica, Matilde had told me everything. I told doña Altagracia that I wanted to cross the border as soon as possible and that Matilde had agreed to go with me to help answer the questions they would surely ask.

I sent word to Matilde that I was staying overnight at doña Altagracia's home. Late in the afternoon the next day, I went to see Matilde to prepare for our trip to the border. To my surprise, Matilde was nowhere to be found. She had left no word of her whereabouts. However, she did tell Edith to tell me she could not go with me to the border because she was afraid she would be arrested for illegally taking me out of the United States.

You could have tipped me over with a feather. I was shocked. She had taken off, leaving me in Tijuana all by myself. Then I remembered doña Altagracia's offer. I quickly gathered my things, told Edith I was going to look for Matilde, and quietly slipped out the back way. One thing was certain—I did not want Rafael to know Matilde had left me all alone; I wanted to be out of there as soon as possible.

There I was, alone at sixteen in Tijuana and once again going to another person's house. At that moment, I did not even think of my birth certificate, all I could think about was what I would do if they didn't let me cross the border. If they didn't believe my story, what would I do in Tijuana?

Full of fear about what the future held for me, I rushed back to doña Altagracia's home. As soon as she saw me, she asked what was wrong. I told her about Matilde being gone and that I had all my things with me. I asked doña Altagracia if I could still take her up on her offer to stay with her. I told her I had to figure out what I was going to do next and how I was going to do it. I had put so much hope in Matilde going with me to the border and her backing up my story that I had not thought about her side of the story.

That was when doña Altagracia told me that right after Matilde and I left for Mexico City in 1945, plainclothes policemen or detectives had come asking questions about Matilde's whereabouts. Matilde had known the authorities were looking for her all these years. In later years, I got yet another confirmation of the same story from another completely independent source. This person said that after Matilde left Tijuana in 1945, the FBI was looking for her and that there was a report she had stolen a baby from the United States. I believe someone in New York may have filed that report.

One thing I need to mention is that Matilde was known in different places by different names. She went by Maria in Mexicali; Rosa in Ensenada, Veracruz, and Poza Rica; and Matilde, her true name, in Tijuana. She also went by the name of Graciela in the different towns she was in while I was in the orphanage and, as I had learned from Mr. Rivera when he addressed her, as Grace or Graciela in New York. God knows how many other names she used. She was able to leave one place and start with a new identity in another. If you were looking for her, it would have been very difficult to find her.

I concluded that the stories about the police, coupled with the neighbor's complaints about Matilde abusing and neglecting me, were among the reasons for almost all the sudden moves in my earlier life. It also explained why she used different names and why she did not put me in school when she could have.

This also explained why my name was spelled so many different ways on the trumped-up Mexican papers Matilde had registered for me. On some papers in Ensenada, my name appeared as Graciela Torres. In Tijuana, it was Graciela Reyes. At the orphanage in Veracruz, my name was Graciela Pilo. Therefore, the records of my confirmation, baptism, and first communion all have the wrong last names. I wonder what name she used when she falsely registered my birth in Ensenada at the age of two. It would be interesting to see all the papers with these lies. I have often wondered under what last name, or names, these papers are registered. Someday, I would like to go to Ensenada and see for myself what records they have for me.

In any case, things were beginning to make more sense. Even though there were some pieces still missing, the puzzle was coming together. I would now have to find the rest all by myself. I had been planning to ask Pablo some questions, but I feared now I would probably lose what little contact I had with him.

Doña Altagracia sensed I was very upset and tried to calm me. She said, "Do not do anything. Your godmother Nelly is coming to see me this weekend, and she can help you cross the border. She lives in Escondido and owns a house. She will do what she can to help you. I will call her and tell her you have gotten a copy of your birth certificate, and that you want to return to the United States."

I believe this was on a Sunday, so I knew I had to wait at least a week. I knew instinctively it would be better for me if I went to the border with an adult who knew me. I thought I would have a better chance of the authorities believing my story.

While waiting for my godmother, doña Altagracia arranged for me to visit my godmother's sister who lived in a suburban neighborhood on one of the hills around Tijuana. She had two daughters, one almost my age. I desperately wanted to be with girls my own age. These were very nice girls, and their parents and friends were very kind to me.

At night, I could see the lights of San Ysidro in the United States from their house on the hill. While staring at those beautiful twinkling lights, I asked myself repeatedly, "How can I get from here to there?" I spent hours looking at the lights. It was such a trial for me to be so close and yet so far.

The weekend came and went, and my godmother did not come because one of her children was ill. She assured me over the telephone they would come as soon as they could. I had no reason to doubt her.

This time, the waiting was made easier. I had my birth certificate in hand, and thanks to doña Altagracia, I had a safe and comfortable place to stay. Moreover, I was with these two girls and their friends. Doña Altagracia asked very little of me and, instead, encouraged me to be with her granddaughters and their friends.

She would tell me often, "Laugh a little more; don't be so serious. You are a young girl; act like one. Youth is gone before you know it."

The truth was that throughout my childhood I almost never smiled. The few photographs I have over my entire childhood, except for the baby photo taken in Brooklyn at age six months, all show a somber expression.

During these few weeks in Tijuana, I was living so intensely it was like being in a fast-moving film. No matter how fast I ran, it was catching up to me. The positive and negative were continually merging.

One evening I was startled by noises at the back of doña Altagracia's house. I looked out to what appeared to be a sea of flashing red lights. I was about to go out when doña Altagracia stopped me. Just then, we heard gunshots. After a while, things quieted down, and I carefully looked out to see the police taking away big, full gunnysacks. Doña Altagracia told me it was probably a drug raid and those were probably sacks of marijuana. I couldn't sleep and lay in fear almost all night.

When doña Altagracia's granddaughter invited me to a party, doña Altagracia encouraged me, "Go have some fun and stop worrying about the future. It will come soon enough." Such kindness I had not known since I was with the Laras, and that seemed a long time ago. So much had happened since; it seemed a lifetime had passed.

Doña Altagracia's youngest granddaughter was turning fifteen, and big preparations were underway for her quinceañera party. She asked me to be one of her fourteen attendants. I wanted so badly to say yes, but I knew I could not afford the dress and accessories that went with it, so I had to tell her that I didn't have the money.

Well, she wouldn't take no for an answer, and before I knew it, she had borrowed a dress in the color she wanted me to wear. Doña Altagracia altered the dress to my size, and I was one of her attendants. I could not believe my luck. It was a wonderful party.

The next weekend I was invited to another party by a friend I had met earlier. On several occasions, this girl had let me wear her gold jewelry and her clothes. Outwardly, I looked like the other girls. I had a wonderful time dancing and singing at the party. Most Mexican people are very generous by nature. They love to enjoy life and do not have to have a reason for a party.

A week later, I was supposed to go to yet another party with this same girl. That evening I missed the bus to her house, and they left without me. On the way to the party, there was a terrible accident, and this wonderful friend was killed instantly. I was supposed to be in the car. Just like a candle, in an instant, the light was out.

One Step from a Dream

At long last, my godmother and her family arrived. I told her all I knew of my background and showed her my birth certificate. She offered to have me come and live with her and her family in the United States and to send me to school as soon as she could. I didn't hesitate to accept.

She drilled me on the questions they would most likely ask at the border and the answers I should give. I tried to memorize the questions and answers without even understanding the meanings of the words.

She said, "When they ask you, 'Where were you born?' you answer, 'Brooklyn, New York.' 'How old are you?' You say, 'Sixteen.' 'What is your name?' 'Grace.'"

I repeated these phrases over and over until I had memorized them all.

The time finally came to leave for the border. I could not contain myself. It was about half past ten in the evening, and my stomach was in knots. I could not stand still for one minute. I kept repeating all the questions and answers to myself. I had gone through so much, and waited so long, for this moment—I didn't want anything to go wrong.

As we said our good-byes, doña Altagracia told me, "Do not worry so much. You know you always have a home here as long as I am alive."

These were very comforting words. Even though I felt deep gratitude toward her for her kindness and help, I do not recall what I said to her, or if I said anything at all. I was too emotionally spent; all I wanted was to get across the border. What was waiting for me on the other side did not concern me at that moment. I would face that in its time.

The border was a short distance away. Yet, driving there was one of the longest drives I have ever taken in my life. It was agonizing. I was paralyzed with intense feelings of hope and fear. My mind was racing in different directions at the same time.

When we got to the border, I was in the back seat with my godmother's children. The U.S. immigration officer asked everyone the same questions, or so it seemed to me. Then the moment of truth came.

He looked at me and asked, "And you, where were you born?"

I said, "Brooklyn, New York."

"How old are you?"

"Sixteen."

Then he asked me a different question from the ones I had memorized, "Where are you going?" He had me.

He asked me to follow him and asked my godmother to wait at the side of the building. All at once fear, tension, and sadness overtook me as I walked with the immigration officer to his office. I had lived for this moment for almost eleven years. This was my lifeline, my impossible dream. If I were to be turned back, what would I do? At that moment, fear was my greatest emotion. The immigration officer left me standing in the cold office. I was alone and trembling. I felt I was in a life and death situation. If I were to be turned away, would I have the strength to go on? I will never forget this moment for as long as I live.

After just a few minutes, it seemed an eternity, he returned. He asked me to sit, and in perfectly clear Spanish, asked, "How is it that you were born in Brooklyn, New York, and you do not speak English? Who are the people you are with? Why are you coming to the United States?"

His questions were coming at me too fast, and I had no easy answers for any of them. I tried to control my fear of rejection with all the force in my being.

I prayed, *God, guide my words so they can make the most sense to this man.*

I took a deep breath and told him, "I was born in Brooklyn, New York, where my mother gave me up to a Mexican woman, named Matilde Flores, who took me illegally into Mexico."

He asked, "Where is this woman?"

I replied, "I don't know. As soon as she knew of my plans and that I had my birth certificate, she disappeared, leaving me alone in Tijuana. I was told she was afraid of the authorities and that she would get in trouble for what she had done."

Then I told him the story of events as Matilde told them to me. Without a word, he took my birth certificate and left the room.

A few minutes later, he came back and asked more questions, which I tried my best to answer. Then he left again. I sat there, trying to hold back my tears. I had just told this officer my life story, and at this moment, I did not know if he believed me or not. I didn't know if I was going to be sent back to Tijuana or if I was going to cross into the United States. It seemed every second in this room was like a year of my life. I got up and paced the room. I was wringing my hands. The waiting was unbearable.

After what seemed an eternity, he returned and asked, "Why do you want to go to the United States?"

I answered him with such force I startled him, "Because it is my country! I want to go to school, to learn English, and to look for my family!"

At this point, he told me, "Under United States law you are considered a minor until you become eighteen years old. If you do not want to stay with your godmother, you will be assigned a guardian, and you will be put in school as soon as possible. Your godmother cannot put you to work for her—you are a minor, and the law will protect you."

I wondered, *Where was this law in 1941 when I was taken across this very border?*

Quickly, I got back to the present. Then he left again. I could hear some typing in the next room. When he came back, he had an inkpad in his hands. He put all my fingers on the inkpad and then pressed them to the back of my birth certificate. At this point, it was still not clear to me whether I was crossing the border or was going to be sent back. All of the talk of being a minor and the law protecting me had almost no meaning. He had not once told me I was crossing. When he was telling me about the state getting me a guardian, it did not make much sense; I was not familiar with United States' laws. In short, I was a *mess* and a ball of fear.

Then he said the words I had waited years, and dreamed countless times, to hear, "Welcome to the United States and good luck to you. If you have any problems, come and see me."

All those tears and fear I had been holding in poured out like a flood. As I write, I am still choked with those same emotions and crying those same tears.

He put his hand on my shoulder and said, "Everything will be all right. I have already spoken with your godmother. She wants to help you. Tomorrow she is going to enroll you in Escondido High School."

He handed me my birth certificate, walked me to my godmother, and said, "Take good care of her."

He said again, to me, "You know you can get help if you need it."

My godmother, her husband, and I got in the car. We all simultaneously let out tremendous sighs of relief. I did not say much; I was in full emotional overload. It was well past midnight, and my godmother's husband had to get up very early to go to work. They had waited more than two hours for me at the border.

My godmother said, "Don't worry, the worst is over now. You can come and go across the United States border. Your birth certificate is your identification, so be very careful not to lose it."

Reality Sets In

As we drove off, I wanted to absorb everything—houses, streets, cars, people, trees—everything. I was struck by how much more orderly it was on this side of the border than in Tijuana. Everything seemed better; to me, it was the most beautiful moment. I wondered if others my age had ever felt the same way as I did then. This was my country. I was filled with so much pride—I had done the impossible. Finally, for the first time in sixteen years, one of my dreams had become a reality.

The next day, on my way to my first day of school, my eyes caught a glimpse of a huge American flag. What a glorious sight—the red, white, and blue moving with the wind—it looked so grand. I felt so very proud; *this is my flag,* I thought. Oh, what wonderful feelings I was experiencing at these sights. I had yearned for this for so long; it was more than a dream come true. I kept discovering more things day by day. The feelings of wonder did not leave me for a long, long time.

My godmother's home had three bedrooms and I shared a room with my godmother's daughter, Maryann, who was younger than me. My godmother did what she could to make me feel welcome. She bought me new clothes and a watch, my first wristwatch, and I was so proud of it. She used a little government pension she got from her first husband, who was in the military when he died. The pension was intended for their daughter Maryann. She was now using this money for me.

In some respects, life was better for me now. I had gained my citizenship, I wasn't being abused, and I was going to school. Moreover,

I was in a good home with regular meals. However, in other respects, life was more difficult. When I first got to the school, I was assigned to a class with students my own age. All of the other students spoke English, and I was completely lost. Most of my classmates had had been in school for at least eleven years, all in English. I, on the other hand, had never completed a single year in school and could barely read or write in Spanish, let alone speak English. In addition, I had been under constant stress all of my life. It was very frustrating not to be able to participate in the classes. This went on for a few weeks until, finally, the school called my godmother. They recommended I go to Belmont High School in Los Angeles. Belmont High had a special class called *The International Group for Learning English as a Second Language.* There were no such classes in Escondido at the time.

Luckily, my godmother had friends near Belmont High School in Los Angeles, and we went to visit. For the life of me, I cannot recall their last name. I think the older lady's first name was Elpidia; I addressed her as doña Elpidia, and her married daughter was Josefi. Josefi had five children; the oldest, a girl, was about thirteen. I think they lived near the housing area called Marabilla.

My godmother asked them if I could stay with them so I could attend Belmont High and they agreed. I had another place to stay. I had lived in five places with people I hadn't known, all within a period of three months. My godmother gave them money for my expenses. I cannot remember whether it was my godmother, or Josefi, who enrolled me in Belmont High.

Building Blocks

"Every blade of grass has its Angel that bends over it and whispers … 'grow, grow.'"

The Talmud

The house I was staying in was big, with very high ceilings and big sliding doors that closed the living room from the rest of the house. I shared a room with the oldest daughter and two of the other children. I slept on a mattress on the floor, just like in Veracruz; in certain respects, some things had not changed for me. In any case, this was not a big problem; I was going to school and that was what was important.

One of the difficult things I had to deal with while living with this family was that every time I tried to say something in English, the children would make fun of me. What could I do but put up with the ridicule? This situation held me back from learning English more quickly.

I could deal with the feelings of not belonging and of being an outsider, as I had lived with this all my life. But now I had to deal with other problems. I was ridiculed at home for not being able to speak English and at school for my lack of clothes and shoes. I didn't have money for lunch at school and, as I was already a burden on this family, couldn't ask for help.

Others my age were focused on what to wear, the latest styles, what party to go to, their boyfriends, etc. I was focused on just the basics of survival. My circumstances made me feel self-conscious, so I spent a lot of time by myself. Not being able to relate to young people my own age was hard. I could not do many of the things others my age found normal. The normality of other's lives made the abnormalities of mine more painfully evident.

I was in a class with an Israeli, a Japanese, a Brazilian, an Italian, a Chinese, a Russian, and an assortment of Latinos. This class was fun because my lack of education did not show as much; all of us were learning English for the first time. When the teacher spoke of grammar, I was lost. I had almost no knowledge of grammar, even in Spanish. At breaks, I especially loved hearing the Italians talk among themselves. I stood near to them just to listen to the music of the language. I felt I was close to my people when I was near them.

My best friends in this group were an Israeli girl and a Chinese boy. I had a crush on him; he was so handsome. When he spoke to me, he spoke so softly, and he seemed so gentle and good. All the Latinos in this class were a lot of fun, but they were always talking about their families' wealth back home. It seemed to me that all of them were from very rich families. Well, anyone in that class was richer than I was, in many ways.

Outside the classroom, I tried to avoid the Latinos because I did not want to be asked about my background. What could I tell them that would not shock them or have them look down on me? Teenagers can be so cruel, and I had little in common with them. Their worries seemed so vain compared to mine. They would worry about what dress or what jewelry to wear, and I would wear the same dress for days. They had the latest styles in clothes, haircuts, and money, while everything I had was outdated. They would eat in the cafeteria, and I would find a cheap piece of bread and milk for my lunch. Life was not easy.

One day I was called to the principal's office. As I entered the office, the principal, Mrs. Swain, said something to me that I could not understand. It was evident she was very angry. She sent for an interpreter who, it turned out, was a nice girl from El Salvador. She told me Mrs. Swain wanted to know why I had not gone to my gym class all these weeks, and why I had ignored the notices that she had sent to my homeroom. I looked at this Latino girl, who seemed so sure of herself, swallowed my pride, and asked her if she would please not repeat any of what I was going to say to anyone outside this office. She assured me that whatever I said would be kept in confidence.

Mrs. Swain was getting impatient. Then I began to talk. I explained, "The reason why I do not go to gym is because I do not have the money to buy gym clothes and shoes."

Mrs. Swain asked, "Where does your family live?"

I told her, "I have no family. I am staying with a family so I can come to this school and learn English. The family has five children of their own, and I cannot ask them for money for myself. My godmother brought me to stay with these people because there was not a school like this one in Escondido."

Mrs. Swain looked at my records and asked me the same questions as the officer at the border had asked, "How is it you were born in Brooklyn and you cannot speak English?"

I looked again at this girl, and she could see the pain and hurt on my face. She reassured me that she would not repeat anything I said outside of the office. I answered Mrs. Swain, "When I was a six-month-old baby, I was taken out of the United States illegally by a Mexican woman, and I grew up in several parts of Mexico. I have been in the United States less than three months."

Mrs. Swain had been standing. Her expression softened, and she sat down. She asked, "Are the people you live with your guardians?"

I said, "No, as far as I know, I do not have a guardian. In fact, I do not understand what it means to have a guardian."

She then wrote something on a piece of paper, said some things to the interpreter, and sent me to the gym teacher. I was assigned to keep the ribbons in order for the ribbon twirler team, and for this, I would be given gym clothes and shoes. After this, I was taken to the dining hall where I was to work for a half hour each day, and for this, I was to get lunch and something to eat at the morning break. I could not believe my good fortune! I could eat a big meal at lunch and not have to eat as much at Josefi's house. My breakfast was the milk and the bread that was given out at the morning break. Now all I had to worry about was my bus fare. I always felt uncomfortable when Josefi gave me money she could have used for her own children.

The next day I was called again to Mrs. Swain's office. The same girl from El Salvador met me in the hall. She must have sensed my uneasiness, as right off she assured me that Mrs. Swain wanted to help me. I was relieved, for I thought I had done something wrong again.

When we got to her office, Mrs. Swain very kindly said, through the interpreter, "Sit down, Grace, I want to talk to you. You are a minor, and you have just turned seventeen. I can become your guardian until you are eighteen. By then, you should have learned English well enough to get a job to help yourself, or if you have the aptitude, I can even help you get a scholarship so you can go to college. As your guardian, I would send you to a doctor for you to have a physical examination and to take care of the problem you have. I would also send you to the dentist. You would live with my family and ride to school and back with me. Would you like this?"

Without any hesitation, I said, "Yes!"

The next day Mrs. Swain made an appointment with Josefi and her mother. She had a big box of canned goods and other things to take to Josefi's family. When we arrived, they were expecting us. We got the big box out and went into the living room. Mrs. Swain explained to them that she wanted to become my guardian and for me to live at her home. She said I had agreed to this, and under the circumstances, it would be better for me.

Josefi said, "If she wants to go with you, it is all right with us."

I thanked Josefi and her mother for their help and said my good-byes to her children. I was on my way to yet another home and another city. This was my third move in the United States. I had averaged a move almost every month, but even though I was a little afraid of the unknown, I knew these were all steps forward.

The medical problem Mrs. Swain had referred to earlier was a tapeworm. The school nurse found this when I told her I was passing pieces often. As far as I could remember, I had never had a complete physical examination; only God knew what else I had.

The Swains lived in San Fernando Valley, California, about three-quarters of an hour from the school by car. On the way to their home, I held my belongings very close, as though to draw some comfort and strength from them. These were the only things familiar to me now. The drive seemed very long, or perhaps I was anxious to face the unknown as soon as possible. I wondered how long it would be until the next move and where I would end up next.

Mrs. Swain tried to keep a conversation going, but I understood very little, and I was preoccupied with my thoughts. Mrs. Swain's daughter, Virginia, was thirteen years old. Mrs. Swain was able to communicate well enough for me to understand her when she told me I could help Virginia with her Spanish. When she said this, I thought to myself, *I could help her with the spoken part, but for the written Spanish and grammar, I needed help myself.*

I was beginning to realize Mrs. Swain assumed that I had had more education than I actually had. I did not want to disappoint her, so I did not say anything. I felt she would know soon enough when she saw my grades. She thought now I would learn English much faster because I would not be able to speak Spanish at home, but I was worried about how we would communicate in the meantime.

I looked up at the sky and thought, *Oh, God, here I go again. Help me to please this lady who does not realize how little education I have had.*

My total months of formal education at this time did not come to the second grade level, and almost all the students in my classes had already been in school ten to eleven years—all of this plus I was just beginning to learn English.

When we arrived at their home, Mr. Swain and Virginia were waiting for us. They were very nice and friendly and talked to me as though I knew what they were saying. I could only catch a word here and there, so I kept saying yes to everything they asked me. Mr. Swain, sensing I was lost, pulled out an English and Spanish dictionary, and we went on from there. When I saw him with the dictionary, I thought to myself how thoughtful these people are to meet me with dictionary in hand.

Their house was Mediterranean Spanish style of brick construction. It had a long corridor from which you could pass every room in the house. The first room was a large living room. Then there was the kitchen, dining room, and all the bedrooms, one after the other. The house was not completely finished, as Mr. Swain was the builder. Virginia's bedroom was the last one, and I was to share her bedroom until the next room was finished. The house had lots of windows that made it light and cheerful. I liked the house very much.

Dinnertime came, and we sat together at a large Spanish-style table. At first, when they asked me to pass the butter, they got the bread. If they asked me to pass the salt, they got the butter, and so on. They were quickly discovering how little English I knew. From then on, when they picked up an item from the table, they told me the name. I would repeat it, and soon they were getting just what they asked for.

After a few days at the Swains' home, Mrs. Swain and I went to the courthouse in Los Angeles. When it was our turn to go before the judge, Mrs. Swain and I stood up. He said something to Mrs. Swain, and she answered yes. Next, I was asked something to which I answered yes. At that moment, Mrs. Swain became my guardian.

The next week was spent seeing doctors. First, I was put in the Los Angeles County General Hospital for two days to get rid of my tapeworm. I was not supposed to eat for twenty-four hours. I was supposed to take in only the medication. The idea was for the tapeworm to be killed by taking in only the medication. Well, none of this was clear to me. The first day I was so hungry I went to the candy machine and got a Mounds chocolate bar. I ate it as if it were my last meal. I would have eaten more, but I did not have money.

The next day a doctor, of Cuban origin, appeared. Addressing me in Spanish, he asked, "Niña, did you take all of the medication yesterday?"

I said, "Yes."

"Did you eat anything after the medication?"

I said, "Only a candy bar, because I was very hungry."

"Ah ha, there is the reason why your friend has not come out. Did anybody tell you that you were not supposed to eat anything at all after you took the medication?"

I said, "If they did, I did not understand them. They talked to me in English, and my English is very poor."

He said, "That figures. Now you are going to take the medication again, and this time do not eat a thing, only what they give you to drink. I promise you, when your friend comes out you can have anything you want to eat, okay? You will feel much better too. Now I will have the nurse examine you and give you your medication again. Remember, no eating."

I was thankful the doctor spoke to me in Spanish. It felt good and gave me a comforting feeling to hear Spanish again.

The nurse came and listened to my chest. When she opened my gown she asked, "How old are you?"

I answered, "Seventeen."

"Boy," she said, "you are well built."

The next day my friend came out! It broke the record as the longest tapeworm they had ever seen. I do not remember how many meters long it was, but it was huge. I even got scared when I saw it for the first time! They kept it in a big jar for show in the hospital. For all I know it must still be there. It had found a permanent home, and I was still looking for one. I left the hospital after two nights and almost three days—a few pounds lighter. I was told that the raw milk I drank in Veracruz and in Jalapa was what gave me the tapeworm.

My next trip to the doctor was frightening. I was not prepared for what was to come. They gave me many tests. Then I was asked to take my clothes off, put this gown on, and get on the examining table to wait for the doctor. When the doctor came in, he told me to lay back and open my legs.

In highly animated Spanish I said, "What? What do you think you are doing?"

The nurse tried to calm me down. I was frightened, and I was embarrassed, and I started to cry, so the doctor called a lady who spoke Spanish.

I asked her, "What in God's name is this doctor trying to do to me? I am not sick!"

She said, "He is trying to examine you. Your guardian requested a complete physical."

Then she realized I had no clue what she was talking about as I had only been to a doctor twice in my life. As delicately as she could, she asked me if I had ever had sexual relations with a man. That was a little too much for me to take in one day. I was indignant.

I said, "No, I am not married! I have never been with a man!"

The doctor shook his head and said a few angry words to the nurse. Then he talked to the Spanish-speaking lady.

Through her, he said to me, "I am very sorry if I scared you."

The Spanish-speaking lady, obviously feeling pretty badly herself, explained that the doctor was going to give me a pelvic examination because that was what had been put in my file. Whether Mrs. Swain requested it or they made a mistake, I have never known, but I will never forget that frightful experience.

Next, I went to the eye doctor, the throat doctor, and the dentist; I was examined very thoroughly. During my visit with the nose and throat doctor, he drained my sinuses and gave me some pills. After taking the pills, I felt like a new person. Before this treatment, I had suffered continuously, for years, from terrible sinus headaches. I also needed dental work, so Mrs. Swain made a deal with her dentist; I would clean his office in payment for his work. I had never before been to a dentist.

I also had chores to do on weekends, such as washing the windows, arranging closets, and doing the dishes, for which I got an allowance—I can't remember how much. As soon as I had saved some money, Mrs. Swain took me to a bank and helped me open a savings account. She advised me always to save part of my pay. She tried to teach me as much as she could in the short time I was with them. She also got clothes for me from her cousin who had a girl about my age.

With the help of the Swains, I was able to learn English at a much faster pace than many of my classmates. I had to communicate all the time in English and after just a few months, the difference was remarkable. Whenever we got to the point where I could not understand, they used the dictionary. They always reinforced what I was learning at the time. This helped me tremendously. Mrs. Swain said all along that this would be the case. She explained the reason I knew so little English when I first came to live with them was that I had always been around Spanish-speaking people, even at school.

That summer, after school was out, I went with the Swains for a glorious week to their cabin in the mountains at Idyllwild, California. Virginia and I enjoyed hikes, swimming, concerts, and theater. During one of the beautiful concerts, I saw Meredith Wilson, noted for the Broadway play, *The Music Man*. I felt great being there, breathing the fresh mountain air, surrounded by the music, arts, and nature. What a marvelous experience to make my spirit soar. Even now, I can close my eyes and transport myself back to that uplifting and marvelous experience. This was my very first vacation, ever.

As the school year had ended at Belmont High, I transferred to San Fernando High School for summer classes. Mr. Swain was a student counselor at San Fernando High. Here, I had very little contact with Latinos. I took arts and crafts and homemaking; in these classes, you were not lectured but shown how to do things.

While I was in summer school, Mr. and Mrs. Swain and Virginia took a short trip, and I was left alone in the house. They had asked their friends to look after me and see that I was doing all right. I was a little afraid but no more than the present circumstances allowed. However, one day when I returned from school, someone had broken in and stolen several things, among them was my pride and joy at this time, the watch my godmother had given me in Escondido. It was a very upsetting experience to see my things all over the floor and all the closets gone through. I was so frightened that I could not stay alone in the house. After the break-in, I stayed in the home of one of the Swains' friends, the nose and throat doctor I had seen during my physical.

When the Swains returned, Mrs. Swain was very upset by the beak-in. She was also upset I had imposed on her friends by staying at their home after the robbery. I tried to explain that I was afraid the robbers would come back while I was there alone. I had never experienced anything like this.

Although all had not worked out perfectly with Mrs. Swain, the summer classes, nevertheless, ended happily and I had done very well; I got all *A*s! I stayed at San Fernando High when the regular school year started. However, I was having difficulty again. My lack of vocabulary in biology, math, and English made it very difficult. In addition, I was yearning to go to New York and look for my family. This was ever-present in my mind and got in the way of my studies. It was as though I believed that when I found my family, everything would be all right.

In some ways, this was good. It helped me to go forward and deal with all of the changes. I had placed so much hope on finding my family that I was always afraid to get too close or too comfortable in any one place or with any one person. I knew change would come, and the separation would be painful. I lived in a state of insecurity and readiness for the next move.

Several things were happening now in my ever-changing life; I was in another new school, the third one in less than a year. I was constantly aware that time was passing by faster than I wanted it to. In the meantime, I had reestablished contact with Pablo and, once more, needed his help.

My eighteenth birthday was coming and with this would come the end of my stay at the Swains' home. They had planned a year-long, around-the-world tour. Just shortly before, Mrs. Swain had been diagnosed with cancer, so they could not continue to take responsibility for me. I was eighteen, yet I would not be ready to get a high school diploma for another two or three years.

I could have gone back to my godmother's or Josefi's house, but I knew I had to move forward and closer to New York to look for my family. For this, I felt I needed Pablo's help. I thought he would know more about the place and my background. With all of this on my mind, I sat down and wrote him another one of those powerful letters. I told him I needed his help in finding my family, and I needed a place to stay as soon as I turned eighteen.

I felt like Cinderella—my eighteenth birthday was when the clock struck midnight, and all I had would turn into a pumpkin. I was under a lot of pressure, and felt that I had let the Swains down in my lack of progress in school. In spite of my best attempts to explain my lack of education to Mrs. Swain, I felt that she never accepted just how little time I had spent in school. I did all I could, but I simply did not have the basic building blocks needed to move forward with knowledge and confidence. Thus, on my eighteenth birthday, I felt as if I were in a race I could not win. Added to all my other uncertainties, this was a demoralizing combination. All I could do was pray for a better tomorrow.

To my surprise, one day, when I came home from school, there was a letter from Pablo. In the envelope was a money order for me to buy a bus ticket to his friends' home in San Francisco. His friends, the Rios, were willing to let me stay with them so I could go to school and get my high school diploma. I was happy, and sad, all at once. Once again, I was headed into the unknown with people I had never met. The insecurity and fear were back again or, I should say, were stronger now. Fear and hope are always with me, even today.

I showed the letter to the Swains. I could see a sigh of relief on Mrs. Swain's face. Mr. Swain, on the other hand, did not feel as good about sending me to people whom I had never met. In this situation, Mrs. Swain was in control, as she was the one who was my guardian. Within days, I received a letter from the Rios, sending their address and phone number and asking me to let them know what bus I was taking so they could wait for me at the bus station. This made the finality of my departure more real. I felt like the world was coming to an end. When I was alone and making plans for my trip, all I did was cry. It seemed my American dream was turning into a nightmare. I did not see I had too many choices, and going back to either my godmother's home or Josefi's home seemed to me like going backward. Yet, going forward was so frightening.

My thoughts went back to my first days of living in the Swains' comfortable home. I remembered so well when I went to bed that first night. Mrs. Swain came to kiss her daughter good night, and she kissed me on the forehead too. When she left the room, I buried my head in the pillow and just sobbed. I had not remembered anyone ever doing that to me before.

The arrangements for my departure were made. Mr. Swain would take me to the bus station. I painfully gathered all of my belongings in one suitcase, said my good-byes, and we left. I had always been afraid of change, but this time it seemed even more difficult. I was a young adult and had been enjoying a more settled life. It seemed that I felt more fear of change and the unknown than I had ever experienced before. It was painful then, and it is painful to remember now.

Mr. Swain and I arrived at the bus station and he waited until the bus left. As the bus left the station, I looked back and could see tears in his eyes. I was trying to hold my tears back so he would not feel worse. As soon as he was out of sight, I put my coat in front of my face and cried for what seemed to be hours. I was crying for leaving this warm and familiar place and the kindness of these people, as well as for fear of the unknown.

Sequestered

As the bus approached San Francisco, people on the bus were excited to see the Golden Gate Bridge at night. My emotional state overshadowed this magnificent and beautiful sight. I did not have the luxury to be in the moment. My thoughts were racing to try to remember the colors of the coats the Rios had told me they would be wearing. I was trying to imagine what they looked like.

The dreaded moment was upon me. As we pulled into the bus station, I put on my coat, suitcase in hand, and stepped off the bus. I could not stop shaking; I felt that my legs would not support me. As I stepped down, I stopped to dry my tears, which, just seconds before, had been pouring down like water from a faucet. I prayed, *Dear God, help me. I feel so hopeless and sad.*

As I started to walk, this big man, with a smile on his face, was coming toward me. A fair-skinned lady with black hair, and a look on her face as though she were angry, said, "You must be Grace."

I just looked at them. I was trying to read their faces. What kind of people were they? Then, as though someone else was speaking for me, I heard myself say, "Yes, I am Grace. How are you?"

Mr. Rio was in his fifties and Mrs. Rio in her forties. Mr. Rio spoke English and Spanish; however, Mrs. Rio spoke only English and was difficult to understand because she spoke with a heavy Irish accent. Mrs. Rio asked me to call her by her first name, Arish. Arish worked at the Woolworth store on Market Street in downtown San Francisco.

Mr. Rio, whose first name was Pacifico, worked in a factory. On the weekends, he was a Pentecostal preacher.

On the drive to their home, they asked a lot of questions, which I can no longer recall because I was too upset. All I can remember is answering yes or no at the time. They lived at Twenty-First and Bryant Streets in San Francisco's Mission District. They had a first floor flat with a living room, two bedrooms, a dining room, a kitchen, and a little porch at the back.

When we first arrived, they asked if I wanted something to eat. I told them I wasn't hungry.

Then they showed me to a portable bed in Mrs. Rio's room. I was to share her bedroom. Mr. Rio slept in the front bedroom. Most of the time, these two people said very little to each other. I was glad the next day was a working day for them, so I could be alone with my thoughts. I had the feeling that perhaps Mrs. Rio did not want me there and that was why they did not talk to each other. It was not a good feeling from the start, and I was very uncomfortable.

The next morning, I asked Mrs. Rio if she knew where the high school was for the area. She wrote the address on a piece of paper. Then she took me outside and pointed in the direction of the school. After they left, I went to the store for her. Then I went to look for the high school.

At the high school, I was told I could not attend because I was already eighteen. They referred me to another school. To attend the other school, I had to take a bus. When I got there, I found out the school was for delinquent youths. They asked me what I had done. I thought they were asking what I had done in the last school I attended. I told them, and then we both realized that this was not the school for me. I had never been in any trouble. Here, someone could get me into trouble in no time. These were tough kids, some from gangs.

The principal of the school referred me to Benjamin Franklin Adult Business School. Benjamin Franklin was even farther away, on Van Nuys Street. Again, I would have to take a bus. The principal also advised me to attend night classes at Mission High School.

I enrolled myself at Benjamin Franklin and went home. That same evening, I walked to Mission High School and enrolled myself in night classes. I was thankful I could walk to Mission High because I did not know how long my money would last. I had close to two hundred dollars I had saved from washing windows on weekends for Mrs. Swain and her friends.

Someone told me I could buy student passes for the bus, which helped a lot. I think it saved me half of the regular fare, and I needed every break I could get. There were even times when the bus driver would not punch my ticket. Some of the bus drivers were kindhearted. Because I was short and wore a ponytail and bobby socks, I looked much younger than I was. I was able to pass for a child when I went to the cinema.

When the Rios came home that night, they were amazed to hear all I had accomplished, especially by myself in a new city.

Mr. Rio remarked, "You really want to get that high school diploma, don't you?"

After dinner that evening, I helped clean the kitchen. I asked Mrs. Rio if I could do something extra around the house to earn money for my bus fare. She said I could do the ironing. Now I had my bus fare covered, so I would only have to think of creative ways to stretch my money for lunches. Most of the time my lunches consisted of milk and the cheapest sweet breads I could buy; I could not afford anything else.

My first day at Benjamin Franklin was as first days go in any new school. In the days that followed, I left the house with Mrs. Rio when she went to work in the morning and returned about an hour before she got back. I set the table and started supper. Supper often consisted of boiled white rice and fish, or meat, in tomato sauce. They were not rich people, so they ate very simple food.

At Benjamin Franklin, I met Cristina Baranda, a Mexican lady who was rearing two daughters by herself. Her mother lived with them. Cristina lived in the Mission District, a few blocks from where I lived. She worked at night in the central office, or clearinghouse, of the Wells Fargo Bank. She asked me all sorts of questions and one day she invited me for dinner at her home. She had been well educated in Mexico and was studying English; she placed high value on education.

At times, when I got discouraged, Cristina would tell me, "You have to get your diploma, Graciela, so you can get a better job. If you quit now, all you can get will be waiting on tables, or worse. You must try to better yourself." She was just the moral support I needed at that time.

During the entire time I was with the Rios, I had an extremely bleak existence. I went to Benjamin Franklin every weekday and to Mission High several nights a week. The rest of the time, except for weekends, I either helped with chores or did my homework on the kitchen table. They had no TV. I was very lonely, as I was not permitted to have any friends to visit, or even to have phone calls. The only way I would see any of my friends or classmates was during the little time when I was not attending classes. My weekends were spent at Pentecostal churches around the San Francisco Bay area where Mr. Rio, a traveling preacher, would be preaching. Arish and I just sat there in these strange churches while Mr. Rio preached. That was my social life. This went on for almost three years.

The one good part of this socially bland existence was that I studied hard and went to school both day and night. By studying with few distractions, I got a diploma, equivalent to a high school diploma, from Benjamin Franklin Adult Business School. I did this with less than five years of formal schooling in my entire life.

I was in a hurry to get my diploma, as pressures were building at the Rios' home. The first, and most troublesome, came one day when Mr. Rio asked me to help him pick out a baby gift for a friend. He drove me to the store; this was on a Saturday, I believe. On the way back, I was sitting in the front seat of the car when suddenly he reached over and rubbed his hand up my thigh and told me I was very pretty. I instantly moved away, as close to the door on my side as I could. I thought, *If his parishioners could only see him now.*

Mr. Rio had also told me once that he became jealous when young men at the church looked at me. On another occasion, he told me the son of one of his friends would be a very good Christian husband for me. I did not give much thought to the part about being jealous and the husband bit, but the leg incident worried me. After that, I made sure I was never alone with him. I did not tell Arish because I did not want to cause any problems for her. I thought they had a very strange relationship as it was. In any case, I was close to graduation and planning to move out as soon as I could find a job.

On My Own

My friend from school, Cristina Baranda, knew I would be getting my diploma soon and asked me if I had looked for a job. I told her no, that I did not know where to start, or what to do. She offered to see if she could arrange a job interview for me at the Wells Fargo Bank. When she saw me at school the next day, she was very excited. She said she had arranged an interview with her supervisor, Mr. Berry, for the next morning. I just hugged her. I could not talk. I thought to myself, *If she only knew how desperate I was to move from the Rios' home.*

Just as I was leaving the house the next morning, Mrs. Rio, noticing my anxiety, asked why I was so nervous. I told her I would be having tests all week. She wished me luck.

I dressed my very best for the interview. I wore a finely tailored dress Cristina's mother had made for me, just for the occasion. Cristina went with me for moral support. God bless her, I knew she sure could have used her time off to rest instead of coming with me. I thank God for kind people, like her, who go out of their way to help others.

Mr. Berry had a kind manner. He received me very warmly and did what he could to put me at ease. He seemed to sense my discomfort and kept the interview short. After just a few questions, he said to me, "I can offer you a position; you can start work the day after your graduation. You will be working as a bookkeeper at the Twenty-Second Street and Mission office. You'll be on trial for six months, and after that, if you do well, you will become a permanent employee. You will start at $280 per month. Would you like to come to work with us?"

I immediately said, "Yes." I was so excited; I felt ecstatic.

Mr. Berry said, "Great, you can have automatic deductions out of your paycheck to be put in a savings account. You can also buy bank stock or United States Savings Bonds. What would you like to do?"

I told him that I wanted to put some in bank stock and some in savings bonds. He asked me to name a beneficiary. I didn't hesitate to name Cristina as beneficiary. I thought she certainly deserved it. He gave me a paper to sign, and that was that. I was hired. I had a job at the Wells Fargo Bank! Cristina was very happy for me. I went back to school—I was walking on clouds!

The next day, I was busy looking for a room to rent. I looked all over the area near the bank, and finally, a week later, I found a place with a Nicaraguan landlady. She rented me a room of her apartment for forty dollars a month. I figured I was doing okay. I would not have the expense of transportation, and I could use her kitchen and store my food in her refrigerator. Things were looking good. I could not move in for another thirty days, which was all right with me. This gave me time to earn my first paycheck to pay for rent and meals.

Finally, graduation day came. Cristina was there to congratulate me, and we had a nice lunch afterward. I did not invite the Rios to the graduation ceremony, as I knew they had to work. I also did not want to tell them I had a job, because this might have put more pressures on me. That first month, while I was working at the bank, I pretended I was still going to school. Since I got home before them, they didn't notice anything different. I prayed no one would see me working at the bank and tell the Rios before I did. I needed the first month's paycheck before I moved out. I was on pins and needles all the time.

One afternoon, as I walked in after returning from the store, Mr. Rio said, "Graciela, I have a surprise for you. Your father is here."

I walked into the dining room and immediately recognized Pablo from photos I had seen. He was a handsome man in his late forties, already with white hair. He approached me, hugged me, and called me daughter. This was the first time in my life I remember seeing him. I felt like a robot when I greeted him. Right away, he was talking of getting an apartment so I could live with him. There was no mention of Matilde.

As I looked at him I thought, *Boy, he is twenty years too late to become my father. Where was he all those years when I so desperately needed a father's protection and care?*

I acted as though I was glad about his future plans. I was in shock at seeing him, and I was still working through my true feelings. I had been through hell and back for twenty years, and all of a sudden, I have a father? I could not forget that he had helped me with money—once for the trip to Tijuana and again for the trip to San Francisco. I never forget those who have been kind to me, and I did not want to hurt him. I thought, *Soon I will be able to repay him the money if he should say anything.*

I knew I could not live with Pablo—he had a drinking problem and I feared drunken people. I used to feel frightened by them as a child, and that fear had never left me. Moreover, how could I explain to people that he was my father when it was apparent he was not? This was a most difficult situation. I knew I had to handle it very carefully.

After dinner, Pablo wanted to take me to the theater. I asked Arish if she would like to come with us, but she said no.

I went alone with him and soon got a taste of how it would be to live with him. This was the 1960s, a time when people were openly very prejudiced toward black people. It looked bad for them to see me, a young white girl, with an older black man. People stared at us and talked among themselves. I even heard derogatory remarks like, "Look at her, can't she find a man of her own race? Is she that hard up?" Some of the remarks were much more hateful and hurtful. It was a frightening experience.

He cheerfully said to me, "Look, they are looking at you because you are so pretty. They can't take their eyes off of you." I knew differently.

On the way home, I asked him if he could give me any information about my mother or even her last name. He told me he did not know anything about her and had only seen her once. He said Matilde was the one who had contact with her.

I said, "Please, I do not care if you have information about my family you think might hurt me. I want to know anything, no matter how painful it might be."

He said, "I swear to you I am telling you the truth. Because of my job, I was away from home most of the time. All I know I have told you already."

My hopes of getting information from Pablo vanished.

When we got back to the Rios' apartment, I thanked Pablo for taking me to the movie. I excused myself and went to bed. I was glad the evening was over. Pablo and Mr. Rio stayed up for hours, talking into the night.

Arish was waiting for me in her room. She asked, "How did it go? Did people stare at you and Pablo? Did they say hurtful things?"

I said, "Yes."

She said, "This is the way things are going to be from now on. You better get used to it." I did not answer anything. I just pretended I was going to sleep.

Arish continued, "You know he wants you to live with him?"

I answered yes and was glad when she did not keep on talking. Thankfully, it was way past her bedtime, and she had to go to work the next day. I lay there silently, unable to sleep.

The next day, I desperately needed to talk to someone, so during my lunch hour, I went to the church about five blocks from where I worked. I asked if I could talk to a priest. No priest was available at the time, so I made an appointment to see Father Bryan. After work that day, I met with Father Bryan and told him my problem with Pablo.

He said, "It is unfair of Pablo to think you could live with him as his daughter. You should not feel obligated to him for two hundred dollars' worth of help. You can be thankful, this is right, but that is all. Tell him you have no intention of moving in with him."

I had no intention of living with Pablo, or with the Rios. I only needed to talk to someone to reinforce my decision. I felt better after talking with Father Bryan. That afternoon I got home just minutes before Arish. Boy, was that good timing. I did not want to be questioned as to why I was late.

The day before payday, I decided to tell Arish I would be leaving the next day. I told her I would never forget their kindness and would be forever grateful to her and to her husband for letting me stay in their home, and if there were anything I could ever do for them, I would do it gladly.

She looked very concerned as she said to me, "You can't think of moving in with Pablo. You do not know what kind of neighborhood he lives in, and he drinks a lot. Besides, you are white. You cannot do this."

I said, "Arish I am not moving in with Pablo. This last month I have been working at the Wells Fargo Bank and I have rented a room with a Latin lady. I do not want Pablo to know where I am living as it will cause problems. I will tell you the address just in case you ever need to contact me. I do not want Mr. Rio to know either, because he may tell Pablo." I asked her, "Can I trust you, Arish? You know what I am doing is best, and besides, you will have your room all to yourself again."

Arish was a lady of few words and did not show much emotion. All she said was, "God bless you. You are a good girl and you deserve better. I will not tell Pablo or Pacifico."

Then I said, "Arish, please tell Mr. Rio after I am gone. I do not want to face him for fear he will be angry and think of me as ungrateful. I will be gone tomorrow before you get home, or if you want me to, I will go now."

She said, "Don't be silly. Tomorrow is soon enough." She left the room.

The next day, with paycheck in hand, I rushed from work. I finished packing and quickly left for my new address. I was almost twenty-one and completely on my own. I gave the landlady money for the deposit and a month's rent—a total of eighty dollars.

I went to my room, sat on the bed, and prayed, *Dear God, what is in the future for me now?*

My room was okay, but the landlady did not want her daughter to associate with me. She thought that because I did not have family, I must not be a good girl, so she did not want people to see her daughter with me. This made me feel very uncomfortable as I knew her daughter was not the saint her mother thought her to be.

In fact, other Latino mothers felt the same way as this lady. They did not like their daughters to associate with girls like me, girls without families and living alone. They thought that because I did not have a family to answer to I must be a no-good. As a result, I always had to make things up about my family to my Latino friends. In fact, I still do—the truth is still painful.

At work, I met Minnie, who was the secretary at the bank. She was a Mexican-American girl who right away introduced me to a group of young people she knew from St. Boniface's Church. At last, I could be with people my own age. I soon settled into life on my own and began to develop friendships. I also started making adjustments between the present and my past. For example, I went to a movie where an orphaned child was waiting to be adopted, just as I had been at the Asilo Veracruzano. During the movie, my two girlfriends could not understand why I was crying so much. They said the movie was sad, but not that sad. They did not know of my past, and if I had told them, they would not have believed me. They came from very sheltered homes, and they had known little in the way of hardships.

By this time, Minnie had asked me if I wanted to move in with her. I told her I would like to, but could not afford the rent. I explained I needed a lot of things, mostly clothes for work and a clock radio to wake me up in the morning. I wanted to build a little savings too. She said, "Well, pay me the same rent as you pay now." So, within only two months, I made yet another move.

Living with Minnie was fun, but on weekends, she would go to San Jose to visit her family and I would be alone. By now, I had met Marlene and some of her friends. They roomed together in a three-bedroom flat where the rent was reasonable, and everyone took turns doing the cooking and shopping. Marlene told me one of the girls, Ginger, was going to get married, and would soon move out. She asked me if I wanted to move in with them. She told me I would get my own room, and food and rent would cost me about ninety dollars a month. I just had to wait until Ginger moved out.

Well, it did not work out this way. I had taken some time to make my decision, and another girl moved into Ginger's room ahead of me. I ended up making the move, but sharing a room with Marlene. Marlene was a delightful girl in her early twenties. She was always happy and always trying to make me smile; often saying I was too serious. She had two younger brothers, and she had grown up in a lovely family home in Bakersfield, California. She was very tall, five foot eleven; I was four foot ten. We were called "Mutt and Jeff."

Marlene had always wanted a sister, so I became that sister. She was like a ray of sunshine. She took me to meet her family, and they took me in too. On my birthdays and at Christmas, they would give me presents. If they sent Marlene something by mail, they would send something for me too. They were certainly a most gracious, loving, and kind family.

We were part of a group of young people who met at St. Boniface Church. We did a lot together. We did volunteer work on weekends, had dances, and went on retreats. This group was like an extended family for me—just what I needed at the time. The priest was my confessor. Things were going well for me.

My twenty-first birthday was approaching and I thought no one knew about it. One day Minnie invited me to dinner. To my astonishment, it was a surprise birthday party, complete with *mariachis*. This was a group of friends from the bank. She chose the day of the party to be ahead of my actual birthday so I would not be suspicious. How in the world could I be suspicious, I had never had a birthday party! When I realized what she had done, I could not stop crying. She could not understand and I simply told her I was crying because I was so happy. Minnie had a beautiful voice and she sang just for me. It was wonderful. She was so thoughtful and she has remained a great friend.

Then, to top it all off, Marlene planned another surprise birthday party for me. This party was on my actual birthday. The parties were great surprises and lots of fun.

During the following year, I was in three weddings of people from the St. Boniface's group. I was the maid of honor at Marlene's wedding, the bridesmaid in Tom's wedding, and in the wedding party for Annie's wedding. It was a lot of fun being in these weddings. The only thing I disliked was the forever-uncomfortable question, "When are we coming to your wedding?"

At each wedding, I could not wait for the festivities to be over so I could wash my hair and take out all of the goo and hairspray that was so much in vogue at the time. I later became the godmother for Marlene's first child, Vikki.

I could have gotten married too, but first I wanted to try to find my family. I even had a fiancé, Carl, a lovely young man who was a college graduate from Yakima, Washington. He was a good Catholic man. There were many girls who would have married Carl in an instant, but he fell in love with me. Even though I loved him, I had doubts and was afraid that if the marriage did not work out, as Catholics, we would mess up our lives. After all, I realized I was not your ordinary girl from Yakima.

When Carl left to go to Washington to finish his studies and to get ready for our wedding, he wrote me every day. The mailman used to call out whatever Carl had addressed the letter on that particular day. On the weekends, everyone who was outside would hear him.

He would announce that he had a letter for "Wonderful Miss Palo" or "Beautiful Miss Palo" or "Adorable Miss Palo." Then he would say, "This guy is nuts about you, Miss Palo. When are you going to marry him and take him out of his misery?" In any case, all of this was good for the morale.

When I went to meet Carl's family in Yakima, I got cold feet and decided not go through with the wedding. Marlene told me she thought I would marry Carl because I felt so alone after she got married. Little did she know that I always felt alone on the inside, no matter how happy I looked on the outside. Carl was too nice of a young man to marry just because I was lonely.

One day, to my surprise, I saw Arish. She told me that a fourteen-year-old girl from the church had complained that Mr. Rio had molested her. He apparently did this when he went to visit the girl's family and found her home alone. She said he was now in a lot of trouble with his church.

I thought to myself, *That girl could have been me if I had not been so careful as to never be alone with him.* After that, the Rios moved away, and I think Arish left him. I have since lost track of her.

Problems in the apartment started when more girls began getting married. The group was breaking up. Every time one girl got married, a new roommate replaced her. All was well until Marlene decided to get married. At that point, we had to give up the apartment because she had been the one who had made it work.

I moved in with a friend from the St. Boniface group and her mother. I think they were from El Salvador. This did not work out, so I started looking for yet another place. I found a rooming house run by an elderly lady, Miss Puccinelli. She was a very strict Italian lady and ran the place like a convent. When I went for an interview, she asked all sorts of questions, wanted references, and gave me a copy of all the rules. I had one thing in my favor; I told her my parents were Italian, and that they were both dead. At the mention of my Italian heritage, she began to warm considerably. Miss Puccinelli's house was on Steiner and California, so I could walk to work.

Until now, I had been a product of a very austere lifestyle. During all of my sixteen years in Mexico, I had lived in a very moralistic, church-driven society, based mainly on the dual standards of men and women. People in general exhibited quite modest behavior. During my year in San Fernando, my days were a mix of a conservative home life and a multi-cultural school life. During my three years with the Rios, I had been almost entirely sequestered from everyday life. Now that I was on my own, I began getting a crash course in what was really going on around me.

By now, I had worked at several branches of the Wells Fargo Bank, and during the time I lived at Miss Puccinelli's, I worked at the Fillmore and California branch. This was near the much-publicized Haight-Ashbury district. To use the expression coined in that era, life there was a *happening*. Visitors came from all over to gawk at the shocking antics of the Flower Children. For these young people of post-WWII years, it was party time all day long.

I often rode the bus to go shopping, and the bus route passed through the heart of the Haight-Ashbury district. As we passed by, I could often see right through the un-curtained windows of the Flower Children's apartments. Sometimes I could see them dressing and undressing or just walking around naked. They had no embarrassment at all. In fact, they seemed to do all they could to shock and display their new free-sex values. Some of the people on the bus laughed at their bizarre behavior, others were shocked.

However, the most shocking incident happened on a gorgeous, bright Saturday morning. I was walking through Golden Gate Park to my friend's house. I planned to meet her so we could go to a tennis lesson. I was strolling leisurely along a beautiful park pathway when I was suddenly confronted by a couple having sex right in front of me. I was shocked at the sight and wanted to run. They, in turn, although they saw me, seemed totally unaffected and uninhibited.

Broken Dreams

Each day after work, I volunteered at the USO Club on Market Street or at a military hospital in San Francisco. At the USO Club, I met a second Carl. We used to talk a lot, and I found out we had many similarities in our backgrounds. I felt he would understand me well.

In December 1963, I said yes when he started to pressure me to get married. His excuse for pressuring me was that he needed to do all the paperwork well ahead of his pending military transfer so I could go with him. We agreed to a civil ceremony at the city hall and we did not live together until we were married in the Catholic Church.

I was twenty-three, lived in the country of my birth, spoke English, had graduated from high school, and had a steady job at Wells Fargo Bank. I was now ready to take steps toward the next major goal from my early childhood—to find my family. However, I had to put these things on hold as I was getting married. I even considered the advice of some friends. They told me that when I had a husband and children of my own I would probably not feel as strongly about the need to find my family. It seemed to them to be such an impossible task because I had so little to go on. For just a fleeting moment, I told myself that perhaps they were right.

I can't remember the date of the civil marriage; however, it was in December. We got married at the city hall. I was on my coffee break, and Susie, a friend from the bank, was with us. Afterward, Susie, because she was covering for me, went back to work. To celebrate, Carl and I went to Chinatown with some of his friends and had dinner. After dinner, Carl went back to his ship and, still a virgin, I went back to my room at the boarding house.

That following April, we got married in St. Dominick's Catholic Church, the family church of my landlady, Miss Puccinelli. Miss Puccinelli took charge of the wedding as if she were the mother of the bride. She used the influence of her long relationship with the church to secure the chapel. She bought all the flower arrangements for the altar and the wedding party. She also sent food to the reception. God Bless her, she was so proud of me.

Toward the end of that year, I had two weeks of vacation. Carl could not get time off, so I traveled to Lehigh, Pennsylvania, to meet his family. After a few days in Lehigh, and knowing Carl had a cousin in the Bronx, I saw an opportunity to do what I wanted most—go on to New York to begin the seemingly futile search for my family.

When I arrived in New York, I stayed with Carl's cousin as planned. I began the search, armed with a birth certificate that was obviously filled with inaccuracies, the two orange cards, and the small photograph of me as a baby. That first morning I got up early and, with ten dollars in dimes, started calling every name in the New York phone book I thought could be related.

Later, I went to the 136 Columbia Street apartment in Brooklyn that was listed on my birth certificate and asked people there if they could tell me where I could find Filomena or Jackie. Finally, at the end of the week, I met an elderly Italian man who was living in the very apartment where my mother had lived when I was born. He knew Jackie's family. He told me he thought Jackie had died in 1957 and had been living with his daughter at the time. He suggested I come back the next day. In the meantime, he said he was going to ask around to see if he could find where Jackie's daughter might be living.

Just as I was about to leave, he asked me, "Do you want to see the apartment where your mother lived?" I said no. I did not feel comfortable going into that building.

I came the next day, and he took me to a house where he was sure people knew of Jackie's family. When we got there, a women and a man were waiting for us. They talked among themselves in Sicilian. Then they looked at me, told me they could not help me, and advised me to just forget about these people, go back to my husband, and have a family of my own. To tell me to forget about *these people* was like telling me to stop living. It was easy for them to be patronizing, naïve, and insensitive when they gave this advice; they knew their families. I was desperately looking into the past to find mine.

The old man felt very badly for me as he was sure these people could give me information about Jackie's daughter. I also had the strong feeling that this Italian couple knew something about my background. In any case, after two weeks of phone calls and knocking on doors in the old neighborhood, my search in New York came to an end. Sad, but determined to come back to search again, I left New York and returned to San Francisco.

Once back in San Francisco, I began to realize that I had made a terrible mistake in marrying Carl. I felt like a failure, and the thing that weighed most heavily on my mind was my obligations to the Catholic Church. I went to talk with a priest and told him all about our marriage. I told him Carl did not want children, and one day when he got drunk, he told me that if I ever got pregnant, he would kick the baby out of me. The priest advised me to give it a little more time to see if I could save the marriage and, if not, to just go ahead and get a divorce and renew my life. He said an annulment would take a lot of time, perhaps years, and would cost a lot of money.

When Carl got orders to go to Norfolk, Virginia, I went with him. The things I remember most about Norfolk were the signs on lawns and streets that said, "No coloreds, no sailors, and no dogs allowed." This discrimination was so hard to take. I spoke with an accent and I was married to a sailor. When I went looking for an apartment, one lady asked me if my husband was black. I was so angry at her ignorance and bigotry I just walked away, leaving it to Carl to talk to her.

Three months later, we were transferred to Charleston, South Carolina, where I met Jeannie and Nancy, friends I keep to this day. Jeannie taught me how to drive, and I got my first driver's license in South Carolina. Nancy and her mom were my moral support. They treated me like part of their family. In later years, Nancy's mom became like a grandmother to my children.

After just short of a year in Charleston, we were transferred to Hawaii. Just after we got to Hawaii, Carl went on a short assignment back on the mainland. When he returned, I found evidence he had been unfaithful. This, coupled with all of the other unhappiness, provoked the start of divorce proceedings. Shortly after, Carl had open-heart surgery and I stayed with him only until he recovered.

Three Years in Paradise

Just after arriving in Hawaii, I got a job as a cashier in the U.S. Navy Officers' Club at Pearl Harbor. Right away, I also became acquainted with a girl, Cheryl, whose husband was at sea on a U.S. Navy nuclear submarine. She told me her husband would be out for three to six months at a time and she sure could use the company while he was away. I moved in with her.

I quickly settled in to living in Hawaii and met several other interesting friends. One was quite interested in fortune-telling and invited me to go with her to see her favorite fortune-teller. She went in first. When my turn came, I no sooner sat down than the fortune-teller asked me for my keys. I thought it would be fun to play a trick on her so I gave her Cheryl's keys. She immediately told me the keys were not mine. I was astonished and quickly gave her my keys.

She proceeded, telling me, "You will be engaged or married before you leave the islands."

I looked at her, contained a nervous giggle, and thought to myself, *This would be impossible. I wouldn't get my divorce decree until I was ready to leave the island. Besides, I was not going with anyone at the time.*

She continued, "I see you surrounded by water, with military men in white uniforms all around you."

At least this part made more sense because I worked at the Officers' Club, which was near the water, and there were military men all around me. This reading happened about seven or eight months before I was to leave Hawaii.

As we were leaving, I told my friend, "This lady's predictions are far off."

My friend said, "I like her, and all the things she has told me in the past have come true."

Time went on and I met Bob, a young lieutenant, at the Officers' Club when he came to cash a check. It was on my birthday. He told me he would like to learn Spanish, but I did not say much as I was used to hearing all kinds of stories from other officers who wanted to date me. I would just listen, smile, and go on with my business. For a time, the hurt and the failure in my life had made me very bitter and I thought all men were alike. Even though I had plenty of opportunities, I would not date anyone. Sometimes I would go out in a group with the people I worked with because I felt there was safety in numbers. After a while, on the insistence of some friends, I dated a few times.

I saw many young officers go off to the Vietnam War, some of them never to come back. Many of them had young families at home. Often, they would call and give their wives or sweethearts the number of the main desk so they would call back, keeping the charges on their home phone bills. I was most often the one who would answer the phone and look for them. For some, this may have been the last time they would talk to their loved ones. If they were happy, I would know it as they would tell me all the good news. Sometimes, however, the news was bad, involving divorces and other problems.

It was a very interesting place to work, but sometimes it was sad, especially when you would hear that so many were missing in action. No matter, you only saw some of these men once before they left for war; it still brought the Vietnam War too close to home.

The management always tried to make the Officers' Club available, even if it was the day off for staff. Sometimes an aircraft carrier would show up in port on its way to the war zone. This was usually unannounced, and if it happened on my day off, I was called to come to work. I, in turn, would then have to call in bartenders and waitresses on their days off. I don't remember anyone refusing to come in.

I cashed checks, made change for the bartenders, answered the phone, booked private parties, took payments, and sold tickets for the different shows the Officers' Club presented. I was busy. I needed to be busy so I would not think of my problems.

Bob kept coming to the Officers' Club and asking me out. My answer was always the same: "No, I can't, maybe some other time."

Well, he did not take no for an answer. This went on for about two months. One of the reasons I would not go out with him was because when I had asked him how old he was, he jokingly told me that he was twenty. As I was twenty-seven, I felt that he was too young for me. He thought that I would know if he were an officer, he had to be older. However, because I never saw him in uniform, I thought he was a civilian or a visiting dependent.

One Sunday evening Bob appeared. All day, everything that could possibly go wrong had gone wrong. A storm had shut the power down, and we were operating in candlelight. When Bob asked me if I would like to go out for a drink, I surprised him with a yes. With the trying day I had been through, I needed to get out.

I told my boss, Mr. Sangster, "I am leaving. I have had it. This has been a most trying day!"

Bob and I drove to the Makalapa Navy Officers' Club, a small, very secluded, quaint, classy, and beautiful place that was not well known. When we first went in, someone was playing the piano. Later, Bob pleasantly surprised me by also playing the piano. I just sat there and enjoyed it all. It was a very relaxing date.

Because Bob lived at the nearby Bachelor Officers' Quarters, all he had to do was walk a few minutes and he was at the Officers' Club. After our first date, he was there every day.

In the meantime, I had given Bob's name, age, and service number to John, a part-time driver for the Officers' Club. John's regular job was in navy intelligence, so he had access to the navy personnel files. He checked Bob's records for me, particularly his marital status. I asked John to do this because I did not want to date a married man, or even a divorced one for that matter. I had understood well all the stories I had heard from my coworkers and friends about other officers who were *married-with-a-single-mind* fellows and who wanted to date. Keeping in line with my life so far, nothing seemed to follow the norm, so I took no chances.

Right before I met Bob, I had met a commander who had Bob's same exact first name, middle initial, and unusual surname. He was also as persistent as Bob in asking me out. Apart from other suitors, I had a lieutenant and a commander with the same names. As usual, I had the commander checked out by my friend who found out that he was a divorced man who lived on Coronado Island in San Diego.

One might think, *Wow, she had everyone checked out.* However, all my life I had always had to look out for myself. When you do not have a soul in the world to look out for you, you devise clever ways of looking out for yourself. Even though I was becoming a divorcee, I was Catholic and didn't want to marry a divorced man. I wanted to start a family and I was looking to marry a man who wanted a family and who would make a good father. Many women my age had help from their family and friends to look out for them. I essentially had no one.

I realized Bob wanted to marry me even though up to then only the commander had actually proposed. One day I was at work when the commander came to see me. He could not understand why I would not go out with him. Then he went over to join a group of his friends. I did what I thought would clearly explain my predicament. Bob was there, so I asked him to go over and introduce himself to the commander. In doing so, he first only showed the commander his identification card. You should have seen the commander's face. The only thing different on his identification card was the rank!

Then the commander came over to me and said, "You knew my intentions were honorable; why didn't you tell me about him?"

I answered him, "Because I did not want to hurt your feelings. I can't marry you. You are a divorced man. Besides, I did not know his intentions before, and now I do."

He wished me good luck and said he thought I had made a good choice. He said his only consolation was my married name would be the same as his. He hoped I would be very happy.

The island of Oahu was a paradise. Our courtship was full of adventure—sailing, walking on the beach, dancing in the best places in Hawaii, ringing in New Year's Eve on top of Punch Bowl, snorkeling in Hanama Bay, picnicking on the windward side of the island, going to Don Ho's shows at Duke Kahanamoku's, and many more fun and interesting things.

We went to a Christmas Eve candlelight service at Kawaiahao Church, a traditional Hawaiian church in Honolulu. The singing in the Hawaiian language was beautiful. The candles were spiritual in their radiance and joined us all. Bob gave me a ring during the ceremony, a very pretty star sapphire with diamonds. He told me it was a "friendship ring."

He proposed to me on February 19, 1968, at the Pearl Harbor Officers' Club. At first, we had planned to marry in California after Bob was out of the service. However, our friends complained that if we got married in California, many of them would not be able to come to the wedding. In ten days, we planned our wedding on Oahu. Bob asked his friends, Mick and Peg, if they would let us get married on their thirty-six-foot sailboat, Kim II.

They said, "With pleasure, but it is in dry-dock, and you'll have to help us finish the work so the boat will be ready in time." We agreed, and Bob and I helped paint the boat. Mick and Peg exclaimed, "You are the first bride we have seen who painted the church she was to get married in."

We asked our good friend, Chaplain Barr, to marry us at sea.

His answer was, "I will marry you anywhere you want." When we told him the day, he was very pleased, as we would be getting married on his birthday.

We had to have alternate plans just in case the weather did not permit us to get married at sea. The alternate plan was to get married on top of Punch Bowl, to which our priest was also very agreeable.

He said to me, "What better place to get married, a magnificent church, the sky, and the sea."

Then came the plans for the wedding reception. I did not have much to do because David, the best man, and Darry, the maid of honor, wanted to make all of the arrangements. All I had to do was pay the liquor bill. Wow, what luck! David was the captain of one of five ocean-going tugboats in the same U.S. Navy organization to which Bob was assigned. When they heard of our wedding, the cooks on the tugs wanted to take care of the finger food and the wedding cake. I was told that the crew of one of the tugs even went shopping in downtown Honolulu for special pans needed to bake the wedding cake. They baked a three-tiered cake, all white with small pink flowers. It was the most beautiful wedding cake I had ever seen. The crews of the other tugboats made delicious finger food. The manager of the restaurant at the top of the Pearl Harbor Bachelor Officers' Quarters decorated the place and even brought beautiful monkey pod serving dishes from his home. It seemed everyone wanted something to do with our wedding. Because we had such a short time to prepare, their help was most welcome.

The best man and the maid of honor did a fantastic job organizing everything. In this wedding, since I had no family, I did not have anyone to tell me what they wanted. Bob had already made his wishes known. He did not want anything traditional at his wedding—not even the traditional mints. He did not want a professional photographer, and he preferred not to pose for pictures. In the end, we decided almost all the pictures were to be candid. We asked our good friends Mike, the staff doctor, Jim, the administrative officer, and Norman, the medical officer, to do the camera work. Norman was one of our close friends and was the one who gave me away. The sailboat was decorated in beautiful baby's breath and pikake flowers. They did a marvelous job with the decorations.

I had to busy myself with the immediate problems of finding a wedding dress, shoes, and wedding rings. Discouraged by not being able to find a dress to fit, I asked a friend in Waipahu if she could make me a dress in a week. She said she had never made a wedding dress but would be more than happy to try. I told her this was not to be a traditional wedding.

I told her Bob gave me a card with my Christmas presents. He had told me he picked the card because the girl on the card looked like me. I showed her the card and asked her to make the dress like the one the girl on the card was wearing. She shopped for the material and made the dress precisely like the one on the Christmas card, right down to the olive green color. Green represented hope, and I was putting a lot of hope in this marriage.

I had a difficult time finding shoes to fit as my size was four and a half. In those days in Hawaii, it took about two weeks to order anything from the mainland, and I only had six days. I finally found a pair of shoes that went perfectly with the dress.

With the shoes and dress behind me, I felt I had things under control. Not so, as we could not find a set of matching wedding bands with one ring small enough to fit me. To have a ring cut to my size would have taken two weeks. We looked and looked. Finally, in desperation, we went into a discount store called Wigwam, where we found just the set of gold wedding bands we were looking for; they fitted us perfectly.

The only thing left was to get the wedding license. This proved to be an embarrassing moment as Bob had called ahead to find out the details of getting a marriage license. They had told him the license would cost three dollars. Well, when it was time to pay, the clerk told Bob it would be five dollars.

Bob exclaimed loudly enough for everyone in the line to hear, "Five dollars! You said it would be three."

The lady calmly explained that when Bob had called he asked only the cost of the license. She said the two dollars was for the registration. Everyone in line was looking at me; I wanted to hide under the table.

The Asian lady who was helping us looked at me, as if to say, *Do you really want to marry this man who is complaining about two dollars?*

I just looked at her and smiled as I knew Bob, who gave little thought to money, was doing this just in fun. He then said to the lady, "Two more dollars. Boy, wives are expensive these days."

With that, he paid the lady the five dollars, and everyone sighed in relief—some even applauded.

The beautiful wedding would not have been possible without the help of good friends who gave so generously of their time and talents. We had to have a blood test. If it had been done locally through normal channels, it would have taken several days. With the help of our friends, particularly the heroic efforts of Jim, it was done at the navy base in less than twenty-four hours. Mike, Norman, and Jim took the wedding pictures and movies. They turned out beautifully. The best part of it all was that this happened so naturally. We were seldom aware the pictures were being taken.

There were only two difficult things in our wedding ceremony. The first was, just before we set out to sea, I had to be confined to the cabin of the sailboat so the groom would not see the bride before the wedding. The other was when the captain asked me to wear tennis shoes. He said the shoes I had on were not safe on the boat. He was perfectly right as the sea was rough, and the small craft warnings had been lifted just minutes before we got under way. However, there was no way I would wear tennis shoes on my wedding day. I managed to compromise by going barefoot.

Following Hawaiian tradition, I wore a lei with seven strands of white pikake flowers and held a beautiful white wedding bouquet. Bob wore his U.S. Navy full-dress, white uniform with a lei of red carnations.

Finally, we were underway. When I got out of the cabin for the ceremony, I looked at David, the best man. He looked the color of my dress, green! He and some of Bob's other friends tried everything they could to get Bob drunk at his bachelor party the night before. Bob was in good shape the next day, but all of the others were suffering from big hangovers. As I looked at David, I felt seasick too. I did not get enough air in the cabin below, and the rocking of the boat in the rough sea made me feel very uncomfortable. When I came out, I still felt queasy. The day before, Mike had given me some medication for seasickness, but it did not seem to be doing any good.

As Father Barr was starting the marriage ceremony, I was praying I would make it through, which I did. Thank God! Right after the ceremony, I was over the rail, but thankfully, the sickness was mild, and I was feeling better in no time. During the ceremony, just as Bob was putting the wedding ring on my finger, the boat lurched and we almost went overboard. David and Darry had thoughtfully attached each of the rings to a string. They did this to keep the rings from being dropped overboard, which almost happened.

Strangely, just at that moment I had a flashback to the times, long ago in Veracruz when I had admired the cadets strolling in the Zocalo and on the Malecon and had told myself someday I would marry a cadet. Just as mysteriously, I recalled the words and the vision that had formed in my mind when the fortune-teller, just a few months before, told me, "You will be engaged or married before you leave the islands. You will be surrounded by water, with military men in white uniforms all around you."

When Father Barr said, "You may kiss the bride," another big wave hit the boat. We were hanging to the side of the rail and almost went into the water. As I said before, nothing in my life comes easy.

Just after we arrived back at the beautiful Alawai Yacht Harbor, we had a small reception with just the wedding party. We opened two magnums of champagne that were made ready for the occasion by Norman, who had been the father of the bride for the day. We toasted our wedding with a traditional Hawaiian fertility cup that one of our friends had given us. Rice was thrown, congratulations were said, and cameras were going all the time.

On our way to the reception at Pearl Harbor Bachelor Officers' Quarters, my thoughts turned inward. I thought how I would have loved to have had some of my family here to share in this moment. A wedding is one of the most important moments in a person's life. I also thought of the people who had helped with this wedding and could not be here to share in the festivities. In any case, I thanked them inwardly, even though I had never met them.

When we arrived at the reception, Father Barr called us aside to sign our marriage certificate, which listed our place of marriage at 157 degrees 52 minutes west longitude and 21 degrees 17.5 minutes north latitude aboard Kim II at 11:21 AM. Technically, because of our location on the sea at the precise time we were married, we had been married in international waters and, because the boat was registered in Canada, on Canadian territory!

The reception went very well and everyone seemed to be having a good time. Food and drinks were plentiful. Darry and David deserve a lot of credit for the success. We were finally ready to leave on our honeymoon.

Just as Bob started the car, we heard a loud whistle and bang, and smoke was coming from under the hood. Someone, I believe David and Norman, had planted a whistle that blew off when the car started. Of course, our guests were watching us from the balcony. They even took a few photos, as they were ready with their cameras. I could hear their laughter as though I were standing next to them. They had fun at our predicament.

Bob quickly fixed the car, and we were under way. They had painted "Just Married" on the windows, and we could hear strange noises coming from the assortment of empty cans and old things they had tied to the back of the car. As we were leaving, several cars followed us, beeping their horns all the way to the gate. Even after we left the base, people blew their horns as they saw us pass.

For our honeymoon, Bob and Norman had found a traditionally styled Hawaiian cabin in a lovely tree-covered setting at Punaluu, on the windward side of the island. The cabin was hidden in a beautiful and very secluded Japanese-style grouping of other small cabins surrounded with lush tropical ponds, bridges, goldfish, coconut palms, banana trees, papaya trees, and an assortment of orchids and tropical plants. All of this, and it was right across the road from a gorgeous secluded beach with magnificent, unspoiled scenery, mindful of old Hawaii.

When we got to our lovely Hawaiian-style cabin, we found groceries and drinks ready for us, even to the little details of the avocados and jalapeños they knew I loved. They had thought of everything. The cabin had a little kitchen, and as I was so tired of eating out, I immediately launched into cooking our first meal. It was paradise. The weather, the sea, and the lush tropical vegetation and fruits were all like those I had known in Veracruz. I felt a familiarity with the place as I have never felt for any other place since. This was a new and colossal beginning.

The next day, we took a short, slow drive in the area. I will never forget the moment we came upon the scene of an old Hawaiian man, sitting on the porch of a lovely old shack, weaving a hat from palm fronds. He seemed not to notice us; his hands never stopping as, from time-to-time, he glanced up at the sea. His eyes seemed to see beyond the distant horizon.

After our honeymoon, we had less than a week before our departure from Hawaii. Here again, our friends, especially Jim, were a tremendous help in getting all the paperwork done in the little time we had left. I thought of how I had hoped these times would never end; we had shared so much and so willingly. To think of them is to think of happy times, carefree times, and caring times. We said our good-byes and were on our way to San Francisco. Bob was to be discharged from the navy, and then we were to go on to Pomona, California, to meet his family.

While in San Francisco, I introduced Bob to some of my friends. After meeting them, Bob told me what a great bunch of friends I had. I also took my girlfriend Marlene to the Officers' Club on Treasure Island. As soon as we walked in, I was paged. I went to the front desk and answered the phone. It was the commander with Bob's same name, the same one I knew in Hawaii, asking me to have him paged to say his wife was at table so and so. I did as asked, and as I was walking back to my table, I saw this blond woman rush out. As soon as she was out of sight, here comes my old admirer to thank me for helping him get rid of his lady friend who, he told me, had become somewhat of a pest. My girlfriend Marlene was quite amused by all of this and wanted to know more about what had just happened.

The commander had to go back to his office. He paid for our lunch and drinks, kissed my hand, and said, "Thank you, my little one." That was what he called me in Hawaii.

After he left, I told Marlene the whole story.

All she could say when I finished was, "A lot of women would love to have your problems. You never do things the easy way; with you there's never a dull moment!"

After a week of honeymoon in San Francisco, Bob told me we were flying to Ontario. I was thinking Ontario, Canada. I soon found out it was Ontario International Airport in Ontario, California! Bob's father and stepmother, Bee, were waiting for us. I was nervous about meeting Bob's family, and he assured me his dad and Bee were the nicest people I would ever want to meet. He was right. Both Bob's father and Bee were very warm and welcomed us with open arms. It so happens, out of all of Bob's family, these two were the ones with whom I immediately felt like I was part of the family. I could see clearly that Bee was the kind of grandmother I wanted for my children. Right away, I loved them dearly. I met the rest of Bob's family, including Bob's mother, at the beautiful wedding reception Bob's father and Bee gave us. Then we left for a three-month honeymoon all over Mexico.

During our honeymoon, we traveled by bus to many interesting sites and visited many people and places from my childhood. In Mexico City, we visited Uncle Gustavo Jr., Uncle Enrique, and Uncle Xavier and their families, all of whom had been so supportive of me during those critical months just before Matilde and I left for Tijuana.

After Mexico City, we went to Veracruz for a few days and then on to Poza Rica where we were guests of Uncle Ricardo and Matilde's half sister, Aunt Mari. I had stayed with Uncle Ricardo and Aunt Mari and their family early in 1957 before going to the United States. At this time, Bob still knew nothing of my story. As far as he knew, we were there on our honeymoon to meet people from my past. I told him we were visiting my relatives.

They received us very warmly, unlike when I had last stayed as a sixteen-year-old girl with Matilde around me. Uncle Ricardo, himself an engineer at Pemex, treated us very well. Normally very frugal, he gave

Aunt Mari extra money to take us out and to entertain us like royalty. I was confused by his obvious change in attitude toward me. This was the same man who had been so indifferent to me when I was last there, a little more than ten years earlier.

Olivia, one of his single daughters, explained, "Graciela, he is very proud of you. You have done what every girl in Poza Rica only dreams of—you married a navy officer who is also an engineer, and you had a fairy-tale wedding on a yacht in exotic Hawaii as we would only see in the movies. Your Uncle Ricardo wants those around him to know his niece is not only well-traveled but has accomplished all of this."

All the time we were there the house stayed full of young people who were curious and wanted to meet us; some even knew me from the time I was last there. One time, I came back from being out with Aunt Mari to find Bob surrounded by more than a dozen pretty, young girls. He was holding his own in Spanish, and they were all asking him questions.

Aunt Mari said, "Look at him with all those girls! Aren't you jealous?" I told her I wasn't. I knew just what was going through their minds. They all wanted to know if Bob had any brothers and they were asking him all about us and about the United States. None of them knew of my story.

Aunt Mari took us to the Pemex Country Club where we had lunch and swam in the beautiful modern swimming pool. She also took us to Papantla and to the beautiful, historic, and interesting pyramid at el Tajin.

Following the glorious visit at Poza Rica, we went on to the city of Veracruz. I easily but painfully remembered the location, Peru and Circunvalación. This was the address where I had endured so much suffering and hardship during my childhood years. We took the same bus ride I had taken so many times in the past. Doña Josefina had passed away. Maria, her daughter from Jalapa, was now living there. Maria invited us to stay and prepared delicious meals for us. Bob even met Rolando.

The conflict in emotions was almost unbearable. I was inhaling the excitement of our recent wedding. At the same time, here was Maria, the same Maria who had treated me so cruelly, and horribly, in Jalapa, extending full hospitality to us. In fact, she now treated me as if I were family. I had never known this behavior from her before. All of this was now happening in the very place where, in the not-so-distant past, I had endured so many hardships from her mother, doña Josefina. When I saw Maria, it also instantly brought back all of those bad feelings and memories of the cruelty and abuse she had so generously inflicted on me in Jalapa.

I had to accept Maria's hospitality gracefully, because Bob did not yet know of my past with her. However, this didn't keep me from thinking about what a hypocrite she was. The feelings I had are best described as bittersweet and conflicted.

Bob and I had a great time going around Veracruz, even though I had to hide the burden of those memories of the past. We swam in the warm water at Villa del Mar, strolled in the Zocalo, and walked in several of the neighborhoods. As we walked on the Malecon and the Zocalo, the sight came fully to my mind of those cadets I had seen all those years before, and whom I had said I would marry one day. Now I was proudly strolling on the Malecon and the Zocalo with my very own cadet. Bob had been to Veracruz during a summer of travel he had taken by himself, some five years earlier. He expressed warm memories of eating breakfast in the Café Parroquia in the area called los Portales. Except for the times I spent with Mrs. Lara and Gabriela Mistral, my memories of the Café Parroquia and of los Portales, were of a much darker nature.

When it came time to return to the United States, the bus passed beautiful Lake Chapala. I remembered that ten years earlier I had seen the same beautiful scene of Lake Chapala fishermen with their fairylike butterfly nets. Then I was with Matilde on the bus ride to Tijuana. I clearly remember the feelings of insecurity I had the first time I had seen this beautiful site and the feelings of security I was having in the present. I was so uncertain of where I was heading the first time; this time I was very certain.

We had been gone nearly three months and only came back when the money was almost out. Well, I should say, Bob's money. Even though I had money of my own, I never told Bob as I wanted always to have my own money, just in case. Besides, I had seen two of my girlfriends' husbands go through their savings in no time. In the world

I grew up in, the man was financially responsible for his wife, an old tradition, but one I still used as a guideline.

We arrived back in Southern California from our honeymoon in June. We stayed with Bob's father and Bee for two weeks. Then Bob got a job at Kaiser Steel and we rented a house and settled in Riverside, California. We had fun setting up our new home.

Tragically, I had a miscarriage in August of the same year. It made me very sad as we both wanted to have a family right away. I had another miscarriage that December. I went to a doctor who diagnosed the problem. He told me to try again and as soon as I knew I was pregnant to come and see him. I could tell within days when I was pregnant. I went to the doctor as he asked. He put me on shots once a month, and I was able to carry my two children.

While I was carrying my first child, I would think and worry because I knew nothing of my family's medical background. The worry was intensified at every visit by the questions the nurses asked me about my family's medical history. One time I got upset at their repeated questions. I asked the nurse to put in my record that I did not know any information about my family's medical history. I told her firmly that I hoped I would not be asked the same questions again. The questions from the nurses stopped, but I could not stop my inner questions about my family medical history. All I could do was pray for a healthy and normal baby.

I was working at a local bank in Riverside at that time. I worked there until the end of January 1971, and our beautiful girl was born in February. This was the first time I had actually seen anyone of my own blood. My feelings were beyond description.

Just as I left the hospital, I was asked if I wanted a nurse to visit once a week to answer any questions about caring for the baby. I readily accepted the offer, and when the visiting nurse arrived, I was full of questions. I explained to her that all we knew was what we had read in our Dr. Spock book. She became very helpful in those first trying weeks. With her help, I think Bob and I did a wonderful job.

Bee offered to come and help, but Bob wanted to take care of us, and he had taken two weeks off to do so. Bob's mother, who was not the grandmotherly type, did not offer to help. She already had six grandchildren and she had told their mothers she did not want to babysit or take care of grandchildren. In any case, she and I had a difficult relationship from the start.

For the next several years, I was busy raising a family of my own and did not have much time to search for my parents and siblings, even though they were always on my mind. Two years later, after my handsome son was born, I again started searching. I started with the New York phone book, writing letters to everyone I thought could help. I waited anxiously for the mailman. Some of the people were kind enough to answer, but no one could give me any helpful information. It was a very frustrating time.

Sometimes, late at night, I would lay in bed, unable to sleep, trying to think of ways of finding my family. At other times, I would cry in frustration and helplessness. I would tell Bob, "My brothers and sisters are somewhere in New York. I must find them, or at least try." One would think that after I had my own children my desire to find my family would subside. This was not the case.

In those close moments when I was breast-feeding my daughter, I wished I could have shared the joy of this beautiful little girl with my sisters or brothers. My drive to find them became increasingly stronger. Even in my busiest moments or in moments of joy or sorrow, my thoughts would turn to them. I have never understood this. I had always been able to walk away from any seemingly hopeless situation and go forward. I think another thing that made me want to find my family was the way Italian families are always portrayed in the movies. They are always depicted as being warm and loving. I so desperately wanted this for my children, but I remained guarded. I knew a loving family would not have abandoned a child as they did me. My husband's family, especially his father and stepmother, were very warm, loving, and nice to me and to our two children, but the rest of the family was not as close. I guess they were all busy with their own lives, while I hungered for close family ties. Life went on and my husband, bless his heart, did everything possible to see that I was happy. He helped a lot with the children. Socially, we were very busy.

Bob was in the Navy Reserve. This gave us two weeks of active duty once a year, which was like an added vacation. Once, we went to San Diego and stayed at the visiting officers' quarters.

One day, as I was coming back from a fashion show at the Admiral Kid Club, the receptionist handed me a bundle of mail, saying, "Here is your husband's mail."

At first, I did not think anything of it. I went to our room and then began to wonder why Bob would be getting so much mail when we were to be here for only two weeks. I took a closer look, and I could see the mail was addressed to the commander I had met in Hawaii that had Bob's same name! I thought it was funny and returned the mail to the front desk. It turned out that he was staying in the same building. It seemed as long as we were in the navy, this would happen again and again. I imagined this would give the commander a sense of pleasure that I was always mistaken for his wife.

At the end of 1973, my husband decided to change companies and was busy with job interviews. The offers started coming, and with each offer, my insecurity grew. Each offer meant leaving our first home, which we had bought only three years before. In addition, it meant we might move away from our children's grandparents. This would be the end of a comfortable way of life; one that I had just begun to enjoy. I did not share these feelings with my husband as I knew he was not satisfied with his job.

He continued to travel to job interviews. Some of the offers involved foreign assignments. Then the request came for Bob to have an interview with a company across the country, in Greenville, South Carolina. Bob went alone to Greenville for the interview.

When he returned, he told me, "No, I would not live there. That place is cloudy and gloomy."

I said to myself, *He said he would not go, and that is probably where we are going to end up.*

Because of my previous bad experiences with discrimination, I was not eager to move again to the South, but the company kept calling. Finally, they made him a great offer, which he accepted. We were to spend a year in France before moving to South Carolina. That was very appealing to both of us. In the end, with an almost three-year-old girl and a six-month-old boy, we decided to move to France.

Before we left, Bob went alone to Long Beach to complete his two weeks of Navy Reserve active duty. I stayed home to sell our house and cars. During this same time, our son came down with severe bronchitis and I had to take him to the hospital. I was so upset, I went only on nervous energy. The finality of our decision, especially in these hurried circumstances, was beginning to take its toll.

Old World Adventure

In February 1974, we celebrated our daughter's third birthday with Bob's father and Bee and, immediately after, left for France. I was very excited about visiting Europe. I was finally going to see the France that Gabriela Mistral had told me so much about. I thought back to those wonderful moments when I was an eight-year-old girl in Veracruz and Gabriela Mistral was telling me all about her travels in Europe and her times in Italy. She would also show me books and pictures of Europe. As occurred often in similar situations in the past, the high expectations and joy of going to Europe were clouded by the constant hurt of yearning for my family.

Looking down from the airplane onto the red tile roofs of our destination, Clermont-Ferrand, a large industrial city in central France, I simultaneously felt a sense of adventure and apprehension. I was remembering how difficult it had been for me to communicate when I first arrived in the United States. Here I was again, going to live in a country where I did not know the language. My husband and I would both have to learn French. I was going to realize one of my dreams, to visit Europe, and I was going to do it with an enthusiastic husband who was as eager as I was. We wrongly thought our two children would be too young to really appreciate and enjoy our travels. However, a year later when we talked to our then four-year-old daughter, she recounted so many of the things she remembered of that first stay in France.

Europe was like an endless museum. I was thrilled every time I saw a painting or a sculpture in the famous museums. I would try to imagine the painter and what he felt as he was painting. Was he pouring his heart and soul out on the canvas? Was he trying to find and express the answers to his deepest thoughts? What moves people to produce such beauty? I did not have a profound knowledge of art; I only knew what moved me, what I liked, and what transcended time. We also visited the famous Catholic shrines all over Europe, and at each, I lit a candle and prayed my fervent prayers to find my family. My inner search was always there.

The Search Goes On

Our wonderful eleven months in Europe went fast, and in December 1974, we returned to the United States and our new home in Mauldin, South Carolina. I rationalized that at least here I knew the language. I was going back to my country, to familiar things. Oh, how naïve I was. I never had culture shock in France or when I came to the United States at the age of sixteen, possibly because I wanted so much to be in these places. However, South Carolina was where I had my biggest cultural shock. In those days, people in the area where we lived were not used to foreigners, and because of my accent, I was called, *the foreigner.*

On one occasion, I went to the bank to withdraw a rather large sum of money. The teller showed some reluctance and asked me if my husband knew how much money I was taking out. Boy, did that get straightened out in short order! When I ordered appliances at department stores, they would take all the information, but they would not deliver without my husband's approval.

I recall an experience that happened when our new house was under construction. Whenever I would tell the contractor to do something, he would say very politely, "Yes, ma'am," but he never did what I asked.

One day, in sheer desperation, I called in the builder, sat him down, and gave him a big glass of California Barbaron wine. After a few sips, I called my husband at work and told him to tell the builder he better do the things I wanted done whenever I asked him. I handed the phone to the builder, and after that, I had no problem with him. I also had a few cases of good California wines that seemed to make it easier for him to understand my accent. Every time he came, I would give him his nice glass of wine, and things got done.

This period remains so fresh in my mind. I was stuck without a driver's license in a strange place and had two small children to care for. When I went to get a South Carolina driver's license, I couldn't understand the officer and he couldn't understand me. I was appalled by their way of treating people who were different from themselves. Today, the South is much more accustomed to having people from all over the world in their communities.

Finally, I thought I would get a break in caring for our two small children, when I learned that Bob's mother and her friend were coming to visit. We had never trusted our children to babysitters, but I really needed a break. Although she had never done this before, I had high hopes that maybe this time she would help me. When they arrived, after cooking for them and showing them around the area, I asked if she could help with the children. Her answer was that she was on vacation and my children made her nervous.

On a previous occasion, Bob's mother had come to our house to recuperate from a bicycle accident she had in Panama. After about three or four weeks, when she was well, I asked her if she would babysit the children so Bob and I could go to Atlanta overnight. She was angry and told me that it was she who should be going with her son. She said I should be the one who should be staying behind with the children.

Just after Bob's mother and her friend left, I had a startling dream. It occurred on May 20, 1977. The night started out just like any other night for a mother of two active toddlers. When my head touched the pillow, I quickly fell into a deep sleep. I began dreaming I was at Bob's father and stepmother's home in California. I was walking toward the tool shed, and just as I was midway there, my father-in-law suddenly came out holding his chest. He took two steps and fell to the ground.

In my dream, I called out to Bee at the top of my lungs. She was only a few feet from me, but she did not hear me! I bent over my father-in-law, tried to comfort him, and continued to call for Bee. I felt I was there in the moment. I could see, talk, and touch in a different and mysterious way, but no one seemed to see or hear me.

Finally, Bee, seeing her husband lying on the ground, rushed into the house and called the paramedics. Then, just as quickly, she was again rushing to his side. She seemed to pass right through me!

I was looking on as the paramedics gave CPR to my father-in-law. I answered all the questions they asked, but they did not hear me. I looked at the rose garden to my left. I looked at the lemon tree to my right. Just then, I looked to the shed. As I turned, the paramedics were sadly telling Bee her husband had passed on. Bee began crying and shaking violently. I was also sobbing.

At that instant, I woke up, gasping for air. I sat straight up and, confused, peered into the early morning darkness. I reached to wake my husband and then quickly withdrew. I realized I had been dreaming. I tried to go back to sleep, but sleep was futile. I slowly groped to the kitchen and made myself a cup of chamomile tea—no help.

Precisely a week later, I awoke feeling irritable, like a caged animal. I called my husband at work. I asked him to come home early because I needed to get out of the house.

Sometime after I called Bob, I went to check on my three-year-old son. As I got to the door of his room, I heard him talking and looking out of the window and asked him what he was doing. In the most natural way, without even turning his head, he said, "I am talking to grandpa. He is there."

His head still straight ahead, he pointed to the front lawn.

I said, "Your grandpa is in California."

He insisted, "No, mama, he is here talking with me."

I turned and walked slowly away, thinking to myself, *This child's imagination is working overtime.*

That evening, when my husband got home, I was waiting outside with the children. He took us to the library. Almost thoughtlessly, I picked out some books. We returned home to put the children to bed, a time I looked forward to every night. Just as we walked in, the phone was ringing. Bee was on the phone and broke the sad news that Bob's father had passed away that afternoon—right to the minute when my son had been talking to him in his room! We arranged the flights and a few hours later, we were on our way to California. After the funeral, I asked Bee where Bob's father was when he had the heart attack. She said that they had given him CPR by the lemon tree.

As she was talking to me, I couldn't stop shaking. She described everything just as I had dreamed it. Nearly three months later, I woke up in the early morning feeling a strong need to talk to Bee. I tried calling her every few hours during the day. Finally, at just before midnight, she answered the phone. We talked about many different things—the family, their rentals, and her pending trip to Alaska to visit with her daughter, Barbara, and her family.

During our call she said, "Grace, this call will cost a lot."

I said, "You are worth it."

We talked for more than an hour then said our good-byes. Five hours later, we got the terrible news that Bee had suffered an aneurism and was in a coma. Sadly, only days later, she passed away. Her passing was a deep loss to me; I had never lost anyone I was as close to as I was to Bee and Bob's dad.

We lost Bob's father and stepmother in 1977 within three months of each other. I missed them and their presence in my life and in the lives of my children. It was after they died that my search became more intense. While they were alive, they helped fill the void within me. We lost them so soon, one after the other, and I felt the loss very deeply. It was a very nearly disabling sadness to know I could not see them or call them again. When I think of them, it is with such fond memories and kindness. Everyone should be remembered this way.

Touching the Past

In my life there is very little I can go back to since I have moved so much and, at times, over such long distances. One day, a very intense feeling came over me—I needed to connect with someone from my past in Mexico. I focused on Gabriela Mistral. I went to the local library in Mauldin and found a book of Gabriela Mistral's poems that were translated into English by an American lady author named Doris Dana. In fact, the book was bilingual, both English and Spanish. In no time, I practically inhaled the book.

I was hungry for more of Gabriela Mistral's books. As soon as Bob came home from work, I asked him to take me to the main library in Greenville, which he did right away. I was able to find another book on Gabriela Mistral, again, written by Doris Dana.

I immediately thought I could make some contact with my past if only I could contact this Doris Dana. I went back to the library, and luckily, through some intense sleuthing, I was able to find Doris Dana's address and phone number. She had apparently moved since she had written the books. With so many names in the library's collection of various New York phone books, do not ask me how I did it, but I went right to the number.

The next day while Bob was at work, I dialed the number, and a lady answered the phone. I asked if she were Doris Dana, the writer and translator of Gabriela Mistral's poetry and books. The voice at the other end said yes.

I continued, "I want to read more books on Gabriela Mistral's poems, but there are only two books in the Greenville Library. I met Gabriela Mistral when I was a little girl in Veracruz, Mexico." There was a long silence. I thought she had hung up on me.

After a long pause and, just as I was about to hang up, I heard a voice asking, "Graciela, *eres tú* (is that you)?"

I was stunned. I was numb. The hairs on my arms stood up, for, with few exceptions, I had seldom been called Graciela since I left Mexico. After I recovered somewhat from my shock, I said, "Yes, I am Graciela, and who are you? How do you know my name in Spanish?" It was a big shock to have a person I assumed to be a complete stranger, suddenly reach so far into the past, and call me by my name. Somehow, I still had not yet associated the name, Doris Dana, with the name of Gabriela Mistral's traveling companion, who I knew from those early days. I now attribute this lack of memory to the tremendous stress I was going through as a young girl in Veracruz.

She told me she had been Gabriela Mistral's traveling companion in Veracruz, and she knew me from that time. She said she had given me some lessons in arithmetic. That explained why I was good at math when I was in Jalapa, even though to that time I had had very little schooling.

As she spoke, my memories of her started to come back—the fog was clearing. Now I remembered her. She had mostly remained in the background whenever I visited Gabriela Mistral in her apartment. In that informal setting, her full name had probably been used very infrequently.

Without hesitating, she invited me and my family to visit her on Long Island. She said she was going to give me some of Gabriela Mistral's books and she could not wait to see me. We talked for a long while and she asked me a lot about my life since she last saw me. She was most interested in how I made it to the United States. Sadly, she told me Gabriela Mistral had passed away in early 1957. I did not think for once, about how much this long distance phone call, quite expensive in those days, was costing; I was in a world of my own. The past was coming to me like a moving picture. The joy I felt from making this connection with the past seemed to overpower a lot of the pain of looking back.

Doris Dana seemed as excited as I was about making this improbable contact. She told me, "I have been asking for a sign from Gabriela Mistral on a big decision I have to make, and out of the blue, thirty years later, you call. You are the sign I have been asking for, only you connect from our past in Veracruz."

Toward the end of the call, I was so excited I could hardly write all the information about her address. I was elated; I had found someone from my past! I told her I could not wait to see her. What an understatement! Finally, she ended the call, saying, "I'm going to write you a letter on how to get to our home. Otherwise, you will get lost on the Long Island Parkway and I may never see you again." She was jokingly referring to the time in Veracruz when Gabriela Mistral and I went for a walk and, like the blind leading the blind, got lost and Doris Dana had had to find us.

When my husband got home that afternoon, I could not wait to tell him what I had done. He became very excited when I told him I had contacted the writer, Doris Dana, and she had extended an invitation to us to visit her at her home in Bridgehampton, Long Island.

My husband looked at me in awe as I told him how I had located Doris Dana and all that had transpired while he was at work. He kept asking, "Now tell me again how you knew what number to call, since Doris Dana now lives in a different town than she did when she wrote the book?" In those days, you could call the information operator and get phone numbers, but you had to know the town.

I told him that somehow I knew because I was guided by a power greater than myself. He said he was convinced I have a guardian angel. I believe here is when he first began calling me his *bruja* (witch). He only shook his head and said, "I do not know how you do it!" He was to repeat this many times.

Doris Dana lived with her cousin, Margit Varga, a prominent New York artist who had been a long-time art editor for *Time Life Magazine*. Our visit was fun and memorable for all of us. They lived in an historic, three-story house on eastern Long Island. The house was filled with antiques and paintings. More interestingly, there was one room filled with relics related to Gabriela Mistral. There were phonograph recordings by the great poet, boxes of her papers and hand-written manuscripts, her books, and her Bible. As I held the Bible in my hand, I was filled with emotions and memories. Doris Dana explained that Gabriela Mistral drew inspiration from the Bible.

The nearby little town of Bridgehampton was so quaint and pretty. At the back of the house, there were acres of potato fields. Our son enjoyed the freedom of their huge backyard and the potato fields beyond. One day Margit Varga even had some of her artist friends over, and we watched them paint beautiful landscapes.

All this time I was very excited, and my thoughts were going back to Veracruz and those precious moments I had spent with Gabriela Mistral. I thought of how wonderful it would have been if I could be with her again. I also recalled more clearly the times when I visited Gabriela Mistral. Whenever she needed to rest, Doris Dana would spend time with me, mainly teaching me math.

Doris Dana and Margit Varga were such wonderful hosts. They welcomed us warmly to their home, hugged our children, and made us all feel very comfortable. We continued to keep in touch by letter and by telephone.

As we left, I began to have very powerful feelings for Long Island, like something pulling me strongly. This was most unusual as I hadn't had these feelings for any place before. I had even been in Mexico, Hawaii, and Europe, all beautiful places, and I hadn't felt this way.

In December 1977, we were to be transferred again to France—this time to live in Cebazat, a small provincial town near the larger industrial city of Clermont-Ferrand. While the movers were packing our personal effects, I was having a difficult time. This was always the case whenever I had to make a move. The movers become the enemy—they were destroying my home and I knew it was best to keep my distance. The anxiety I felt at seeing our things packed was not because of leaving Mauldin, but was a result of the trauma I experienced, as a child, from moving so often. I couldn't even discuss this with my husband because I couldn't make sense of it myself.

Finally, the idea came to me to go by myself to Long Island to visit Doris Dana, or for her to babysit me, until the ordeal was over. Bob was relieved with the idea and agreed to stay back with our children to finish the packing.

Strangely, when I arrived at JFK Airport, the strong feelings toward Long Island came back. In any case, I had a very warm and meaningful stay. I especially enjoyed the moments Doris Dana and I spent together, going over the many interesting and historically important items from Gabriela Mistral's estate. In her will, Gabriela Mistral named Doris Dana as executrix for her estate. Doris Dana had spent years organizing and documenting the huge collection. We listened to phonograph records with original recordings of Gabriela Mistral reading her own poetry, enjoyed discussing the beautiful set of Deruta dinnerware Gabriela Mistral got from Italy, and went over original manuscripts and many other facets of this truly great poet's life. Doris Dana made me aware of the Adoptees' Liberty Movement Association (ALMA). She also introduced me to her wonderful friends, many of whom were important artists and writers living in the quaint and beautiful town of Bridgehampton.

After the movers were gone, my husband and children left South Carolina to join me in New York and onward to Europe. Doris Dana drove me to JFK Airport. Along the way, the sky went dark with migrating geese. They were flying just above our heads in a huge, noisy formation. I had never witnessed such a site. At last, we joined Bob and the children. In what seemed like only minutes, we were off on our flight to France.

Our second stay in France was as enjoyable as the first. Maybe more so, because we all spoke French, our children were older, and I did not have to worry about baby food and diapers. Our son could see almost all the places he missed on our first trip when he was too young to remember. Greece, almost all of Spain, Morocco, and Italy were especially memorable for the children. At all of the shrines we visited, I lit candles and prayed, *Please God, grant me a way to find my family.*

After almost two years in France, we were back in Greenville, South Carolina. I not only had the blues about being back, but I also had to live in a hotel with my two rambunctious children. It seemed the realtor we left to manage our house decided to be charitable at our expense and had failed to evict the tenants, who had stopped paying the rent several months earlier. We had to go to the magistrate's office ourselves to have them evicted.

Finally, we were settled into our house, and once again, I began to resume the search for my family. Based on an ad in the *Genealogical Helper* magazine, I contacted a private detective, experienced in genealogy, to help with my search. After discussing what I wanted him to do, he wished me luck and told me I did not have enough information to go on. He said I would be wasting my money. Once more, another hope vanished.

My search was not going anywhere. To distract myself, I took a course at Greenville Technical College. On my way to class one day, I was stopped by a professor and told to follow a group of students. We were taken to a conference room where the professor explained that we were brought there for our own safety. He said Iran had taken Americans hostage and the school administration feared repercussions against us.

I thought, *Against us?*

When the professor finished, I spoke out. I said, "I am an American. I speak with an accent, but that does not make me Iranian."

The professor apologized, saying, "I can see we have made a mistake, but you do look Iranian."

I acknowledged that they had truly been trying to do the right thing. As I was leaving, in an effort to ease the fears of the Iranian students and to show clearly I understood how they felt, I smiled and said, "I am a citizen of the world and so are all of you."

Sometime later, my husband, who was project manager to build a large tire plant near Columbia, South Carolina, told me we had to move to be closer to the plant site. This meant another move, but I thought this would be a welcome change.

We bought a house in a very nice subdivision in Irmo, South Carolina, a quaint bedroom community, just minutes from beautiful Lake Murray. Here my need to find my family became very intense. At times, I would lie awake thinking of ways to find my family. Bob would often be awakened by me crying in the dark and would ask what was wrong. It was always the same answer. He would comfort and assure me.

I joined a group named Triad, which helps adoptees find their natural parents. I met the leader of the group at her home, and she gave me forms to fill out. I told her some of my story and, because I had not been legally adopted, she could see I did not have much to go on. To her credit, she acted positively and told me where the meeting was being held. So now, I felt I would at least be with people who could understand my strong need to find my family.

I went to the first meeting of Triad, and instead of making me feel I belonged, I was confronted with the realization of just how little information I had to go on and how fortunate these other people were because they had been adopted. They at least had legal records, which I did not.

The only useful piece of information I had was Jackie, the name of the man Matilde told me my mother was living with when I was born. Most members of the Triad group had a lot going for them. For many, it was just a matter of time before they would make contact with their natural parents. Some of them even had the help of their adoptive parents. I, in turn, had nothing in the way of information that compared to what they had. Once again, I was on the outside looking in. I felt pretty low when I left that meeting. I believe my meeting with Triad happened in April 1981.

I was desperate to try any means to get information on Jackie. Since we lived near Columbia, South Carolina, the state capital, I made an appointment with a representative of one of South Carolina's United States' senators. I thought he could help me get information from Social Security or other governmental agencies. I will never forget this meeting. I explained to this complete stranger, all the details of how, as a baby from Brooklyn, New York, I was taken to Mexico. After I finished telling this man my story, I told him I needed the senator's help in getting information about Jackie, possibly from Social Security or the Census Bureau.

To my surprise and horror, in an arrogant and laughing manner, this insensitive, callous individual said, "Why, you're a nobody. You cannot prove who you are related to and therefore have no right to records or to invade privacy!"

When the senator's representative so cruelly made this outburst, it was like a knife going through my heart. He showed no understanding, compassion, or humanity. I had just trusted this bigot, supposedly a public servant, with my life story, and his behavior was detached, cruel, and indifferent.

I thought, *How is it Jackie's rights were being protected when he was highly instrumental in taking every right away from me?* In fact, what he did was criminal. Jackie had coldly turned me over to the most irresponsible woman in the world to endure a childhood of physical and mental abuse, hunger, indifference, and cruelty. His rights, though his was a criminal act, were being protected, and I had been stripped of all of mine! I walked out of that office feeling horrible, humiliated, and depressed. Another door closed on me; another hope vanished. Now where do I go from here?

Something in me would not let go. I was not about to give up, even though my case now seemed more hopeless than ever. I went home and told my husband the outcome of my meeting with the senator's representative. I can still see the anger he expressed at the callousness this person had shown. His face was filled with hurt over the cruelty this miscreant had so needlessly inflicted on me. In his most loving way, my husband told me not to give up. He had become very proficient in pursuing his own family's genealogy and family history. He said we would go to the local library and look at the microfiche films of the census. He told me even then, there were many other things we hadn't yet tried. My next stop was the library, to explore other possibilities.

Through all of this, I got support from our many friends, especially two friends named Jackie, at the Union United Methodist Church, and Analies and Rudy, who kept our children whenever we had to be away. At that time in my search, their support played a major role in helping me endure the constant disappointments.

I was also encouraged by the help I got from the Brooklyn Public Library. They promptly and graciously sent copies of the pages of the phone book for 1940, and other information, which I had requested. It seemed there was not much else I could do to help my search, except wait for a miracle to happen.

To make matters worse, I had a neighbor who, a bit too enthusiastically, said that she could trace her family back hundreds of years. In fact, so could my husband. Here I was with nothing but a baby picture taken in Brooklyn, two orange hospital visitation cards, a birth certificate with mistakes, and the story Matilde had related to me—apparently nothing—to prove who my parents were.

In the middle of May, I returned from shopping and found my husband home. I asked him if he were feeling ill. He asked me to sit down. He said he had quit his job but not to worry as he already had some job offers. He knew I liked Columbia better than I liked Mauldin and our children were in one of the best schools in the state. My reaction was, more than anything, fear of moving. He told me he would try to stay in the area so we would not have to take the children out of their excellent school.

I told him, "As soon as the school year ends, I would like to go to Brooklyn and walk the neighborhoods to see if we could find someone who might help us make connections. This is a great opportunity to do this now that you are not working. I would like very much if you would help me."

At this same time, my son began to ask piercing questions like, “Mommy, who do you come from? Why don't you have a family? Who is your mommy?” All of these questions from my seven-year-old touched me deeply and were very painful as I had no answers. Far from discouraging me, this renewed and solidified my resolve to continue my search.

The Picture

Only the Dead Know Brooklyn

Thomas Wolfe, *The New Yorker*, June 15, 1935

My husband and I began to piece together a more effective plan to search for my family. We came up with the idea of trying to contact the widow of Mr. Rivera, the man who, some thirty-five years earlier in Veracruz, had offered to take me back to Brooklyn to live with his family. We went to the Greenville Public Library and started with the New York phone book. We found a very long listing of Riveras. On a whim, I resorted to running my finger down the pages at random. I said we'd call whatever number my finger stopped at. It stopped on the name, Vincent Rivera. We called the number, and to our total surprise, the very Mrs. Rivera we wanted to contact, answered the phone! After some further introduction, she told us she knew all about my birth, and she had even been a babysitter for me a few times during my infancy. Mrs. Rivera was quite excited and offered us a place to stay in her apartment in Brooklyn. I considered it very kind of her to do this. As the call ended, I asked Mrs. Rivera why her telephone was still listed under her late husband's name. She said she had kept his name in the phone book in his honor. We made plans to leave for New York.

As luck would have it, Bob's sister had made plans to visit us just at this crucial moment. I asked him to call her to see if she could change her arrival date and come a week later. I did not see any problem with this because she was not working, her children would be out of school, and her husband was not traveling with her. She was immovable. She said she was coming—she had made her plans and she was not going to change them.

I told Bob I was leaving for Brooklyn, with him or without him. He called his sister again and told her this was something we both felt we had to do now and we were going. He told her she could use the car and the house. She said she would come and even offered to keep our children while we went to New York. She did not know much of my background, so I could not tell her why it was so urgent for me to go to New York now and why it could not wait another week or month. I just had this strong urge, and something in me told me I had to do this now.

She arrived at night. I had plenty of food in the house, and everything was ready for us to leave the next morning. On our way to New York, we stopped near Washington DC. I could see my husband felt bad about having to leave his sister and family so soon after they arrived. So again, I told him if he wanted, he could take me to the next bus station so I could continue on to Brooklyn by myself and he could go back to be with his sister. In any case, I knew I had to go on. I told him I must do this, with him or without him. He told me yes, he felt bad, but there was no way he was going to let me go to Brooklyn alone. The urgency within me would not subside; in fact, I think it got stronger.

The next day, we arrived at Mrs. Rivera's apartment. We were greeted very affectionately and welcomed with open arms into the home of an almost complete stranger. I was full of questions. Right away, I asked her to tell me what she remembered from 1940. Mrs. Rivera sat us down. She started to spill out bits and pieces of the story that connected her and her long-deceased husband to what was, in her clear and lucid memory, a small baby she said she held in her arms on a number of occasions so long ago. She said she knew nothing about my natural mother. She added that it was her husband and Pablo who were friends. They came from the same town in Puerto Rico, and they had worked together on ships.

She said, "I met you when Matilde ask me to take care of you while she went out."

Actually, I was very sad to hear this as I had hoped she could give me more information that would help me find my family and my mother.

Mrs. Rivera brought out a small, tin box obviously holding some of her few prized possessions. She carefully lifted out a three- by five-inch photograph of a baby girl, identical to the photograph I had so strongly protected for so many years. Amazingly, for some forty years, she had kept this picture of a baby she had seen only a few times. Bob could not believe his eyes.

He looked at me and asked, "Why would this woman keep this picture all these years?" The feeling came over each of us that we had just witnessed a miracle. This was to be another in a series of miracles in our desperate drive to join the past to the present, through a fog of disinformation, denials, and lies—each for its own selfish want to keep the past buried.

We spent the better part of the afternoon asking deep searching questions and did uncover some leads that just as quickly ended in either someone who would have known my family but had died, or to frustrating lapses in knowledge of key points.

Mrs. Rivera graciously offered us her apartment as a home base for our search. We really began to enjoy her friendship and her kindness. She called her daughter and son to meet us, and the three of us told them the story. Vicente, her son, commented, "Homer and his odyssey have nothing on you." The next day Vicente offered to help us search the neighborhood in the area around Columbia Street. We accepted the offer and launched into an inside-look at present-day Cobble Hill and the Columbia Street waterfront areas of Brooklyn. The neighborhood had been primarily settled by Italian families in the early 1940s, but as time marched on, the Italians became more affluent and moved to newer neighborhoods. This left a lower cost area to be bought up by a succession of newly arrived ethnic groups, each eager to start, just as the Italians had, in their move up the American dream ladder.

Vicente enthusiastically joined in the search. He took us to darkened apartments where Puerto Rican revolutionaries draped flags of an independent Puerto Rico on the walls. We went to other, somewhat scary apartments, such as that of a lonely widower who warmly accepted our inquisitiveness into a past he had lived in 1940s Brooklyn. I was thankful we had a place to rest our feet after the long walks we made all over Brooklyn and, in particular, on Columbia Street. We talked to everyone who would listen to us. We went into some places that were pretty sad looking.

Matilde had told me that Jackie was a longshoreman. We visited the very nice Longshoreman's Union Building where we were greeted warmly. We began asking for anything on Jackie related to the sparse information I had in hand. I told them that as a baby I had been taken away. This must have struck a sympathetic note as it seemed they could not do enough for me. From here, we got a lot of cooperation from the supervisors and clerks. At one point, the whole office stopped what they were doing so they could help look for records. With no helpful result, they encouraged us to go to their main office in Manhattan, where they maintained the records of longshoremen who were no longer living.

We arrived at a plush office in a very old building in Manhattan. Here again we found the gentleman who greeted us to be warm, most helpful, and kind, dispelling the myth that New Yorkers are indifferent.

Finally, back in Brooklyn from the Longshoreman's Union offices, we went to a nearby funeral home to see if they had any records that could be helpful. We thought they could give us a clue as to the address of members of the family I was looking for. When we finished with the records, I asked the attendant if he could give us any more ideas of where to go. He told me not to worry but to leave it to him.

He said very confidently, "We have ways."

He looked to Bob and I like someone out of *The Godfather*, pinstripe suit and all.

When we got out of the funeral home, my husband said to me, "I bet he has *ways*!"

I believe my husband's knees were shaking so badly I could hear them. He had lived a somewhat sheltered life. Now seeing him with me in the streets of Brooklyn, going to all the places, talking to all the people we talked to, and walking along Columbia Street among some run-down places, made me respect him a lot. He is a very special and wonderful person.

At the end of the day, we returned to Mrs. Rivera's apartment, tired and worn out, to rest and to get ready for the next day. Mrs. Rivera had cooked a traditional Puerto Rican dish, *pasteles*. *Pasteles* (much like Mexican *tamales* but made from *platanos*, the big bananas many Latinos use for cooking. Pasteles are stuffed with meat, steamed, and wrapped with banana leaves). She also made us *coquito* (a drink made of milk, egg yolks, and liquor). Coquito is out of this world. I guess while we were out on the street, Mrs. Rivera was in her kitchen cooking all these delicious Puerto Rican dishes. They were so good Bob asked her if he could have another *pastilla*. We all laughed, as Bob had used a similar-sounding but incorrect word and actually asked her if he could have another *pill*. We were very appreciative since most of the time, we did not stop to eat because we wanted to cover as much territory as we could in the little time we had.

On the third day, Mrs. Rivera or my husband came up with the idea of putting an article in the local newspaper. Bob asked Mrs. Rivera which paper she would recommend. She did not hesitate to give us the name of the popular local newspaper in Brooklyn.

I immediately called the newspaper. The man who answered told me they did not do that type story. My husband was sitting across from me and he could tell I had run into another dead end. I told my husband what the man had said. Bob took the phone from me and told the man that he was probably passing up a very good human-interest story, and the least he could do was to send someone to listen to the story and decide from that. My husband must have been very convincing, because when he gave the phone back to me, the man told me he was sending a reporter and a photographer before noon. He asked us to stay home and wait. I put my husband back on the line so he could give the man the address.

By now, I was numb, and at the same time full of hope, but very afraid that this was probably the last thing I could do to find my family. I had made inquiries to the Departments of Health and Welfare in New York and California, the Local 1814 International Longshoremen's Association in Brooklyn, the Brooklyn Public Library, the *Genealogical Helper* magazine, the South Carolina senator's office, the Cumberland Hospital in Brooklyn, Triad and ALMA (the adoptive associations), and the private investigator. In addition, I had sent countless letters and made numerous phone calls to potential relatives in New York and, lastly, my two earlier trips to New York had so far come to a dead end. Psychologically, I was putting a lot of faith into the newspaper article.

I also had to come to a decision. I could no longer go on with this heavy burden robbing me of the joy in my life. In some ways, I was afraid to have the article printed. If this should turn out to be just another dead end, how would I fill the emptiness, the hole in my heart? I prayed, *Oh, God, help guide me and give me the strength to go on searching.*

We were all very tense, and waiting for the reporter and the photographer seemed interminable. I was a nervous wreck—I could not think clearly and was afraid I would say the wrong things. Here again was the very strong feeling this was something that had to be done, no matter what. I now wonder what was going through my husband's mind at the time. He must have known, or sensed, how desperate I felt.

All I remember is him telling me, "It will turn out all right; you will see."

Just then, there was a knock. Bob opened the door for the photographer, a man in his late forties, and the reporter, a woman in her early thirties. They introduced themselves and started asking questions. The photographer asked me to pose by the phone book. At the end of the interview, and after the photographs had been taken, they assured me the story would be in the next day's paper. Finally, they asked for our address and phone number and said they would call me whenever they felt they had a legitimate response to the article.

I asked, "Why don't you just put my phone number in the article, so they could call me directly?"

The lady reporter laughed. She told me, "Do you know how many nuts there are in this world? Many people would pretend they are the ones you are looking for. We have to screen the calls carefully, asking them key questions no other person would know."

I guess I seemed naïve. It never occurred to me people would do that. As they were leaving, they told me it was a great story, and that it would be in the paper as soon as they could get back to their office to complete their write-up and develop the photographs.

The photographer said kindly, "I hope you find your family."

I just looked at him; I could not utter a word! After they left, we drove to the church nearest to Columbia Street, the Sacred Heart of Mary and Jesus Catholic church. We went in, and I asked at the main desk if I could see the church record books for baptisms, marriages, and deaths. We were told that these records are normally only available for specific requests. We asked to see a priest.

When the priest arrived, in a kind voice he asked me, "Why do you want to look at all these records?" Then he turned to my husband and asked him, "Why are you helping her?" I guess he was trying to make me feel more at ease. He could tell I was getting pretty frustrated from all the looking and coming up with nothing so far.

He also asked me, "How are you going to be able to tell if the names you find in the records are the person you are looking for?"

I anxiously blurted out, "Please let me look at the books. I will know the names when I see them."

At this point, Bob talked privately with the priest for a few moments. The priest came back, just shook his head, opened the big locked bookcase, and wished us good luck. We poured through those books as if they contained the answers to my whole life history. The only name I was somewhat sure of was what Matilde had told me was the name of my alleged father, and I didn't find anything about him. I also didn't know my mother's married name and wasn't even sure of her maiden name, and as far as I knew, there were some errors on my birth certificate. After what seemed like a long time of looking and coming up with nothing, I went back to the priest. He took us to an office in another room.

The priest looked at me and said convincingly, but with no possible way of really knowing, "You are *Calabrese*, and you must not give up; you should keep on looking."

I wondered, *What is a Calabrese?* Somehow, this priest was sure I was Calabrese. He explained that Calabreses, people from the southern Italian province of Calabria, are known to be very determined and hardheaded.

Discouraged and sad, I asked the priest, "In the 1940s, if a family broke up in this part of Brooklyn, where would they have put the children?"

He said, "At that time, it would have been the Angel Guardian Home. Today, however, the Angel Guardian Home provides different services."

I asked, "Where is the Angel Guardian Home and how can I look at some of their records?"

He wrote the address and the telephone number on a piece of paper and told me the name of the person to contact. He told me I would have to call them first. I used the church office phone. The contact person was on her break, and I was told to call back later. Bob and I left with the priest's blessings.

On the way, we decided to visit Brooklyn's famous and historic Greenwood Cemetery, high on top of Park Slope. I stood on the highest point, under a cloudless sky, looking all around at the beauty of this magnificent city. I said to myself, *I love this city. Will it ever love me back and reveal the information I seek? I have wondered for forty years who am I? How long must I remain no one's child?*

On the way back to Mrs. Rivera's apartment, we stopped at a phone booth where I again anxiously called the Angel Guardian Home. Finally, I got the lady on the phone. I told her who I was and that I was looking for my brothers and sisters, who were put in a home in the late 1930s when the family broke up, most probably here in Brooklyn. I told her the names of my mother that were on my birth certificate. I said her other children were born up to the end of 1938. I asked her if I could please look at the records of the Angel Guardian Home.

She told me that because of their privacy policies, I could not just look at the records and she could not give me any information over the phone. She said I would need to write a letter requesting the information. I told her I was returning home to South Carolina the next day and that I would write her as soon as possible. I felt I was facing another roadblock. After I hung up, I told my husband I could not just request the records. They had to have my request in writing. I was terribly disappointed and sad. So, tired and discouraged and, with no more leads, we left for Mrs. Rivera's apartment to pack for our return home.

Early the next day, just before we left, I went to the local store and got the newspaper. I could not find the story. I went back to the apartment and told my husband they had not printed the story as they said they would.

He said, "Maybe they did not have room, so it probably will be in tomorrow's paper."

We expressed our thanks to Mrs. Rivera, said our good-byes, and left for South Carolina. By now, I was missing my children terribly—I wished the car would fly.

The Picture Again

"There are only two tragedies in life: One is not getting what one wants, and the other is getting it."

Oscar Wilde

We arrived in South Carolina late in the evening on Father's Day. I was afraid even to think about all that had happened during the previous five days. As we pulled in the driveway, my sister-in-law met us at the door holding a paper over her head and making light of a phone call she had gotten that day.

She said, "This woman, Cristina, called. You wouldn't believe the wild story this woman told me. She said she was your lost half sister."

I hadn't told anyone in Bob's family of my childhood. I could not blame Bob's sister for not knowing this may be a true story, but the way she was teasing me with the paper brought out decades of anger and frustration. My whole being, years of struggle, were focused on this moment, and she was making light of it.

With the force of the anger and the frustration, I said, "Please give me the paper."

She continued laughing and teasing me with the paper held over her head.

My husband told her forcefully, "Please give her the paper."

She continued to tease and still didn't give me the paper! This time my husband was firm, grabbed her arm, took the paper. I rushed to my bedroom to call the number.

As I started dialing the phone, I had strong expectations that I would now finally find closure to all my questions and my life-long feelings of emptiness. I wanted time to fast-forward. I dialed the phone so fast I had to redial. Finally, I was connected, and a woman answered.

I asked, "Cristina?"

She answered, "Yes."

At that instant, what went through my mind was, *My God, I have done the impossible!*

Cristina told me, "Early this morning I sat down to have my coffee and read the paper. When I saw the story at the bottom of the second page, I said to myself, I know who she is! My father is her father!" She continued, "I immediately called the newspaper. They carefully interviewed me and told me you had already left for your home in South Carolina. Then they gave me your phone number."

All that had happened to this point in the phone call was colored by that fateful showdown I had with Matilde in Poza Rica, twenty-five years before. Until this moment, essentially all the information I had about my father was what Matilde had told me.

As soon as we had confirmed who she was, I very impatiently asked, "Cristina, please tell me all you know about my mother. Do you know where she is? Do you know her married name?"

Cristina said, "I know nothing of your mother."

Her words were like putting a dagger through my heart. In an instant, I went from elation to deep despair. All these years I had put so much hope in the thought that if I found anyone connected with Jackie's family I would then find my mother's family; in an instant, that hope had vanished.

We made a date to meet the first part of July. She said she would get all the family together for our reunion. I again eagerly asked Cristina if she could tell me the whereabouts of my mother or at least her married name. She said she did not know where my mother went. She said she had only seen my mother twice, when she had visited her father, and knew very little about her or her background. Cristina said that she visited her father again right after I was born. By then, my mother and I were gone, and her father did not talk about it after that.

In the midst of my pain and disappointment, I regained my composure and was very careful not to let Cristina know how I was truly feeling. I told Cristina that I was very anxious and happy to meet her and her family. We decided on a date for the reunion.

I tried to take a positive view. I told myself that maybe a member of her family could give me a clue as to my mother's whereabouts. I said a little prayer and started getting excited about our trip to Long Island. I hoped for the best.

It turns out the story had appeared in the newspaper, just as the reporter said, but was not printed with my picture. This is why I hadn't seen the article the same morning that Cristina read it. She had called several times during the day as I was on my way home from New York. So here, I had the first piece to the puzzle. I could hardly contain myself. My husband was so happy for me that he glowed.

I was counting the days until the reunion. My sister-in-law and her three children stayed with us for another week and then left to meet her husband in Washington DC, to continue their vacation. Angry as I may have been at her insisting on the date of her visit, I will always be grateful to her for spending those days of her vacation as the only adult with five children, so Bob and I could make that fateful trip. It was difficult to enjoy their visit as I felt I could not yet share any details of my past life. In fact, as I write this, they still do not know my story. In my heart, I would rather have been in New York, but I had chosen to stay home so my husband and our children had time to visit with his sister and her children.

I went through the motions, but inside I was a nervous wreck. No sooner did my sister-in-law and her children leave than I started packing for our return to New York, this time with our children. I felt like I had beaten all the odds and had accomplished the impossible. Many people, who knew of my search and saw how little I had to go on, had advised me to forget it and move on with my life. They said my chances of finding my family were one in a million. Well, I felt like a million!

In the meantime, the newspaper printed another article about us making our connection. They printed the photographs they had taken of me during the interview in Mrs. Rivera's apartment along with the baby picture Mrs. Rivera had kept all those years. The article announced our pending reunion.

We arrived at Cristina's home on Long Island in the early afternoon of June 29, 1981. I was forty years old. The house was full of people:

my half sister Cristina and her husband, Frank; Cristina's two married daughters and their husbands and children; Cristina's aunt; and my half brother, Vinnie. I could hardly feel anything. I was afraid to feel. The same reporter and photographer, who had assisted us before, were there. They took many photographs and asked me how I felt. All I could say was a tearful, "I feel great!"

I was not even aware of what my children were doing at that moment. All this time my husband was taking pictures, and he had the look on his face that said, "We made it! We made it!" He was so right; we had made it. I was even glad he was not working so we had the time to do all of this. Was this meant to be?

Well, my joy came to a very abrupt halt when Cristina's aunt told me in a low voice that they were not sure I was Jackie's daughter. I had already known about this doubt because Matilde had hinted at the same thing. What hurt me most was the insensitive timing of this woman's remarks. I have always thought she was very jealous and most certainly did it to hurt me and may have even not had any other real reason to say what she did.

I was stunned. I looked deeply in her face and had an instant flashback. I realized that this was the same woman I had spoken with in 1964, when I came to Brooklyn to look for my family. I knew without a doubt that this was the same woman.

I remembered in detail when I went to her home with the elderly Italian gentleman who knew these people were well acquainted with, if not related to, Jackie. They were obviously well acquainted with this man because when we knocked at the door, we were invited in with no hesitation. There were several people in the room, including this woman. They looked me over very carefully and then went to another room where they spoke with the old man at some length, all in Sicilian. Then this lady came to me and told me, "We don't know anything about Jackie or his married daughter. Go back to your husband, be happy, and forget all of this."

I was dismayed and very angry. I told her, "You are the woman who turned me away in 1964. You told me then that you didn't know anything about Jackie or his married daughter and here you are related to them."

Just at that moment, we were interrupted. She quickly took the opportunity to move away and avoided me the rest of the afternoon.

The lady reporter came to me. She wanted me to tell her more of my story. She even offered to write a book about it. I declined her offer, my reason being that I had not yet found anything about my mother. In my mind, I was still not certain Jackie was my natural father. If he were my father, why hadn't anyone in his family taken me in?

The biggest disappointment came when I pressed Cristina again about my mother. She repeated all she had already told me on the telephone. She told me again that she didn't know my mother's name or anything about my mother's family.

She said, "Me being his daughter, out of respect, I couldn't ask anything more. In those days, it was an uncomfortable and shameful situation. We just couldn't talk about it."

I cannot adequately express the sadness, the anger, the feeling of defeat, and the sheer disappointment that came to me at that moment. I had a very strong, sick feeling in the pit of my stomach. I could not believe what I was hearing. I had looked for Jackie's family in the hope of finding out about my mother and her other children. Now that I had found his family, I had come up empty-handed.

So, I asked, "Why didn't you take me?"

She told me she didn't know of their plans for me. And, in any case, she could not have taken me because she had three little girls of her own, the youngest being six months old when I was born.

During the next few days, I learned that Jackie had immigrated to the United States from Palermo, and that we had been a hair's breath away from finding him through the Longshoreman's Union records. In fact, we may have seen his records and not known it. I have since learned more about Sicilian family beliefs at the time I was born. In those days, an illegitimate child was no one's child. Even after thirty-six years in America, this Sicilian-American family was still deeply immersed in *la vita vecchia* (the old ways).

As I now reflect on this reunion, I am aware that Cristina and her family had been fully accepting, warm, and generous toward me. I had every reason to feel happy and grateful to have found such a wonderful person as Cristina to be my half sister. However, in spite of being fully aware of this, I was still not able to react as I should have. I believe

Matilde's explanation that Jackie had been so callous in rejecting me, when she had brought me back to my mother, had a lot to do with my feelings. This, coupled with the fact that no one in Jackie's family had offered to take me in, formed a barrier that I still find difficult to overcome.

I had not yet seen either the first or second newspaper articles. When Cristina showed me the second article, there it was again, this same baby picture. It was above a picture the reporter had taken of me by the phone book at Mrs. Rivera's home in June. For a long while, I did not look at or read the article. My eyes were fixed on the baby picture. For me the saying "a picture is worth a thousand words" is certainly true. The two newspaper articles, though containing some errors, had made the connection.

Later, after we ate, Cristina brought out yet again another copy of my baby picture. Cristina too, had miraculously kept the photograph all these years. The photograph had been among Jackie's things after he died. It was exactly the same photograph as the one Mrs. Rivera had kept for forty years, and the same one I had found in Matilde's basket in Veracruz when I was eight years old!

My husband just shook his head upon seeing it. He found it hard to believe these two women, Mrs. Rivera and Cristina, had kept my picture for more than forty years. I was intrigued at this picture reappearing, now for the second time, and how all these years I had clung to this same picture for dear life. The picture seemed to have a power over people. I could understand the power over me, but to these people, it could have meant nothing. Nevertheless, over and over, it kept showing its power and exerting its force. As I lay down that night, I cried myself to sleep. I could not believe I had come so close and was yet so far.

After several days of very gracious hospitality, we left to return home. On the way, I could no longer pretend to hide my tremendous disappointment at not getting information about my mother or my brothers and sisters. Tears were rolling down my cheeks as the song *Jesus Christ Superstar* was playing on the radio. As I listened to the words, a peace came over me. My husband said at the very same instant, "I have the feeling we are going to make this trip to Long Island many more times in the future."

All I could think was, *How could he think that? Doesn't he sense my tremendous disappointment? I guess he is doing his best to cheer me up.*

On the way back to South Carolina, we had arranged to meet with my sister-in-law and her family in Washington DC. The next day, we all went to the National Mall for a Beach Boys concert and other Fourth of July celebrations. My sister-in-law was full of questions about my family, and I had to pretend I was very happy to have found them. I did my best to hide the pain of not finding anything about my mother or my siblings.

When we finally got back home, it hit me hard. I seemed to have run out of things I could do to find my mother, and I could not come up with any new ideas. That feeling of defeat and lost hope was something I did not know how to deal with. I have always had faith and hope, but now I found myself weak in both areas. My husband was still busying himself with job interviews. I felt I could not put more stress on him or our children, so I did my crying where they could not see me.

Some days later, when I was all alone in the house, I got on my knees to cry and to pray to God with all my heart. I asked Him that if I was not to find my family to remove my obsession to keep looking. I knew finding them would take a miracle, and that was His department. I also asked that if there was a chance for me to find my family to show the way, to help me not to lose hope, and to keep my dream alive. I had a cleansing cry from the heart. I thanked Him for my blessings, for my two children, and for my husband. I felt so weak; I had difficulty getting back on my feet.

I went to my desk, and as I sat down, I remembered the Angel Guardian Home in Brooklyn. I had forgotten to write the letter requesting information on my mother and siblings. I rushed to look for all the notes we made while in Brooklyn. I found the address of the Angel Guardian Home. I wrote the letter and mailed it immediately. As I recall, this was sometime in August. I did not mention this to my husband because I did not want to get my hopes high. This too, would probably come to a dead end, but I had to try.

The Picture Full Circle

"What's ahead of me and what's behind me are nothing compared to what's inside me."

Jean Shapiro

At about noon on September 11, 1981, I was outside waiting for the mail delivery. I had no reason to be waiting for the mail and normally did not do so, except on this day. My husband was in the garage working on his fishing boat. He could see the mailbox very well. So again, there was no reason for me to be out there. Something kept me by the mailbox, and when the mailman arrived, he handed me the mail. I casually started to sort through the envelopes and circulars. I halted abruptly. I was stunned by the sight of a letter from the Angel Guardian Home. I froze and stood there just gazing at the envelope. Fear overtook me. I was fearful of its contents—fearful it would be just another door closed. I feared this would be the last chance I would have to find my mother's family.

I quickly went to my husband, handed him the unopened envelope and said, "This will probably be just another disappointment; look at it." I walked away.

He quickly opened the envelope and read the letter.

He slowly looked up and asked me, "How did you do it?"

He was so overwhelmed that he let the letter go from his hands. He mumbled, "This is a miracle; I can't handle it," and walked away, leaving me standing there with this letter full of information about my siblings.

He took off, and still in disbelief, I took the letter inside to my desk and looked intensely at the names and dates. For the first time, I was seeing my mother's married name and my sister and brothers' given names! There are no words to describe what I felt and I couldn't even share these feelings with my husband.

I remember I was full of doubts. Could there be another woman with my mother's name? Are these truly the names of my sister and brothers? I was preparing myself for the possibility of great disappointment. Before this moment, I hadn't even known how many siblings I had or any of their names or ages.

I sat at my desk, for what seemed the longest time, until my husband got back. Then he read the letter again and said, "I do not know how you did this, but here in this letter are the names of your mother, your sister, and your brothers."

I was filled with emotion, hope, and at the same time, apprehension. What if they don't want to meet me? This was a very strong possibility, as I had been born out of wedlock.

Many things went through my mind. I reasoned that if they didn't want to meet me, I would figure out a way to meet them without their knowing.

I was ready, or trying to make myself ready, for rejection. After all, Jackie had rejected me, my mother had rejected me, and their rejection now would not surprise me at all. At least I would have the satisfaction of knowing who they are. I reasoned I would have to be satisfied with whatever the future had in store for me.

I asked Bob, "What if they don't want to meet me?"

He said, "Sure they will want to meet you. Get on the phone and start calling."

I had to look in the New York phonebook and try to find the right people as there were pages and pages with the same last name. I didn't even have an address, and there were many with the same initials. I concentrated in the Brooklyn area. I had tried to call my sister, Luisa, but I could not get her right number. I knew she was likely married and would have a different last name. I looked up all the people with the same last name. I was beginning to think I was losing my touch in finding numbers. Then I tried my youngest brother, Giovanni.

On the first number I dialed with the given name Giovanni, someone answered. To my complete amazement, it was just the number I was looking for. My brother Giovanni was not home at the time, so I talked to his eighteen-year-old son, who was also named Giovanni. This was the first time I had made contact with my mother's side of the family. I told my nephew that I was possibly a distant relative of his father's, and to make sure, I had to ask him some questions.

My first question was, "Is your grandmother's name Filomena?"

He said, "Yes."

"Do you have an aunt named Luisa?"

Again, he said, "Yes."

Then I asked him if he could give me Luisa's telephone number, which he did. I continued by asking him about his uncles and everything checked out perfectly with the information from the Angel Guardian Home. I told him I would call later when his father was home.

He asked me what relative I was, and I told him a very distant relative to his father. When I finished the call, I was elated and so proud to have such a polite and cooperative young man for a nephew.

It turned out that my sister was married and had an unlisted number. Now, armed with her number, I called right away. My brother-in-law, Harry, answered the phone. I asked for Luisa. He said she was out and asked me to call later. I hung up and called back a half hour later. Harry again answered the phone but this time was a bit more insistent I tell him who I was. I gave Harry the same story I had given my nephew Giovanni, but he was a little more difficult to convince. Then, Harry began to ask more questions, and I started to tell him my story. I told him I was Luisa's sister. He asked me more about my family, especially my husband.

Harry was very impressed that I was married to a professional man. He also asked me if I owned my own home and other questions that were so probing you would think I was being checked for a credit rating. I could sense he was very protective of my sister. I told him more of the story about who I was and how I was taken out of the country—in short, the story of my life. I told him I wanted to meet my sister, but if she did not want to meet me, I would understand and would meet her without her knowing it.

He told me yes, he was sure she would want to meet me. He said that Luisa had always wanted to have a sister. We ended our call, and I waited two long hours. I called again, and she was still out. This time Harry told me he would leave the phone off the hook until she got home so I would not be wasting my money on long distance calls.

Finally, Luisa got home, just before midnight. Harry told her as soon as she got home that she had better sit down as he had something to tell her.

After he told her, all she could say was, "Wonderful, I have a sister!"

When she finally answered the phone, I asked, "Do you want to ask me any questions to make sure I am who I say I am?"

She said very confidently, "No, I believe you; it feels right."

Though I have nothing to base it on, I have always felt Luisa already knew of my birth. I asked when we could meet. She said she had to talk to Harry as she was concerned about how he might feel with the commotion of having my two young children in their house. I told her that would not be a problem as we could just stay in a nearby hotel. Later, she called back and we made a date for the following week, on September 15.

This meant I had two days to get us ready for the trip back to Long Island. I was running on nervous energy, and I needed neither food nor rest. I was about to realize the remaining part of my lifelong dreams. I had triumphed over the impossible! After so many years of endlessly painful struggles, I was finally going to meet my mother's family and maybe even my mother!

The second time I talked to my sister I asked about our mother, "Is she still living? If so, where is she?"

She told me she did not know, but she gave me the phone number of our Aunt Mary, our mother's half sister, who lived in Texas. I could not believe my sister or brothers did not know if their own mother was dead or alive and, if living, where. I felt very sad when she told me this. Right after I finished talking to my sister, I dialed Aunt Mary's number. Aunt Mary answered the phone and the first thing she did was to deny being related to my mother. She told me she was not related to these people and she had nothing to tell me. Wow, what a blow! Sadness began to overwhelm me as this woman denied she was related to me. The feeling of rejection, so deeply engrained in my soul, took away some of the feelings of joy I should have had at this moment.

I said to myself, *Grace, you must prepare yourself, this might happen again in Brooklyn and in Long Island.* I felt like something had just been taken out of me. I could sense she was being evasive. I hung up the phone and cried. I felt she knew where my mother was and she had refused to tell me.

I called my sister back. I asked her, "Please double-check the phone number for Aunt Mary." She gave it back to me—it was the same as before. I told my husband to stand by; I was going to call Aunt Mary again.

When Aunt Mary answered the phone, I told her, "Please do not hang up. I am not asking for anything more than the whereabouts of my mother. I feel very strongly you know where she is. You need never hear from me again after you tell me where she is. I do not want any material things from you or from any of your relatives. All I want is to find my mother."

My husband, seeing I was too emotional and not getting anywhere, took the phone from me. He asked Aunt Mary if he could talk to her husband. Her husband came to the phone. I can't remember all that went on, but my husband got results. Aunt Mary's husband gave us the address they had for the nursing home where they thought my mother was staying. Bob thanked them and said good-bye. I found out later that Aunt Mary might have been afraid we were after an inheritance, part of which should have gone to my mother.

In any case, using the address, he called information and got a number. We immediately called the home. The lady that answered told me she had to look at the records because she thought they did not have anyone with that name. She asked me to call back.

I said, "No, I will hold the line."

The lady told me it would take a while. Several more ladies came to the phone while I was waiting. I asked the last lady to hurry because I was calling long distance and this was very urgent. She asked me why it was so urgent. I told her Filomena was my mother and that I was taken away from her when I was a baby.

She said, "Please hang on. I will see what I can do."

After what seemed an eternity, she came back to the phone and said she did not have the exact address but only the town, Patchogue, Long Island, where my mother had been transferred a few years earlier.

Then she said, "I hope she is still alive and that you two get to meet. Good luck."

I immediately called information and got the phone numbers of several nursing homes in Patchogue, Long Island. I very anxiously called the first nursing home number and asked to speak with Filomena. I waited on the phone for about five minutes and then, for the first time in my life, I heard my mother's voice!

She had no idea what was happening. She was upset, asking repeatedly, "Who are you? Who are you?"

I was speechless; I couldn't talk. A flood of emotions poured out. The strongest was anger.

I wanted to reproach her. My mind raced with thoughts, *Why did you get rid of me so uncaringly? Why didn't you think of me?*

So much anger welled up in me that I could not speak, and at the same time, I was elated at actually hearing her voice. All I really wanted to do was hang up and deal with my feelings until we got to New York. I could tell she was having difficulty speaking, so it would not have done much good to continue.

Mercifully, the nurse took the phone and told me that Filomena had difficulty speaking and that she was suffering from dementia. I told her that I would be coming to see her soon. The nurse assured me this would be very good as she almost never had visitors. She asked me who I was, and I said I was the daughter of a high school friend of hers. I was sad to know I might not ever be able to communicate with my mother. I thanked the nurse and hung up.

I asked our children to tell their teachers that they would be absent for about a week. Our son, caught up in the excitement, told his teacher and classmates that he was going to New York to meet his grandmother, who had been lost for forty years, and his uncles, who were the Guardian Angels in Brooklyn. This prompted a call from the teacher who said our son had a vivid imagination. She explained what our son had told the class. I handed the phone to my husband to explain to her.

We eagerly made our arrangements and arrived in New York on September 15. As we pulled into the driveway of my sister Luisa's home, our faces lit up; there in huge letters on the garage door was a banner saying, "Welcome Home Grace and Family!"

My sister Luisa and her two beautiful teenage daughters, our nieces, met us at the door. They warmly welcomed us into their beautiful home. The large, well-landscaped home was built on a picturesque canal in a very upscale neighborhood in quaint Massapequa, Long Island. It was a glorious reunion—beautiful meals, warm conversation, and, especially, family. They were very open and accepting.

I can still hear my sister saying, "We are family; we are family!"

That was truly music to my ears. My sister's husband, Harry, was a very nice and very special man. Though blinded by a degenerative eye disease, he and Luisa had built up a very successful business employing several dozen people. In conversation with him in his office, one could not easily detect that he could not see. As we became better acquainted, we came to know he was held in high regard and many people sought his wise counseling and thoughtful advice. He was always up on current affairs and was a joy in conversation. He could hardly believe the things about my childhood. My sister and Harry were great hosts.

The Gift of Our Sister Grace

Though never a word was spoken
nor our faces did she see
She knew only of siblings—
but not of where we all could be

A score plus years of searching—
with no trace of a clue to guide her
Her being yearned to see the day—
sister and brothers would be beside her

Then came the dawn—a priest gave a hint—
pointing the way to the family tree
A letter arrived, revealing the name—
unfolding in a flash the past mystery

One night a voice was heard from a far distant place
A startling announcement was made "I am your sister Grace!!"

Sister, spouse, and children came,
weaving a cloak of love and security
In gratitude we gather together—
for she made of us a close-knit family

Mother no longer cries for her children—
separated no longer—our lives we share
Now we are a family that truly cares—
this the answer to fervent prayer

The bond of our family unity extends far beyond this
time and place
A sign forever—of healing Divine—
in the gift of our sister Grace.

L. B.
September 1981

A poem by my sister Luisa composed just after we first met.

As soon as we met and talked for a while, I told my sister I was very anxious to see our mother.

She had a hurt look on her face as she told me, "I do not know where she is."

I told her, "But I do. I have the address, and she is in nearby Patchogue!" She seemed shocked to hear this. We all got into the car, and Bob drove us to Patchogue.

On the way she asked, "Grace, how did you get all this information about our mother? Who gave it to you?"

I told her, "It was not easy, but I did it. My husband got a start toward finding her from Aunt Mary."

Luisa asked, "Why hasn't Aunt Mary ever told me?"

I answered, "Why didn't you ask her? You had Aunt Mary's phone number."

As we drove on, my emotion-filled mind raced with thoughts of finally getting answers to questions that had consumed my life. At the same time I was filled with these thoughts, I strongly braced myself for the possibility of great disappointment and rejection. All my life I had walked with one foot in the positive and one foot in the negative. This was my guard against the intense pain that had repeatedly visited me in the past. So often, just at the very instant when I could almost reach out and touch glorious possibilities, I would be dashed to the depths of despair.

From the moment we finally arrived at the nursing home to the time we left, my mind was a blur. I was almost paralyzed by emotions. A cascade of feelings filled my being. I felt anger, hate, love, joy, and pity all at the same time.

We entered the large, open, and well-lit nursing home where we were greeted by a lady administrator named Rosa. We asked to see Filomena, and she immediately accompanied us to the dining room and pointed to a woman with pepper hair and very white complexion sitting at a table. At that instant, a surge of emotions and very intense feelings of accomplishment filled my being and touched my soul. No matter what would happen next, I had done more than the impossible, and this could not be taken away from me. My mother had just finished eating lunch. She wore a cotton housedress, light blue, with a floral pattern.

We walked slowly toward her and I greeted her rather stiffly. She was not very talkative and had a look of fear. Rosa took us to her room, which she shared with another lady. My mother sat on her bed and stared at me, her hands one in the other on her lap, but she did not, or could not, seem to communicate. Rosa told us she could often communicate with my mother, especially about the past, even though my mother struggled to converse at all.

In the next instant, I realized the precarious possibilities for what was to come. My mother might accept me or unbearably and painfully reject me again. I approached her rather guardedly.

I believe I said to her, "I am Grace."

She looked at me with a look of incomprehension. Instantly, just as so often in the previous weeks, I went from the peak of elation to the depths of sadness. I knew I was too late. Right away I realized what I wanted most from her was not possible. She was a shell of her past, and in my mind, I just knew she would not be able to share any of it with me.

I turned away to hide my deep disappointment. I walked, almost ran, out of the room and out of the building. I remember holding onto the rail as my tears were blinding me. My tears turned to sobs. I covered my mouth to mute the sounds so I would not alarm other visitors. I cried alone and walked until I could control my sobbing. After some time, I finally regained my composure enough to go back.

Rosa suggested we all go with her to a small conference room where we could have more privacy. We all sat on folding chairs at a large table. I sat on my mother's right, my husband and Luisa sat across from us. My mother was obviously, and understandably, frightened and uncomfortable.

I showed my baby picture to my mother; I told her I was that baby. I pointed to Bob and said he is my husband. I told her about my children. She looked and listened but never uttered a word. Again, I showed her my baby picture, thrusting it into her hands. She took the picture and looked at it very intensely, taking a long time. She was reaching back forty-one years in her troubled life. She slowly turned her head toward me and back again to the photograph. Then her eyes slowly lifted to mine and fixed on me with a piercing stare that burned indelibly into my memory. I felt as if she were looking deep into my inner self. At that instant, there was no doubt she had made the connection.

I told my husband, "I got what I wanted; she knows who I am."

I looked across the table at Luisa. To my surprise, she had a very angry, pained expression I could not understand. I expected this to be a moment of joy. I realized then that Luisa was dealing with her own feelings. Most importantly, I also knew I could not share my thoughts or my feelings of this moment with her. She was trying desperately to deal with this in her own way. Here I was in the pivotal moment in my lifelong search, and I couldn't communicate with either my mother or my sister.

Later, it became clear that my sister too, was rediscovering her mother. She said she had last seen her as a young child. My sister was about five years old when she and her three brothers were put into foster care. I asked her if she remembered anything about this time or about our mother and their home life. She described her father as a very cruel and abusive man. She told me these memories were very painful. Mainly she said she was too young to remember. I was surprised, because I knew I could remember things, even horrible things, from when I was three. From the letter, I knew how old she was when she was put into the Angel Guardian Home. To this day, none of my siblings or the extended family has ever shared the details of this time with me.

We talked with Rosa about how my mother's care was being funded. Just before leaving to come to the nursing home, Harry had warned us of his fear, that as Filomena's family, we might somehow incur her past and ongoing expenses. Rosa assured us that all of her care was already being covered and we had no financial responsibility. After this first meeting with my mother, we were all emotionally spent. We decided to leave and return to my sister's home.

As we drove back to Luisa's home, we made plans to go on to Brooklyn to meet my four surviving brothers: Michael, Francesco, Vicenzo, and Giovanni. We decided to go to my brother Francesco's home first, then to my brother Giovanni's home, and hopefully to meet my oldest brother, Michael. Francesco, my second oldest brother, would not go to Giovanni's home as they had not been on speaking terms due to some old issues between them.

At Francesco's home in Brooklyn, he and his family greeted us warmly with a delicious traditional Italian meal. I felt that they were trying to feed me enough to make up for the past forty years.

During the lively discussions at the table, Francesco suddenly lit up. He looked at me very carefully, paused, and exclaimed, "You are the lady in the newspaper I read about in June!"

The room went suddenly silent. All eyes were on Francesco.

He continued, "I cried when I read the first story and was so happy when I read the later story because you found your family. Little did I know I was looking at my own sister; a sister I did not know I had! Something about that baby picture brought tears to my eyes. I just could not comprehend how anyone could give away such a pretty baby."

Here again, the baby picture proved I was that very baby in Brooklyn, more than forty years before. A memorable visit ended and we said our good-byes. Now I was anxious to meet the rest of my brothers.

My youngest brother Giovanni, his pretty wife Connie, and their two sons gave us a wonderful welcome. When we walked into their home, the table was filled with people and set with a beautiful traditional Italian feast. I looked around the room. My eyes immediately locked on my oldest brother, Michael. He looked back and then away. Under his breath, and as if talking to no one in particular, he said in a soft voice with a quiet air of disbelief, "She looks just like her!"

As he said this, I knew there was no doubt in his mind that I was his sister; this meant a lot to me. I knew at first that when Giovanni had called him and told him about me that he did not want to meet me. All this time, my husband was taking pictures and the expression on his face said it all! He was so happy for me.

During the dinner, I asked Michael if he had known about me. He looked at me as if not wanting to answer my question. I asked him again. Then he told us our mother had visited him in the early 1950s. While at his home, she had started crying.

Michael said he had asked her what the matter was. She said, "I am crying for my little girl."

My brother, thinking she was crying for my sister Luisa, told her, "Don't worry; my sister is doing all right."

She answered, "No, I am not crying for Luisa. I am crying for my daughter Grace."

Then she told him all about me. My brother said he had never told anyone until now. Just then, I recalled what Matilde had told me of the Italian women who came to visit and bring me presents. Ever since he told me this, I have had the feeling that not only did he know of me, but the relatives also knew. I believe the reason he never told anyone was that I had been born out of wedlock. In those days, according to Southern Italian traditions, an illegitimate child was a great shame on a family. An illegitimate child was no one's child.

The conversation remained lively and the whole setting was made all the more memorable by the beautiful table that was set in the Italian tradition of never running out of food. There was so much food that I thought perhaps Giovanni was making sure I never went hungry again.

I was so excited I could barely eat anything from this fantastic, beautiful banquet. The centerpieces at the table were made of traditional Italian cold cuts, cheeses, and seafood arranged beautifully in colorful wheels on giant platters. The table was filled with many other traditional Italian dishes and desserts. The delicious *calamares* (squid) and marzipan candies had been longtime favorites from my childhood in Veracruz. I was surprised to discover these same delicacies are also favored by Italians, especially Italians from Southern Italy, even more specifically, Calabria and Sicily. My children sure enjoyed all of this and at the same time were wondering what was happening to their mother.

During all of the lively discussions at the dinner table, I brought out my baby picture. When my brother Giovanni saw it, he was immediately taken aback, shocked. He exclaimed, "I know that picture!" Instantly, all eyes in the room zeroed in on him.

In a flash I shot back, "How do you know this picture? Do you have a copy?"

He took a few seconds to compose himself, replying, "No, I used to see it often whenever I passed by Roubain's Studio on Columbia Street on my way to work. It was a big picture. They kept it in the window as an example of their work. It remained there until they closed the studio. I was married with two boys during this time. I was always attracted to that photo, and I could not understand why. I reasoned that I probably wanted a daughter. Now I know I was looking at my own flesh and blood and didn't know it—I was looking at my sister." This was the fifth time this photograph had magically surfaced to tie me to the past. Indeed, the picture had now gone full circle.

Just before dark, I asked my brother Giovanni to go for a walk with me. I wanted to talk to him alone, and I wanted to see if I could ease my tensions by walking. He took me all around his neighborhood and we talked. I asked questions, but he did not have much to contribute about the family tree or our family history. He told me he had been born two years before me and had been put into the Angel Guardian Home at the tender age of two weeks. He was the lucky one; he was put into a foster home where the family raised him as if he was one of their own.

The family that took Giovanni also took two of my other brothers, Vicenzo and Francesco. Vicenzo was five years older than Giovanni and Francesco was eight years older than Giovanni. Francesco told me the family they were living with never introduced Vicenzo and him as Giovanni's brothers. To them, Giovanni was their own baby. Giovanni lived with his foster family until he got married. Talking to Giovanni, he had nothing but good memories of his childhood. I am very thankful for that.

When we came back from our walk, I asked my oldest brother, Michael, if we had any aunts, uncles, or relatives in Brooklyn.

He said, "Yes, we have an Uncle James, close by."

I said, "What are we waiting for? Let's go see him!"

Michael made a call to Uncle James's house, and we were on our way. I was on a roll and I didn't want to stop.

We arrived at our Uncle James's house, and as I walked in the door, my Uncle James exclaimed, "Filomena, you have lost so much weight!" Uncle James was in his late seventies, and since no one had told him about me, he thought I was his sister Filomena, my mother!

The hall was not well lit so my oldest brother, Michael, explained, "This is not Filomena; this is Grace, Filomena's daughter."

Uncle James said, "She looks just like Filomena!"

After Matilde and Michael, Uncle James was the third person to say this to me. Somehow, I always knew my looks would erase any doubts.

We talked, and I asked Uncle James if he had any pictures of my mother when she was young. He answered, "Unfortunately, no, those photos were lost in a flood." Uncle James brought out pictures of his family and put them on the table. He pointed to one of a lady in her late fifties. He told me she was Grace. I told him I was Grace. I thought he was a little confused.

Then he said again, "This is Grace, your grandmother."

So here for the first time I learned my maternal grandmother's name. The picture was not very clear or I was too nervous to remember what my grandmother looked like, but at least I knew I was named after her. This gave me a good feeling. Before this, I never liked my name. I felt it probably was just a name picked out of the air at the last minute to fill a space in a birth certificate. I was to find out later that the name Grace followed a long trace of Italian naming tradition in my family, all the way back to the 1700s.

We were ready to leave Uncle James's house when I looked closely at his wife, another Aunt Mary. Suddenly a feeling welled up from deep inside. When I heard her voice, I immediately recalled I had spoken to her on the phone in 1964, when I first came to New York to find my family. I said to her, somewhat forcefully and with no doubt whatsoever in my mind, "You are the one! I called you in 1964, and I asked you about a woman named Filomena that went by name of Maria, with your same last name. You told me you did not know anyone with that name."

She was startled by this but did not deny what I said. She answered, somewhat defensively, "You did not mention Filomena's married name. That is why I was confused."

I realized I had come so very close during my search in 1964, and this was the second time during that search I had been diverted from the truth—both times for each person's own unexplained and selfish reasons.

We left Uncle James's home and went back to my brother Giovanni's home. We had more to eat and drink and got to know one another a little better. My brother Michael was a very entertaining storyteller with a great sense of humor. Everyone around the table prodded him to tell the hilarious stories of their past. Long into the night, after a warm and loving gathering, we all decided to make the two-hour drive to my sister Luisa's home on Long Island. Everyone drove back with us. It was a great time. Looking back, I think of this time as my shining moment in

Camelot. It seemed possible, if just for a moment, that this fragmented family might finally be reunited.

Now I wanted to visit my mother again. The next morning, Luisa was with us as we drove to the nursing home and met again with Rosa. She took us to see our mother. Rosa had become quite interested in what, apparently to her, seemed to be a developing, dramatic story. After a few moments, Rosa asked us to accompany her to her office. Inside the office, she asked a few more questions and then looked at me and, as if a light had turned on, excitedly exclaimed, "Why, you're her daughter! You're her daughter! I knew it from the first moment I saw you!"

Excitedly, she asked a staff lady to bring my mother to a smaller room just behind the main office. We stood together, waiting uncomfortably. When my mother came into the room, she stood, facing me at arm's length with Rosa, Luisa, and my husband Bob at our sides. Rosa tried to entice my mother into telling me about my father. Then, in an increasingly excited way, said, "Filomena, this woman is your daughter, for God's sake! She is from you and Jackie." Then she asked her, "Is Jackie her father?" She repeatedly prodded my mother, asking her this same line of questions.

Finally, my mother looked down at the floor and, as if the word was being exorcised and brought up from the depths of her soul, breathed loudly, "Yes!"

Unstoppable streams of tears flowed from me and from everyone in that room. All of this was captured by my wonderful husband's camera. Rosa was ecstatic; we all were.

My mother moved closer, her arms were around me. I had finally accomplished what had, for so long, seemed impossible. Not only had I returned to my country of birth and found my family, but I had returned to the very point where I had left off very nearly forty-one years before—in my mother's arms.

Made in the USA
Lexington, KY
18 July 2013